P9-CTB-146

PRAEGER SPECIAL STUDIES IN
INTERNATIONAL ECONOMICS AND DEVELOPMENT

Problems and Prospects of the Alliance for Progress

A CRITICAL EXAMINATION

Herbert K. May

FREDERICK A. PRAEGER, Publishers
New York · Washington · London

338.
917308
M466

HC
125
.m35

The purpose of the Praeger Special Studies is to make specialized research monographs in U.S. and international economics and politics available to the academic, business, and government communities. For further information, write to the Special Projects Division, Frederick A. Praeger, Publishers, 111 Fourth Avenue, New York, N.Y. 10003.

FREDERICK A. PRAEGER, PUBLISHERS
111 Fourth Avenue, New York, N.Y. 10003, U.S.A.
77-79 Charlotte Street, London W.1, England

Published in the United States of America in 1968
by Frederick A. Praeger, Inc., Publishers

All rights reserved

© 1968 by Herbert K. May

Library of Congress Catalog Card Number: 68-14161

Printed in the United States of America

71962

CONTENTS

9   THE ROLE OF U. S. BUSINESS   105

10   THE ROLE OF U. S. LABOR   120

       The Need to Increase Union-to-Union
           Relationships   124

       The Need to Expand the Functions and
           Resources of the American Institute
           for Free Labor Development (AIFLD)   130

11   THE ROLE OF THE U. S. PRESS   135

       The Need to Transmit More Complete
           Information to Latin America   136

       The Need to Transmit More Complete
           Information About Latin America to
           the United States   142

12   THE ROLE OF THE U. S. GOVERNMENT   146

       The Need for Broader Relationships
           with the Military Leaders of Latin
           America   146

       The Need to Publicize and Dramatize the
           Achievements of the Alliance for Progress 150

       The Need for Long-Term Scholarships for
           Graduate Studies in the United States   155

       The Need to Help the Formulation of
           Specific Development Projects   158

13   THE ROLE OF OTHER FREE WORLD
           COUNTRIES   164

       The Need to Improve European Procedures
           for Collaboration on Latin American
           Problems   167

       The Need for Broader Expression of
           European Involvement in the Alliance
           for Progress   172

       The Need for European Participation in
           the Alliance for Progress Machinery   177

ABBREVIATIONS

AFL-CIO	American Federation of Labor - Congress of Industrial Organizations
AID	Agency for International Development
AIFLD	American Institute for Free Labor Development
CIAP	Inter-American Committee for the Alliance for Progress (Comité Interamericano para la Alianzo para el Progreso)
CSUCA	Superior Council of Central American Universities (Consejo Superior Universitario Centro-Americano)
DAC	Development Assistance Committee
ECLA	Economic Commission for Latin America
GNP	Gross National Product
IA-ECOSOC	Inter-American Economic and Social Council
IBRD	International Bank for Reconstruction and Development
ICFTU	International Confederation of Free Trade Unions
IDB	International Development Bank
IFPAAW	International Federation of Plantation, Agricultural, and Allied Workers
OAS	Organization of American States
OECD	Organization for Economic Cooperation and Development
ORIT	Inter-American Regional Workers' Organization (Organización Regional Interamericana de Trabajadores)

UDN   National Democratic Union of Brazil (Uniao
                Democratica Nacional)

UNIAPAC   International Union of Catholic Employers
                Associations (Union Internationale des
                Associations Patronales Catholiques)

USAID   United States AID Mission

USIA   United States Information Agency

INTRODUCTION

Although the Alliance for Progress has had a much better record of accomplishment than is generally realized, the record is not as good as many of its supporters had hoped for, and expected. Perhaps even more important, there is now a widespread disenchantment with the Alliance throughout Latin America, a deep skepticism that it will accomplish the fundamental improvements in the economic and social conditions of that area that were earlier expected of the Alliance. This disenchantment was reflected in the joint statement issued in April, 1966, by the Organization of American States (OAS) Panel of Experts, the so-called Nine Wise Men of the Inter-American System. That statement, which was issued at the time of their collective resignation, included the comments that the Alliance "is passing through a period of crisis" in which "there are symptoms of discouragement, skepticism, and despair" which make it "indispensable" that there be "clear demonstration of a firm (inter-American) determination to overcome the crisis in accordance with the spirit of the Charter of Punta del Este."

This and other problems of the Alliance were considered at the Fourth Annual Meeting of the Inter-American Economic and Social Council (IA-ECOSOC) in April, 1966, in Buenos Aires, and at the Special Meeting of that Council in Washington, D.C., in June, 1966. The Buenos Aires meeting was held for the specific purpose of evaluating the Alliance at the end of its first five years, and the meeting produced several important suggestions for strengthening it. The Washington meeting was convened for the purpose of considering possible revision of the Charter of the OAS, and agreement was in fact reached for revision of the "Economic Standards" and "Social Standards" of that Charter so as to reflect more fully the objectives and requirements of the Alliance. The more important recommendations of those meetings will be summarized at the end of this introduction, together with certain other recommendations which others have made for strengthening the Alliance. The fact that greater attention will not be devoted to those recommendations in this volume should not be interpreted as manifestation of a belief in their unimportance.

1

On the contrary, I consider most of them important and worthy
of full analysis. That analysis will not be provided in this volume because, for one thing, it would require considerable expansion of the text, but, primarily, because I believe that the
recommendations in question touch only indirectly on what I
consider to be the principal problems of the Alliance.

It is now abundantly clear that if the lofty goals of the Alliance are to be achieved to a reasonable degree, much more
will be needed than improvement of intergovernmental economic relations--the aspect of the Alliance which has so far received almost all of the attention of the Alliance leaders and of
the nongovernment community in the United States and Latin
America. Much more will be needed than improved trade relations with and among the Latin American nations. Much
more will be needed than continued or even expanded foreign
financial assistance to Latin America. Much more also will
be needed than continued enthusiasm, intelligence, and hard
work on the part of those governmental and intergovernmental
officials responsible for administering the Alliance. Much
more will be needed than a serious determination--even a
greatly expanded determination--on the part of the separate
Latin American nations to pursue the self-help and reform
measures called for by the Alliance. All of these will be
needed, but they will not be enough.

The critical truth is that the Alliance poses an ideological
challenge which is more intricate and more difficult than that
of any international economic and social program ever before
initiated by the Free World. The text of this volume will be
devoted to analysis of that ideological challenge and to certain
recommendations which I consider essential for meeting it.
First, however, it will be useful, for background purposes,
to summarize just three case histories illustrating different
aspects of this challenge:

1. In 1961, the Government of Colombia, under the Presidency of the outstanding statesman Alberto Lleras Camargo,
enacted two important laws. The first modified Colombia's
income tax structure by sharply increasing tax rates at the higher
income levels while reducing the tax rates at the lower income
levels. The second created a land reform institute with broad
powers to buy large estates and distribute the land among the
peasants. Each law was unquestionably a major step in the
right direction, richly meriting the label "reform" and help-

ing qualify Colombia as one of the countries most actively pursuing the goals of the Alliance for Progress. What is more,
the Colombian Government had put together a long-term development program which received the approval, in 1962, of
the Panel of Experts of the Organization of the American
States; and the program was buttressed by a long list--very
rare in Latin America--of development projects approved by
(in fact, largely formulated by) the World Bank. Moreover,
each of the country's two major political parties--the Liberals
and the Conservatives--was firmly and publicly committed to
support of the Alliance, including vigorous support of domestic
and foreign private enterprise, and the Liberal-Conservative
coalition seemed to be securely in control of the country's political leadership for years to come. It is small wonder, then,
that Colombia was widely considered to provide one of the best
examples in Latin America of how well the Alliance was working.

Yet, the Alliance is not faring as well in Colombia as any
of its supporters would have liked. Economic and social disturbances became increasingly aggravated during the term in
office of President Guillermo Leon Valencia and continued
during the initial months of President Carlos Lleras Restrepo's
term, while the early enthusiasm in Colombia for the Alliance
has clearly abated. A full explanation of what has gone wrong
would be beyond the compass of this book, but a synopsis of
some of the principal factors will reveal part of the complexity
and difficulty of the challenge of the Alliance, even when it is
operating in a highly auspicious environment:

(a) Although the income tax reform law of 1961 commend-
ably sought to reduce the regressivity of the tax system as
a whole, one of its major consequences was to provoke a
decline of total tax revenue by over 200 million pesos in
1962 since the increased tax rates on higher incomes yielded
far less than enough revenue to compensate for the drop of
revenue derived from the lower income groups. One of
the unintentional results of the tax reform law, therefore,
was an aggravation of inflationary pressures in Colombia,
even without taking into account the Government's need for
an increase of peso revenue to finance implementation of
the development program.

(b) Colombia had been running a current account deficit
in its international balance of payments for several years

--a deficit provoked by a sharp decline during recent
years of its export earnings resulting from the drop in
the world price of coffee and by the perpetuation of inflation along with overvaluation of the foreign exchange value
of the peso. With sufficient determination and more political pain, the Colombian Government could have permitted
the exchange rate to reach a more appropriate level, but
there was little that the Government could have done alone
to increase world coffee prices and, therefore, its earnings from coffee exports. In any case, the balance-of-
payments deficits persisted, thereby impairing Colombia's
"creditworthiness" as a recipient of loans from abroad
and impairing the climate for foreign private investment.

(c) While the newly created land reform institute had broad
powers to buy and redistribute farm land, it proved to be unable to exercise its powers. It was required to buy land
which was being inadequately utilized, but had great difficulty establishing clear standards by which to determine
"inadequate" utilization. It was required to pay a "fair"
price for any land it bought, but was unable to establish
generally acceptable standards and procedures for determining "fair value." Furthermore, the administrators of
the institute were fully cognizant that distribution of land
to the peasants would not in itself meet their economic or
social problems inasmuch as they might well be unable to
produce efficiently and even to hold on to their farms unless they were quickly given technical assistance and
relatively easy access to low-interest credit for the procurement of living quarters, farm tools, seed, etc. The
technical problems associated with implementation of the
land reform objectives of the institute accordingly proved
to be almost paralytic in their over-all impact. In addition,
the institute was severely handicapped by the Government's
shortage of pesos with which to buy land, or even to pay
for the initial installments.

(d) The shortage of pesos was, in fact, one of the major
impediments to implementation not only of the land reform
efforts but of the development program as a whole. For-
tunate as Colombia was in having sound projects within that
program, it nevertheless had considerable difficulty in
bringing those projects to fruition because of the scarcity
of pesos. Even when a given project called for a very large
component of imports and when foreign lenders were dis-

posed to provide the necessary financing of those imports, substantial amounts of <u>pesos</u> were also likely to be necessary; and the inadequacy of such <u>pesos</u> would alone serve to delay the project, if only because few foreign lenders have been willing to provide enough foreign exchange to cover the local costs of any project. Most foreign lenders have considered the raising of necessary <u>pesos</u> through noninflationary means to be one of the principal manifestations of "self-help" on the part of a loan applicant. They have generally doubted the wisdom, furthermore, of lending enough money to cover an excessively large percentage of the costs of any project in another country on the principle that the borrower should assume a substantial part of the financial risk of the venture, preferably by covering all of the local costs, if only to provide maximum assurance that due care will be taken to avoid incurring unnecessary local costs and to administer the completed project as efficiently as possible.

I do not wish to overstate the weakness of the Alliance in Colombia. When the newly elected President of Colombia, Guillermo Leon Valencia, took office late in 1962, he appointed the brilliant and vigorous Carlos Sanz Santamaria, then Colombia's Ambassador to the United States, as Finance Minister. Sanz Santamaria succeeded, despite serious political difficulties, in persuading the Colombian Congress to enact legislation permitting him to increase tax revenues substantially. He also very much improved the exchange-rate structure and obtained a stand-by agreement with the International Monetary Fund for balance-of-payments support. He was successful, furthermore, in obtaining loans from the World Bank and from the United States Government and other governments to help finance some of the more important projects of the Colombian development program. On the other hand, substantial budgetary deficits and balance-of-payments difficulties continued (though less seriously than would have been the case except for Sanz Santamaria's efforts), and many important projects and the land reform program have not moved forward as had been anticipated.

2. The course of the Alliance for Progress in Brazil will, in the long run, be the most important single index of the success of the Alliance as a whole. Brazil occupies half of the area of South America, and the 80 million population of Brazil is one-third of that of all Latin America. It is accordingly of

great importance that the Alliance did not receive even the
most perfunctory of lip-service support from the Brazilian
Government until a military coup d'etat deposed President
Goulart and brought a new Government into power on April 1,
1964, under President Castelo Branco.   Furthermore,
the Alliance has had little effect in Brazil even since the new
Government took office and despite that Government's manifest desire to play an active role in support of the Alliance.
The problems confronting that Government in its sincere efforts
to promote the economic and social development of Brazil in
accordance with the objectives of the Alliance are similar in
important respects to those confronting the Government of
Colombia, as described above, and indeed are similar in important respects to those of the Goulart Government. In other
important respects, however, the problems are very different.
A summary of some of the more important problems confronting the Alliance in Brazil since its inception will therefore reveal additional aspects of the complexity and difficulty of the
challenge of the Alliance:

(a) The Charter of Punta del Este, which formally inaugurated the Alliance for Progress, was signed on August 17,
1961, just eight days before the startling resignation of
President Janio Quadros. The Vice President, Joao
Goulart, then took over the Presidency after a few days of
turmoil during which most of Brazil's principal military
officers sought to prevent his taking office because of
their fear that he would be dominated by his Communist
associates. As matters turned out, President Goulart
proved in fact to be very much influenced by the Communists, several of whom he appointed to high-level positions
in his Government. I do not believe that President Goulart
was himself a Communist, nor that all of his Cabinet officers were Communists. However, it became evident
very soon after he took office that neither he nor any of
his principal subordinates (with the exception of Roberto
Campos, his Ambassador to the United States) were
kindly disposed toward the Alliance. It was evident that
the Goulart Government could not be expected to support
the Alliance, and that, on the contrary, it might very possibly try to lead the rest of Latin America in opposition to
the Alliance.

It should not be assumed, however, that the Alliance
would have had easy sailing in Brazil even if Quadros had

not turned the Government over to Goulart. The course
of the Alliance in Brazil might have been just as difficult
if Quadros had remained. For certain underlying problems in Brazil would have been working against the Alliance under the Presidency of Quadros or Goulart or anyone else. And Quadros's conduct during his seven months
in office was hardly such as to encourage confidence in his
ability or willingness to overcome those problems, as described below:

(b) Nationalism and antagonism toward "foreign trusts"
had long existed and had long been growing stronger in
Brazil, being endorsed not only by the Communists and
other leftists in Brazil, but also by the military as a
whole and by many of the most important business groups
in the country. The motivations of the Communists are
well known. The motivations of the others are much more
complex, very often being based upon a sincere belief that
foreign-owned companies are always so rich, and therefore
so strong, that the Brazilian Government cannot protect
its national interests against their depredations, and/or
that it is the remittance abroad of the "huge" profits
earned by the foreign companies that is responsible for
Brazil's balance-of-payments difficulties, and/or that
Brazilian businessmen must be protected from the unfair
competition of foreign companies that are so rich and so
powerful that they can stifle the growth of Brazilian-
owned enterprises.

It would be of little use to state--though it is true--
that any objective and well-informed analyst could demonstrate the inaccuracies of those beliefs. The point is that
the inaccuracies had never been demonstrated to the Brazilian people, and the beliefs had long been held deeply and
sincerely by a great many Brazilians. Indeed, a strong
emotional attachment had developed around those beliefs.
I well remember, for example, the following colloquy which
took place as far back as 1948, during a meeting in Rio between the Brazilian and U.S. labor advisors of the Joint
Brazil-United States Technical Commission (on which I was
serving as the U.S. fiscal advisor). The subject being discussed at the meeting was the means whereby technical
training for Brazilian laborers could be improved, when
suddenly one of the Brazilians stated, apropos of nothing,
though he was clearly thinking about the agitation then

taking place in Brazil for a law (which soon thereafter was enacted) reserving for the Brazilian Government all rights to explore for, and exploit, Brazil's petroleum resources: "That's all very well. But, O petroleo e nosso!" ("The petroleum is ours!").

The U.S. labor advisor was obviously surprised by this sudden and irrelevant outburst, and (though it was U.S. policy to try to avoid arguments with Brazilians on this subject) replied:

"Of course the petroleum is yours. But what good does it do you to keep it under the ground?"

The Brazilian's reply was simply: "Better ours under the ground than yours above the ground!" Many misconceptions surrounded this statement and similar statements appearing at that time throughout the Brazilian press. But the fact that they were misconceptions did not lessen the significance of the fact that they were very widely held in Brazil, even among the country's military and business leaders (as reflected in the fact that the bill calling for a Government monopoly of petroleum exploration and exploitation was spearheaded by the UDN--the political party representing the more conservative business interests of Brazil).

I do not wish to convey the impression that the climate for foreign investment as a whole has long been unfavorable in Brazil. For there was, in fact, a great influx of foreign capital into Brazil following the end of World War II (the inflow of U.S. private capital alone amounted to approximately $1 billion), most of which took place during 1953-59. The need for additional private foreign investment was generally understood, and new investments were welcomed and even encouraged. It is important, however, to recognize that the nationalistic and "antitrust" concepts mentioned above, lay under the surface during this period, and that their influence existed even before Goulart came to power. For example, the first expropriation of American and Foreign Power property in Brazil took place in 1959, during the Presidency of Kubitschek, not Goulart. It is especially significant that each of the two principal candidates in the Presidential elections of 1960 (Janio Quadros and Army Marshal Teixeira Lott) asserted vigorously and

repeatedly during the campaign that Brazil must take steps
to protect itself from "improper conduct" by foreign investors. Each claimed that the "huge" profits being remitted abroad by the foreign-owned companies were "bleeding the economy" and each held those companies at least
partly responsible for many of the country's other ills,
including inflation.

(c) Those who were distressed by the manner in which
Quadros led the Government during his seven months as
President and who were then shocked by his irresponsible
resignation on August 25, 1961, should be careful to avoid
the easy conclusion that the Brazilian people were at fault
for having elected him. It should be remembered that his
principal opponent, Marshal Lott, was strongly supported
by the Communists and other leftist groups. Quadros was
the candidate of the conservatives, including most of the
businessmen and, indeed, the middle class as a whole.
Quadros and his supporters made a great point during the
campaign of emphasizing his reputation as having been a
serious, businesslike Governor of the State of Sao Paulo,
who had even succeeded in balancing the budget of that
State. Marshal Lott's campaign, on the other hand, was
characterized by a great deal of demagogy, and I believe
that the Brazilian public showed considerable maturity
when they elected Quadros by a landslide.

Once in office, however, Quadros quickly began to
prove himself to be a very different man from the one whom
the Brazilian people had thought they were electing. To be
sure, he did take some steps toward cleaning up the financial mess he had inherited from the Kubitschek regime, although he did a poor job even in this respect. However,
the most important fact of Quadros's incumbency was that
he--not Goulart--initiated a radical, a truly revolutionary,
change in Brazil's world posture.

President Kubitschek, Quadros's immediate predeces-
sor, had consistently pursued Brazil's traditional role as
the best friend of the United States in Latin America, despite what he considered the inadequate level of financial
support extended to his government by the U.S. Government and despite the cold shoulder which the U.S. Government gave to his 1958 proposal for an "Operation Pan
America." He rejected all recommendations for resump-

tion of diplomatic relations with the Iron Curtain countries, and his domestic, as well as his international,
policies were always firmly pro-West, anti-Communist,
and proprivate enterprise (despite the expropriation of
American and Foreign Power property by the leftist
Governor of the State of Rio Grande do Sul during Kubitschek's term of office). And it is significant that, while
Kubitschek pursued these policies and while his financial
policies were calamitous, he remained extremely popular
in Brazil. There is virtually no doubt that he would
have been reelected if the Brazilian Constitution had not
prevented him from succeeding himself.

Quadros, on the other hand, quickly let it be known
that he would not pursue Kubitschek's pro-West and anti-
Communist orientation. He announced that he was prepared to resume diplomatic relations with the Soviet
Union and other Iron Curtain countries, and stated that
he would support entry of Communist China into the United
Nations. He publicly praised Fidel Castro and (during
his last days in office) gave Brazil's highest award, the
Cruzeiro do Sul, to Castro's Minister of Industry, "Che"
Guevara. He even announced that he would support le-
galization of the Communist Party of Brazil. And he
nominated several leftists to high public office.

I believe it would be a mistake to call Quadros a
Communist. In fact, I am inclined to share the general
belief that one of his objectives in the adoption of policies
such as those described in the preceding paragraph was
to gain sufficient support from Brazil's leftists and
nationalists to neutralize the opposition they might otherwise have given to the conservative economic and financial
policies he was intending to adopt. However, I have no
doubt that he had a basic anti-American bias (deriving
principally, according to a widespread rumor among
Brazilians, from the discourteous treatment once accorded to him by a U.S. Customs official). I have no
doubt also that he intended by his "independent" policy
to play the Free World off against the Iron Curtain in the
expectation that he would thereby gain the maximum advantage for Brazil from its dealings with each of them. Probably, too, he felt that Brazil should demonstrate its importance as a nation by severing all international ties which
might be interpreted--however inaccurately--as committing

Brazil to follow the foreign policy lead of any one other
country or any combination of other countries.

In any case, and whatever his reasons, Quadros
severely weakened Brazil's ties with the United States
and with the inter-American system as a whole. In so
doing, he severely weakened the prospects for the success of the Alliance for Progress as a whole, and particularly in Brazil.

(d) While President Kubitschek had undeniably kept his
country firmly wedded to pro-West and anti-Communist
policies, and while Brazil's rate of economic growth during his term of office had been impressive, his mismanagement of Brazil's financial affairs contributed greatly
to the economic and social ills which are still tormenting
that country. Inflation, which had been a serious problem in Brazil even before Kubitschek took office, then
became even more serious, galloping at the rate of more
than 30 per cent per year during his last two years in office. The inflation, plus the maintenance of an artifici-
ally high foreign exchange value for the cruzeiro during
this period, contributed greatly to a very sharp deterioration of Brazil's balance of payments, although the drop
in the prices of coffee beginning in 1955 certainly had a
great bearing on the Brazilian situation, just as it did on
the balance-of-payments situation of Colombia and, indeed, on that of almost all of the fifteen Latin American
countries producing coffee. Under the Kubitschek Government, the accumulated gold and foreign exchange reserves of the Bank of Brazil were completely exhausted,
and while the large inflow of foreign private equity investment which had begun in 1953 continued through 1959,
Brazil's foreign indebtedness increased even more rapidly, laying the foundation for the frequent debt "reschedul-
ings" which have had to be negotiated with foreign credi-
tors since then and which have greatly impaired Brazil's
creditworthiness in the eyes of foreign lending agencies.
Brazil's need for balance-of-payments assistance in one
form or another has, in fact, been so great and so persistent ever since early in 1958, that most international
lenders have been extremely shy in considering any new
loans to Brazil, including any loans which would help
promote the objectives of the Alliance for Progress.

In my opinion, one of the most distressing features of
the inflationary situation, which was so bad under Kubitschek and Quadros and which became even worse under
Goulart, has been the fact that even today almost every
important sector of Brazil is opposed to one or more of
the measures necessary to stop it, despite the great
harm it has done and is still doing. Very few businessmen understand or will accept the need for credit restrictions at the Bank of Brazil. Very few laborers understand or will accept either Governmental restraint on
wage increases or action by the Government to reduce the
hugely swollen payrolls of the Government-owned and
heavily subsidized railway and shipping lines. Very few
coffee producers or exporters understand or will accept
the need to reduce the prices paid by the Government for
coffee it then deposits in warehouses with little prospect
of ever selling. There is a general sentiment that while
"something" should be done to reduce the rate of inflation,
that "something" should not be painful to anyone. The
fact that inflation has caused a serious distortion of investment, has been a serious deterrent to various types of
basic investment, has impaired Brazil's international
creditworthiness, and has caused many forms of social
distress and disturbance is either not understood or is
dismissed with the argument that "Brazil is different
from any other country. The foreigners are wrong in
trying to apply their orthodox and textbook theories to
Brazil. For, after all, Brazil has had a lot of economic
growth despite, and maybe even because of, its inflation."
Few Brazilians understand that the economic development
of their country would have been very much greater and
very much sounder if it had not been for the maladjustments
provoked by inflation, and few understand that most of them
will have to endure some temporary pain if Brazil's economic and financial house is to be put in order. The
Alliance for Progress is badly handicapped in Brazil by
the fact that few Brazilians understand the necessary ingredients of self-help.

(e) Economic development has long been Brazil's number
one objective, and the need for social reforms has in general
had little--and half-hearted--attention. In fact, President
Kubitschek's delegation to the Bogota Conference late in
1960 initially opposed the U. S. delegation's proposals for
the joint advancement of economic and social reforms, tak-

ing the position that meaningful social reforms could take
place only after a high rate of economic development had
been achieved and that it would accordingly be a waste of
energy and resources to try to achieve the two simultaneously. President Quadros likewise placed his emphasis
upon economic development, and even Goulart--despite
his loudly avowed zeal for giving preference to the welfare of the labor and peasant groups of Brazil--failed to
promote either legislative or administrative reforms for
that purpose, although I do not know which was the more
responsible for his inaction: lack of genuine interest or
inability to determine the necessary courses of action.

It is important to observe, in this connection, that
even the groups which stand to gain most by meaningful
social reforms have had few ideas as to the specific
measures they should seek. The peasants, for example,
have not had the kind of leadership which has wanted to,
or could, make specific and constructive proposals for
land reform. Instead, the principal peasant organizations
during the terms of Kubitschek, Quadros, and Goulart--
the Peasants Leagues of the Northeast--were created and
led by an avowed Communist, Francisco Juliao, whose
objective was revolution, not reform. The labor unions
likewise were heavily infiltrated, and often led, by
Communists. But whether or not Communist-dominated,
the unions were--and continue to be--far more concerned
with the possibility of bettering their lot through political
pressure than with what we in the United States have come
to consider the "normal" functions of a union. Among
other things, the Brazilian unions have no concept of how
to utilize their organization for any sort of social action
of their own. Some indication of the kinds of problems
faced by the Alliance for Progress in these circumstances
may be given by the following account of a conversation I
had in February, 1963, with Amino Afonso, then Brazil's
Minister of Labor:

I pointed out that one of the objectives of the Alliance
is to promote the social, as well as the economic, welfare
of Latin America's laborers and that I would therefore
appreciate knowing why he was so outspokenly critical of
the Alliance instead of working within it. He replied that
the Alliance (which he incorrectly spoke of as a U.S. aid
program) had done nothing to help Brazilian labor because

the Latin American regional organization (ORIT) of the
International Confederation of Free Trade Unions called
all of the Brazilian union leaders Communists, and was,
therefore, preventing the U. S. Government from helping
any of the unions. He said that if the U. S. Government
were really interested in helping Brazilian labor, it
would have been doing so without regard for ORIT, and
that since it had not done so he could hardly be expected
to be enthusiastic about the Alliance. I told him, first,
that the U. S. Government believed that those union leaders
who were Communists were acting against the interests of
Brazil as well as the United States and that any help to them
or their unions would accordingly be contrary to the objectives of the Alliance and that, second, the U. S. Government
valued ORIT's judgments on the political orientations of
Brazil's labor leaders, but that, third, the U. S. Government made its own decisions on such matters and did not
follow ORIT's opinions blindly and that, fourth, in any case,
Brazil was just as much a member of the Alliance as the
United States and should be trying on its own to promote
the social, as well as the economic, welfare of its laborers
through specific reform and self-help measures. I asked
whether he was sponsoring any such measures, and if so
whether there was any way in which the U. S. Government
could be helpful. He stated after some discussion that he did
not have any specific measures in mind, but he added grudg-
ingly that if he thought of any he would get in touch with the
Alliance.

        I was convinced from our conversation and other evi-
dence that Amino Afonso did not have the vaguest idea of
any specific social reform or self-help measures that
should be taken for, and by, Brazil's workers. He had been
a Communist collaborator while a Federal Deputy and had
continued to work very closely with the Communists after
being designated as Minister of Labor by Goulart, either
because of his ideological convictions or because of his own
ideas of political opportunism. I doubt that he had the true
interests of the workers at heart. And I had obviously failed
to impress him by my frequently reiterated point that Brazil was as much a member of the Alliance as the United
States. I suspect that he was immutable in his fundamental
orientation, and that nothing could have been done to obtain
his collaboration with the Alliance.

The present Minister of Labor is, of course, a very different man from Amino Afonso, and he is undoubtedly anxious to support the objectives of the Alliance in Brazil.   However, the Alliance still faces great difficulty in formulating specific reform and self-help measures to better the welfare of Brazil's laborers.   For while the Communist leaders of the unions have been removed by the Castelo Branco Government, the unions have not yet developed the attitudes and skills necessary for the formulation of the specific kinds of social measures which would be in the best interests of their own members.

3.   Generalissimo Rafael Trujillo had been dictator of the Dominican Republic from 1930 until his assassination on May 30, 1961.   His assassination was evidently effected by a group of military officers and civilians whose patience with the tyranny and corruption of the Trujillo regime had been exhausted and who were no doubt influenced by the action taken by the Organization of American States late in 1960 in ejecting the Dominican Republic from the Organization and recommending that each of its members break diplomatic relations with, and impose economic sanctions against, that country until it ceased being a threat to inter-American peace.   For a time after the assassination there was considerable turmoil within the Dominican Republic and there was some doubt as to the kind of government which would ultimately prevail.   However, free elections were finally held in December, 1962, with Juan Bosch the victor, and high hopes were held within the U. S. Government that the Dominican Republic might soon become a model demonstrating how well the Alliance for Progress could work under a Government genuinely concerned with economic and social development and generously assisted by the United States and the other countries and agencies associated with the Alliance.

The Alliance did in fact have some initial successes in the Dominican Republic.   However, the high hopes that many of us had had for quick, major, and demonstrable successes were not realized, and the political disturbances which soon came to dominate that country wiped out such progress as had initially been achieved.   The following were some of the principal difficulties confronting those who were seeking to promote the success of the Alliance in that country after the demise of Trujillo:

(a) The establishment of free elections and Bosch's assumption of office in March, 1963, did not usher in a
period of political stability, as had been hoped. Perhaps it had been too much to expect that any people,
suddenly thrown on their own politically after more
than thirty years of dictatorship, would quickly settle
down into the kinds of political discipline called for in
a successfully functioning democracy. Or perhaps political passions were excessively inflamed by Bosch's
enormous conceit and the violent temper and intransi-
gence he displayed during his frequent radio addresses
and on other occasions, when he felt that his opinions
or motivations were being questioned. Or perhaps his
tolerance of the political activities of the Communists
and other leftists of the Dominican Republic was too
frightening. In any case, there was serious political
unrest in the country almost from the day he took office, and finally he was deposed by a military coup
d'etat on September 25, 1963, after only seven months
in office.

(b) For all of his intellectual brilliance, Bosch was an
extremely poor administrator. He had virtually no concept of the need to delegate authority or the need to allocate the different responsibilities of government among
his Cabinet officers as sharply as possible, so that each
Minister would have a reasonably clear idea of what he
was expected to do. Bosch surrounded himself with a
large number of separate personal advisors (each of
whom thought he alone was the truly important advisor),
and Bosch retained the right to make all decisions, even
the most trivial; his Cabinet officers had little authority
and little morale. Perhaps they did not warrant more
confidence and more authority. However, I suspect that
Bosch would have had little confidence in any subordinates. I remember, for example, a conversation with him
early in 1963, just after he had been elected, but before
he took office. I was asking him how he proposed to allocate certain specific responsibilities among his Cabinet
officers, and his reply to every question was, "That's an
important subject. I will handle it myself." The Alliance
for Progress is a highly intricate venture, and I am convinced that its prospects for success in any country will
be handicapped unless a large number of different talents
are brought to bear on it.

(c) A shortage of specific projects--projects formulated in sufficient detail to permit the intelligent expenditure of funds--plagued both the Bosch Government and the military junta which succeeded Bosch. The Trujillo Government had had little interest in either economic or social development and even that part of the bureaucracy which stayed on after Trujillo's assassination had neither training nor experience in the formulation of the necessary projects.

(d) It has been estimated that only about 40 per cent of the population under Trujillo was literate. The bearing of this fact on the Alliance for Progress may be seen in the fact that the economic development of a country is dependent above all else upon the development of the people of that country. Education is not only one of the major social objectives of the Alliance. It is also one of the principal prerequisites for economic development, and education cannot be achieved quickly, however intensively any government works for its achievement. This problem is serious almost everywhere in Latin America, but the problem in the Dominican Republic is among the worst.

The intricacies and inherent difficulties of the Alliance for Progress, some of which were illustrated by the foregoing case histories, have led me to the conclusion that much more must be done than has yet been done if the Alliance is to move forward as it should, and as the security and well-being of the entire Free World require. It is essential that several nongovernmental sectors of the Free World involve themselves deeply in promoting the success of the Alliance. It is essential that a major drive or series of drives be undertaken to promote achievement of a consensus of agreement among and within the countries participating in the Alliance concerning certain of the concepts upon which the Alliance is founded. It is essential that the Latin Americans themselves accept responsibility for making the truly critical decisions pertaining to implementation of the Alliance--and by "truly critical" decisions I do not mean the ultimate decisions as to which countries should get how much foreign financial aid.

In the United States and in most other countries of the Free World, the public at large insists that the role of the federal government be limited only to those activities which are necessary. Disputes are constantly taking place over the question of

whether any specific activity by the government is, or is not,
"necessary," but few dispute the general thesis that the government must not be allowed to undertake activities which private
citizens are able and willing to do better, or even as well, if
left to their own devices. Yet no significant sector of the
American public (or that of any other Free World country)
has shown any disposition to take an active part in furthering
the Alliance, despite the fact that there is a great deal that
the public can do to further the Alliance that the U.S. Government cannot do as well and, in many cases, cannot do at
all.

To be sure, the public's failure to play its proper role
in the Alliance has doubtless been due, in very large part if
not entirely, to the fact that the complexity and importance
of the Alliance has not been understood even in the United
States, and the public has not appreciated the nature and significance of the role it should be playing. I hope that this
book will help clarify the issues at stake and help galvanize
the American public into active and effective support of the
Alliance. I know of no area where it is more critical that
the public transform its faith in private initiative from lip
service into vigorous action.

Public involvement in the Alliance is critical, above all
else, for the indispensable support it can give to the ideological foundations of the Alliance. There is no quarrel anywhere
with the need for the more rapid economic and social development of Latin America. And there has been remarkably little
disagreement, except among the Marxists, over the measures
to be employed for achieving that objective, as spelled out in
the basic inter-American documents which established the
Alliance. However, those measures were necessarily phrased
in fairly general terms, and considerable disagreement and
uncertainty have prevailed over the specific measures needed to
implement the Alliance. It has proven all too easy to dismiss
such disagreement and uncertainty as being "merely technical" in character, the implication being that satisfactory decisions on the questions at issue would be expected to follow in
fairly short order either after the technicians had completed
their job or after confusion among the technicians had demonstrated that political leaders were, after all, sufficiently well-
qualified to "brush away the details" and to resolve these matters once they set their minds to doing so. Unfortunately, the
truth of the matter is that disagreements over "technical"

matters have for the most part reflected disagreements over basic policy alternatives rather than over mere details. The disposition on the part of many of the Alliance leaders to sweep such disagreements under the carpet has no doubt helped prevent acrimonious debate, and may even have been politically necessary during the formative stages of the Alliance. But if the rate of progress under the Alliance is to accelerate, it is critical that the differences among and within the Alliance members over basic policy issues be faced and resolved. And various sectors of the American public can do a great deal to help assure satisfactory resolution of those issues. More specifically, they can do a great deal to help clarify the meanings of such concepts as "self-help" and "reform." No one can oppose the desirability of those concepts in the abstract any more than anyone can oppose the desirability of justice, but determination of the specific measures which would constitute self-help and reform has been a highly controversial and almost completely unresolved issue of the Alliance.

Ultimately, however, the basic policy issues of the Alliance can be resolved only by the Latin Americans themselves, even though ideological assistance to them from foreign governmental and nongovernmental sectors will be indispensable. The success of the Alliance depends upon the fullest possible assumption of responsibility by the Latin Americans for that success. And this will entail, above all, assumption of responsibility by the Latin Americans for resolving the basic policy issues now dividing them. It is the Latin Americans alone who can effectively determine, for example, the specific degrees of income tax progression which are both politically feasible and appropriate for achievement of tax equity and other objectives in each of their countries. It is they alone who can effectively determine the specific financial, trade, and other policies appropriate in each of their countries for promoting economic integration of the region. It is they alone who can determine the specific measures which are both appropriate and politically feasible in their separate countries for creating a climate in which private investment is likely to flourish.

It is only when the Latin American leaders of the Alliance squarely face these and many other equally difficult "technical" issues and make a really serious effort to resolve them that the accelerated economic and social development of Latin America through appropriate self-help and reform measures will be as-

sured. Furthermore, it is only after meaningful standards by
which to measure self-help and reform have been established
that foreign governments and financial agencies will have satisfactory gauges by which to measure the level of financial assistance which might appropriately be extended, under the broader
Alliance concepts, to each of the Latin American countries.

I do not mean to suggest that the success of the Alliance
depends exclusively upon resolution of technical issues. Though
it is true that technical issues lie at the base of many of the Alliance's difficulties and must be resolved, it is also true that
the heart of the Alliance is essentially spiritual. Thus political
turbulence in Latin America has derived in large part from the
economic and social distress prevailing throughout that region,
and Marxist concepts have increasingly acquired adherents as
despair has increased over the apparent inefficacy of democratic institutions and international democratic alignments to
overcome that distress. A war of ideologies between Marxism
and the Alliance for Progress is raging in Latin America and
it is crucial for the Free World that the Alliance be victorious.
I hope that the analyses and recommendations of the ensuing
pages will make a contribution toward that victory.

The most important suggestions which others have made for
strengthening the Alliance and which deserve full analysis elsewhere, are summarized briefly below:

1. On April 12, 1965, four outstanding Latin Americans--
Raul Prebisch, Director General of the Latin American Institute
for Economic and Social Planning; Jose Antonio Mayobre, Execu-
tive Director of the United Nations Economic Commission for
Latin America; Felipe Herrera, President of the Inter-American
Development Bank; and Carlos Sanz Santamaria, Chairman of the
Inter-American Committee on the Alliance for Progress--sent to
each of the Latin American presidents and the President of the
United States their "Proposals for the Creation of the Latin
American Common Market." These Proposals, which received
favorable consideration at the IA-ECOSOC meeting in March-
April, 1966, included recommendations of trade policies, invest-
ment policies, and monetary policies to be adopted by the Latin
American governments and the Inter-American Development
Bank for the establishment and smooth functioning of the common market. In addition, various recommendations were pro-
ferred concerning the principle of reciprocity, the treatment
to be accorded to the relatively less developed countries of

Latin America, the measures needed to deal with the internal
dislocations that might arise in the process of liberalizing
trade, and measures designed to stimulate Latin American
private enterprise within the common market. Finally, the
Proposals included various recommendations for the establishment of institutional machinery for coordination of the
types of action necessary for creation and operation of the
common market.

2. Many Latin Americans have long argued that the
United States Government should extend preferential import
treatment to the export products of Latin America comparable
to the import preferences extended by the United Kingdom
and the European Common Market countries to the export
products emanating from other parts of the world. Considerable attention was devoted to this idea at the Buenos
Aires meeting in March-April, 1966, and the Washington
meeting in June, 1966. The subject was also discussed
at the meeting of the Presidents of the American nations,
held in April, 1967.

3. Latin Americans have frequently urged that the
United States Government "liberalize" the conditions which
it has established for obtaining and utilizing AID and Export-
Import Bank loans. Particular emphasis was placed on this
subject at the Buenos Aires meeting where the argument was
made that AID has been unrealistic in its demands for Latin
American "self-help" as a prerequisite for loans and that both
AID and the Export-Import Bank should relax their barriers
to the utilization of loan dollars for purchases other than in
the United States.

4. On May 10, 1966, Senator Robert Kennedy proposed
on the floor of the Senate that there be various revisions of
United States Government policy toward Latin America, including a proposal that the level of aid to that area be increased
to approximately the level of the postwar U. S. aid to Europe
under the Marshall Plan.

PART

I

THE NATURE OF THE CHALLENGE

CHAPTER 1 THE ANTECEDENTS OF THE ALLIANCE

World War II was not the cataclysm for Latin America that it was for the rest of the world. However, its effects upon that area were nonetheless profound in many respects, especially psychologically. It changed the way Latin Americans looked upon themselves and upon their relationships with the rest of the world. It gave a powerful impetus to deep economic, social, and political changes in almost every country of the area. Ultimately, it made an Alliance for Progress a necessity if Latin America was to be preserved as part of the Free World.

Before the war, Latin America was very much on the outskirts of world affairs. It was affected by developments in other parts of the world--as reflected, for example, in the sharp decline of world markets for Latin American products during the 1930's--but it had little influence upon such developments. The Good Neighbor Policy of President Franklin Delano Roosevelt had succeeded in overcoming many of the strains previously existing between Latin America and the United States, and inter-American relations were generally good, although many Latin Americans felt stronger bonds of kinship within some European countries, especially Germany and Italy. Europe accounted for a larger percentage of the foreign trade of several of the Latin American countries than the United States, and European private investments exceeded those of the United States in several countries. Income levels were low throughout the region and the general public appeared reconciled to the perpetuation of low income levels, except in Argentina and Mexico. There was political unrest everywhere, but dictatorships were the rule rather than the exception, and the political unrest rarely posed any threat to the fundamental economic and social structures then prevailing. Marxism had many converts among the intellectuals, but had not yet captured a foothold among the general public, again excepting Mexico.

25

The war changed all that. Trade with Europe was suddenly severed. The United States became the purchaser of almost all of Latin America's exports and the supplier of almost all of its imports. All of the Latin American governments broke off diplomatic relations with the Axis countries and then declared war on them, despite the fact that some of them had earlier been sympathetic to the Axis. The Brazilian Government sent an expeditionary force into action in the Italian theater, and while none of the others became involved in actual combat, Latin America as a whole had the sense of active and important participation, if only through the enforcement of "economic warfare" measures such as the establishment of various types of control over the conduct of the German-, Italian-, and Japanese-owned companies within their borders. They felt also that they were making an important contribution to the Allied cause by their exportation to the United States of copper, manganese, quartz crystals, and other critical raw materials (all at U.S. price ceilings) as well as by their exportation (again at U.S. ceilings) of sugar, coffee, and other consumer goods in great demand during the war.

Supply shortages and rationing abroad plus shipping difficulties kept Latin America's imports at a very low level during the war. As one important result, most Latin American countries experienced substantial balance-of-payments surpluses which led to the accumulations of large gold and foreign exchange reserves. Perhaps even more important, some Latin American countries learned that they could profitably produce certain commodities which they had previously been importing. Their aspirations for industrialization no longer seemed unrealistic. Indeed, extravagant notions of the feasibility of rapid industrialization became widespread.

None of the Latin American countries eliminated the import or foreign exchange controls that were in effect at the end of the war. The latent demand for imports was huge, due to a wide variety of interrelated facts, especially: the accumulated demand for consumer goods (including automobiles, refrigerators, etc.) which the Latin Americans themselves had not yet begun to produce; the need to replace worn-out machinery parts; the wartime expansion of monetary incomes and savings combined with a general reluctance to permit depreciation of the foreign exchange values of their currencies; and the need for capital equipment to expand industrialization. The fact that war-induced scarcities and war-induced controls had facilitated the wartime industrialization made a deep impression, leading the people of many countries to believe that their governments could and should facilitate continued industrialization by carefully planned rationing of the accumulated gold and foreign exchange reserves and in other ways. The concept of government planning for economic development had become much more popular than it had been before the war.

In fact, the pace of industrialization did step up rapidly, though unevenly, after the war. Despite the much-criticized erosion of the purchasing power of the accumulated gold and foreign exchange reserves because of the postwar price increases in the United States and other countries, and despite the generally poor administration of the import controls, there is no doubt that much of the postwar industrial investment in Latin America was financed out of the accumulated reserves. Much of it was financed also by the large increase in the level of Latin America's export earnings as the prices of many of its major export commodities escalated. Moreover, there was a tremendous increase in the scale of foreign private investment in several countries of the area, resulting largely from the fact that U.S. and other foreign businessmen saw the profit opportunities in the government-sheltered internal markets just as clearly as the Latin American businessmen saw them.

Meanwhile, the attention which the United States Government had directed toward Latin America during the war very largely withered away. Our preoccupation with the military and political threats of Communism in Europe and the Far East led to mammoth grants of economic and military aid to those parts of the world while we saw little need to help Latin America. To be sure, we sent large numbers of Government employees to Latin America to provide technical assistance under our "Point Four" program, and that assistance was both helpful and appreciated. Moreover, the Export-Import Bank of Washington greatly expanded its lending activities for economic development projects in Latin America. However, the dimension of such loans was tiny as compared with our grants to Europe under the Marshall Plan, and many Latin Americans focussed with considerable displeasure on this comparison as well as on the fact that the assistance to Europe was in the form of gifts whereas the Latin Americans were expected to repay the Export-Import Bank loans despite the relative poverty of the Latin Americans.

Although the growing coolness of many Latin Americans
toward the United States during the fifteen years following the
war must be ascribed to many factors, I believe that the growing feeling of something like unrequited love was paramount.
While recognizing that their role in the Allied war effort was
relatively minor, most Latin Americans felt that their role
was nevertheless important. Moreover, they felt that they
had contributed all that could reasonably have been expected of
them and that their contribution had been appreciated. At the
same time, they were greatly impressed with the virility and
power of the United States and by the high moral qualities of a
nation that, during the midst of a terrible war, could dedicate
itself as we did to the creation of a postwar world based on
justice and freedom from want. Their pride in the wartime
partnership was great, as were their hopes for the continuation
of that partnership after the war. Hence their deep disappoint-
ment--their feeling of having been cast aside--when they perceived that, the war being over, the United States had little
further interest in maintaining any partnership with them.
Imagine their chagrin at finding that the United States was far
more interested in promoting the reconstruction of even the
defeated members of the Axis than it was in promoting the
development of Latin America!

It would be a gross distortion to say that the Latin Americans measured our postwar friendship for them in terms of
our aid to them as compared with our aid to other parts of the
world. Most Latin American leaders understood our concern
over the Communist menace in Europe and the Far East, and
respected us--even admired us--for the assistance we gave to
the countries threatened by that menace. However, it was a
difficult psychological strain to accept the fact that the United
States was unwilling to distribute any significant portion of its
immense bounty of the early postwar years to the Latin Americans, who felt that they had been our true friends and who
accordingly considered themselves to be as deserving of help
as the people of Europe. They welcomed our efforts to promote the reconstruction of Europe, but pointed out that the
success of those efforts would increase the already large dis-
parity between the income levels of Europe and those of Latin
America unless we also tried to promote the economic development of the latter.

More was at issue, furthermore, than just the question
of aid. Deep psychological scars were left also by the many

other ways in which the United States Government rejected
Latin American overtures for economic and political collaboration.   Thus, we refused to participate in any of several
proposals to help stabilize the prices of the major raw material export commodities of Latin America, despite the
sharp downturn which many of those prices experienced
after their initial postwar rise; in an inter-American economic conference in 1954, for example, we rejected a Latin
American proposal to help stabilize such prices on the
ground that accepting any such proposal would be a threat
to private enterprise.   Until 1958, furthermore, we consistently rejected every proposal for an inter-American bank
on the ground that none was needed.   And we threw buckets
of cold water on the 1958 proposal by President Kubitschek
of Brazil for an "Operation Pan America" in which the United
States would collaborate economically and politically with
the twenty Latin American republics in a joint effort to promote
the economic development of that area.

     The offhanded way in which we rejected the Latin Ameri-
can proposals during that period was in some respects even
more painful to them than the fact of rejection.   We uniformly manifested the attitude of being annoyed by the importuni-
ties of the Latin Americans.   We conveyed the impression that
our negative responses were virtually automatic and could be
reversed only by pressure, not reason.   We repeatedly stated
that the problems of Latin America were of its own making,
that private foreign and domestic investment would overcome
those problems, if only the Latin Americans would stop discouraging such investment.   We were ungracious even in the
cold manner with which we approved the very helpful loans
extended by the Export-Import Bank.   In general, our eyes
were turned toward Europe and the Far East, and the American
public as a whole seemed to be taking it for granted that the
alignment of Latin America with us and the rest of the Free
World would continue forever.   Our news media devoted very
little space to Latin American affairs except for coverage of
the more violent political upheavals, which were generally interpreted as being in some sense endemic to the area and of
little fundamental significance.

     The violently unfriendly reception accorded to Vice Presi-
dent Nixon in Peru and Venezuela in 1956 and the Castro takeover
in Cuba in January, 1959, provided a rude awakening of the
people of the United States as to what was really taking place in

Latin America. It was as though a veil had been torn away, revealing an unhealthy and frustrated continent where revolutionary forces were at work which not only could pull that continent away from the rest of the Free World, but also could pose a serious threat to the peace and security of the United States. We suddenly became aware of the fact that the postwar boom had subsided in many countries and had been replaced by economic stagnation, with the exhaustion of their gold and foreign exchange reserves and the decline of their export earnings; that inflation was widespread, aggravating the serious social and economic tensions; that Marxist concepts had captured the minds of a large portion of the leaders and the people of many countries; that powerful movements were afoot to collaborate with the Iron Curtain countries politically and economically or "only" to adopt "neutralist" or "independent" foreign policies; and that the bounds of allegiance to Pan-Americanism and the rest of the Free World were near the breaking point. We suddenly realized that we might have to pay a very high price for our longtime neglect of that region.

Our reactions to our newly acquired knowledge were impressive, though uncoordinated. In August, 1958, Under Secretary of State Douglas Dillon announced the readiness of the United States to join in the creation of an inter-American bank, reversing our long-standing opposition to such a bank; the Inter-American Development Bank accordingly was established in April, 1959. Then, in July, 1960, President Eisenhower announced that the United States Government would be willing to help finance social development projects in Latin America to help relieve the social inequities of the area, thereby moving away from our traditional emphasis upon economically productive projects and private investment. This was followed at an inter-American conference in Bogota, Colombia, in September, 1960, by the commitment of the United States delegation (headed by Under Secretary Dillon and Assistant Secretary of State Thomas Mann) to provide loans and grants totalling $400 million for social development projects; in turn, the Latin American delegations committed their governments to institute reforms in agriculture, housing, taxation, and education so as to permit effective utilization of the U.S. assistance.

The Republican and the Democratic candidates for the presidency each gave considerable emphasis during the 1960 campaign to the need for a much more vigorous and imaginative program of action in Latin America. Then, on March 13, 1961, President Kennedy convened the Latin American ambassadors at the White

House where he announced that the United States would like to join with the countries of Latin America in a new "Alliance for Progress" dedicated to the economic and social development of Latin America and the strengthening of its democratic institutions. He stressed that a major ingredient in this Alliance would necessarily have to consist of the measures taken by the Latin Americans to help themselves, but he implied that the United States Government was ready to commit itself to facilitate the success of those measures through the extension of large-scale financial aid over a period of several years.

President Kennedy's proposal of an Alliance for Progress electrified the continent. Coming as it did within six weeks after his inauguration, it was taken as evidence of a sharp revision of U.S. policy and as the augury of a great improvement in inter-American relations. The Council of the Organization of American States quickly resolved that the proposal should be considered at a Special Meeting of the Inter-American Economic and Social Council. Preparations for the meeting were undertaken by officials of the U.S. Government, officials of several Latin American governments, staff members of the OAS, the President of the Inter-American Development Bank (Dr. Felipe Herrera), and the Secretary of the United Nations Economic Commission for Latin America (Dr. Raul Prebisch). The Ministers of Finance or Economy of the United States and the twenty Latin American republics, plus the representatives of the various inter-American organizations and many nongovernmental representatives, then convened for the Special Meeting of the IA-ECOSOC at Punta del Este, Uruguay, during August 5-17, 1961.

On August 17, the chief delegates of the governments of the United States and nineteen Latin American republics (all except Cuba) formally inaugurated the Alliance for Progress by approving its basic documents: a "Declaration to the Peoples of America" and "The Charter of Punta del Este Establishing an Alliance for Progress within the Framework of Operation Pan America." No one who was present could have failed to be impressed by the excitement of the occasion. A new era was dawning, and everyone knew it. Some of the delegates may have been skeptical about one feature of the Alliance or another, but there was no question about the general enthusiasm for the Alliance as a whole.

To be sure, the Cuban delegation--headed by the outspokenly pro-Communist "Che" Guevara--did not share the general enthusiasm.

Cuba did not subscribe to either the Declaration or the Charter.
It is interesting to note, however, that despite the flamboyance
and extravagance which characterized all of Guevara's many
statements during the meeting and despite his scorn for the
Alliance's emphasis on private enterprise, he steadily avoided
any attack on the Alliance, per se. He never denied that the
Alliance would be helpful, limiting himself instead to the claim
that adoption of socialism and close collaboration with the Communist countries would permit more rapid achievement of the
Alliance objectives than reliance on private enterprise and collaboration with the United States. In fact, it was not until the
final day of the meeting that he revealed that Cuba would not
join the Alliance. And it is especially noteworthy that he did
so only after he had pointedly asked Secretary of the Treasury
Dillon (the United States chief delegate) whether Cuba would be
eligible for U. S. aid if it joined the Alliance and after Secretary Dillon had replied that Cuba would not be eligible for such
aid as long as it remained a Communist country and a threat
to the security of the hemisphere.

The fact that the Cuban people are not participating in
the Alliance is deplorable. But their present Government could
not have adhered to the Alliance in good faith even if the other
governments had welcomed its adherence. Among other things,
Fidel Castro and his Government could hardly have subscribed
to the statement, expressed in the Declaration to the Peoples of
America, that

> This Alliance is established on the basic principle
> that free men working through the institution of
> representative democracy can best satisfy man's
> aspirations, including those for work, home and
> land, health and schools. No system can guar-
> antee true progress unless it affirms the dignity
> of the individual which is the foundation of our
> civilization.

Nor could he and his Government have agreed with the declared
goal of the Alliance, as likewise expressed in the Declaration,

> To stimulate private investment in order to en-
> courage the development of Latin American coun-
> tries at a rate which will help them to provide
> jobs for their growing populations, to eliminate
> unemployment, and to take their place among the
> modern industrialized nations of the world.

CHAPTER **2** THE BEGINNING
OF THE
CHALLENGE

Examination of the understanding reached at Punta del
Este will reveal that the Alliance for Progress represents an
innovation of tremendous significance in inter-American relations. It has restored the wartime partnership, but this time
the common enemy is poverty, insecurity, injustice, totali-
tarianism, paternalism, and personal indignity in Latin America. The Latin Americans have dedicated themselves to the
arduous and painful recomposition of their separate and collective economic and social structures, and to the strengthening of their democratic institutions. The United States has
dedicated itself to support the Latin Americans in that effort
and in doing so has cast aside its long-standing and patroni-
zing attitude that all the Latin Americans need to do is to
emulate the economic and political policies which have worked
so well in the United States. The role of the United States
in the Alliance is very important and the people of the United
States subscribe as fully to the fundamental objectives of the
Alliance as the people of Latin America do. But Latin American
inspiration permeates all of the major mechanisms and instrumentalities of the Alliance, and it is the Latin Americans themselves who carry the ultimate responsibility for its fate.

It is small wonder that the Latin American representatives
at the first IA-ECOSOC's annual review of the Alliance for Progress during October, 1962, in Mexico City, were frequently
heard saying: "This is our Alliance. We must make it succeed."
I was deeply impressed by the almost unanimous voice with which
the Latin Americans expressed their devotion to the Alliance because of its critical bearing upon the welfare of their separate
countries and because of its significance for inter-American relations. The official report covering the proceedings of that
conference accurately reflected the spirit shown there when it
stated that,

> For the first time in the history of the inter-
> American system, the countries participating
> in the Alliance have met in an open forum to
> examine and discuss each other's economic
> and social programs, and their policies and
> problems, in a spirit of mutual confidence
> and cooperation. This precedent of mutual
> review of the progress made and the difficul-
> ties encountered will, in the coming years, spur
> countries into common action for solving
> common problems.

The Alliance has, in fact, chalked up many impressive and encouraging signs of forward movement. However, it cannot be said that all is going well with the Alliance. [1]

In November, 1963, the Ministerial representatives at the second annual review of the Alliance in Sao Paulo, Brazil, stated that "The region as a whole has continued to advance toward achievement of the goals of the Charter of Punta del Este," but that

> however important may be the outlook for
> production, investment, and trade--crucial
> means in determining the success of the Alliance--
> it is equally important to evaluate the direction
> in which the countries are moving socially
> and politically. In this connection, only a
> cautious optimism is in order; for, however
> great may be the efforts already made in
> some countries and however encouraging it
> may be that all members of the Alliance are
> trying to meet the obligations they assumed
> in Punta del Este, one cannot but be con-
> cerned with the slowness with which many
> countries are overcoming obstacles to the
> profound changes in institutions, policies,
> and internal structures that will be necessary
> to make the Alliance a living reality.

It is an important fact that the situation described at that time is as true today as it was then. Almost all of the speeches delivered at the fourth Ministerial review of the Alliance in Buenos Aires in March-April, 1966, emphasized the need for increased political support for the Alliance with-in the Latin American countries, and included statements

such as the following by Edgardo Seone Corrales, outgoing
President of the IA-ECOSOC:

> The progress which has clearly been obtained is
> nevertheless not a tendency which has been gen-
> eralized in a satisfactory degree and appears
> to be threatened by forces which are tending
> to debilitate it ... (among other things) per
> capita food production increased (during
> 1961-65) by only 3 per cent. This indicates,
> if one takes into account the very low indices
> of nutrition of the great majority of the Latin
> American population, that without a great and
> decisive effort, misery, particularly in the
> rural areas, will make every development
> effort fail and will put the peace and security of
> the continent into jeopardy . . . The retardation
> of the agricultural sector has an intimate rela-
> tionship to the prevailing disequilibrium in the
> structure of landholdings. . . . (The Secretariat
> data) show that agrarian reform... virtually has
> not begun in Latin America.

By Juan Carlos Pugliese, incoming President of the IA-
ECOSOC:

> Five years of Alliance have permitted only timid
> advances along the road of solid construction.

By Jose A. Mora, Secretary General of the OAS:

> The Alliance for Progress must abandon its
> predominantly academic position, essentially
> governmental and technical, by translating it
> into the language and interpretation of the
> common man. ... We must aspire that the
> doctrine have a continuous replanting and
> that it be thought of and evaluated not only
> within economic, social, or cultural scopes,
> but also within political scopes. ... The es-
> sential element of all development is the
> formation of human resources, simultaneously
> with the formation of capital. In this sense,
> the situation of Latin America continues to be
> critical. The efforts being made are insuffic-
> ient.

By Roberto Campos, Brazil's Minister of Planning and Economic Coordination:

> The original ambition of making of the Alliance a
> "nation mystique" has not been realized.

Since the time of the Punta del Este conference, military coups have overthrown the governments of Argentina, Peru, Ecuador, Guatemala, Honduras, the Dominican Republic, Brazil, and Bolivia. The fact that democratically elected government subsequently came to office in some of these countries and that free elections have been promised in the others has not fully compensated for the damage done by the coups to the image of the Alliance. Nor has the image of the Alliance been promoted by the political turmoil which has continued to prevail in some countries or the tyranny which has continued to prevail in Haiti. Revolutionary sentiment is important to a greater or lesser degree in almost every Latin American country, and the Alliance for Progress has nowhere become identified in the minds of the people as a practical mechanism, or as the most attractive of alternative mechanisms, for satisfying their aspirations.

In September, 1962, the Alliance's Panel of Experts sent a deeply perceptive report to the IA-ECOSOC depicting what they called the Alliance for Progress "crisis" and recommending various measures for overcoming it. The following comments about the "crisis" remain as accurate today as they were then and deserve to be quoted at length:

> Reading the editorials in the most important
> newspapers of the hemisphere, listening to
> the opinions expressed in the national con-
> gresses, judging from the comments made
> by the responsible leaders of economic ac-
> tivities or enterprises in all the countries,
> noting the scarcity of favorable expressions
> of public opinion in the hemisphere, heeding
> the critical opinions expressed at the Con-
> ference on Tensions Affecting Development
> in Latin America, held in Bahia, and, finally,
> considering the skeptical or critical attitude
> taken by high government officials one may
> well conclude that the Alliance for Progress
> is indeed encountering serious difficulties...
> (It) has not yet had the political and psycho-

logical impact that it should--whether because
the problems are extremely complex, because
the situations of the Latin American countries
are more difficult than they seem, because
the program in itself does not have popular
support, because external aid has not been as
quickly effective as hoped, or because the
governments are not in a position to fully
carry out their obligations....

None of the earlier programs of international cooperation had stated the problems af-
flicting Latin America more accurately or with
greater understanding. Nor had any of them
approached the problem in such an all-in-
clusive way or included among means of action
so many solutions that incorporate the thinking
of government leaders and statesmen of Latin
America. The objectives of the Alliance for
Progress respond to the most deeply felt
needs of the people of Latin America. Nevertheless, an atmosphere of frustration, and a
sense of "crisis" has grown up around it.

It seems all too clear that the Free World is confronted
by a crucial challenge. After many years of having kept its
eyes and ears closed to the problems of Latin America, the
U.S. Government has entered into a truly inspired Alliance
to bring about the economic and social development of that
region. As a whole, the separate partners in the Alliance
are sincerely trying to fulfill the responsibilities they assumed at Punta del Este--and with some success. Yet, there
has been widespread criticism that progress on fundamental
reform has been disappointingly slow and that the Alliance
has had little political or psychological impact. There is a
growing concern, which I share, that unless and until the
people of Latin America take the Alliance to their hearts, the
danger will continue to persist that Marxist or other totalitarian
and illusory "solutions" to the problems of the area will be
adopted. It is very important not only that the ultimate objectives of the Alliance be furthered as rapidly as possible, but also that the people of Latin America acquire reasonable confidence in the achievement of those objectives. The perpetuation
of Latin America within the Free World is at stake.

I had been associated with the Alliance for Progress from
the time of its inception until mid-August 1963, when I joined
a private business firm. In September,1961,I had returned to
Washington as Director of the Latin American Division of the
Treasury Department after having served six years as Financial Attaché of the American Embassy in Rio de Janeiro and
after having been a member of the U.S. Delegation to the Punta
del Este Conference in August of that year.   Then, in May,
1962, I was transferred to the State Department where I held
two concurrent positions, one as Deputy Assistant Secretary
for Inter-American Affairs and the other as Deputy Assistant
Administrator of the Agency for International Development (AID)
with responsibility for economic coordination of AID's Alliance
for Progress activities.   My sense of the high privilege I had in
serving in those capacities was constantly reinforced by my
appreciation for the profound devotion to the Alliance which was
demonstrated by my superiors and by my other colleagues in
the U.S. Government as well as by a great many officials of
the Latin American governments and the various inter-American
institutions.   At the same time, however, I was constantly
distressed by the high percentage of our time which we all found
it necessary to spend putting out fires instead of building for
the future--a fact which certainly distressed the very able U.S.
Coordinator of the Alliance, Teodoro Moscoso, no less than it
distressed me.

The economic, social, and political troubles which had
been shaking Latin America for many years did not subside when
agreement was reached for an Alliance for Progress.   Indeed,
some of those troubles were actually aggravated by the impetus
which the Alliance itself has given to changes, albeit peaceful
and democratic changes, in the status quo.   Accordingly, it was
not surprising--though it was disturbing--that so much of our
time and energy had to be spent in trying to alleviate or overcome
the troubles which often appeared to be headed toward dangerous
economic or political crises during that period.   It also was not
surprising that a growing sense of frustration and disappointment
began to disturb many Americans and Latin Americans as they
perceived the difficulty of attaining quickly the fundamental reforms called for by the Alliance.   In fact, doubts became current
as to whether it is "practical" to expect the achievement of fundamental reforms over the opposition of vested interest groups, and
as to whether it is possible even to talk about such reforms without
discouraging private investment in the affected countries.

I admit that I have often shared the widespread feelings of frustration and disappointment over the fact that the Alliance has not progressed more rapidly. I believe that a number of measures must be taken to strengthen the Alliance. However, I believe also that--properly strengthened--the Alliance still is likely to be the salvation of Latin America and of Latin America's partnership in the Free World. I am convinced that it is completely "practical" to expect achievement of the reforms necessary in Latin America and to encourage--not discourage--private investment at the same time.

I am more worried about the Alliance now than ever before, but only because I sense a growing impatience among those who want to see "proof" that it is succeeding and among those who seem ready to interpret almost every sign of new trouble in Latin America as evidence that the Alliance is failing. This impatience is understandable, but it is not justifiable. If allowed to persist, it may undermine the prospects for the ultimate success of the Alliance more effectively than any of the substantive obstacles which confront it. If allowed to persist, impatience can lead to despair and, eventually, resignation to defeat. Short of that, impatience can provoke excessive shuffling of personnel, organizations, and even specific programs of action. All has not gone well with the Alliance, but many good starts have been made and much valuable experience has been gained. This is not the time for the American people to resort to desperate measures to "save" the Alliance. It is the time to redouble our efforts to spur the Alliance forward in the directions in which it is already moving, though too slowly.

This book has three principal objectives:

One is my desire to demonstrate that great patience and perseverance will long continue to be necessary if the critically important Alliance is to succeed. Chapter 3 accordingly describes the aspects in which the Alliance represents a movement which is more complex, more ambitious, and therefore less easily attainable than any comparable movement ever before undertaken by mankind. Chapters 4 and 5 are devoted to a description of the principal problems which must be resolved if the Alliance is to achieve its ultimate objectives.

My second objective is to propose certain specific measures which should be pursued in order to assure the success of the Alliance and, particularly, to assure victory for the Free World in the "war of ideologies" which is raging in Latin America. Some of these measures are necessarily governmental in character. However, my major emphasis is upon the measures which can and should be performed by various nongovernmental sectors of the United States and other parts of the Free World.

The Alliance for Progress is more than an undertaking of the twenty governments which subscribed to it in Punta del Este. It is an undertaking of the peoples who were represented by those governments. Its success depends in part on the conduct of the governments, but even more on the conduct of the various groups--especially the businessmen; the laborers in industry, agriculture, and commerce; and the students--who comprise the nongovernmental sectors. It is reasonable to ask of our Government that it work effectively with the governments of Latin America, but it is not reasonable to require that it accept full, or even predominant, responsibility for influencing the minds and conduct of the people of Latin America. This latter task (which is discussed more fully in Chapter 6) is one which various nongovernmental sectors of the United States are especially well equipped to handle and to which they should be, but are not, devoting a large portion of their minds and their energies.

During my twenty-one years of Government service, I heard and read--and often sympathized with--many complaints about the excessive centralization of responsibility in Washington. In the United States, as in other countries, there are people who almost instinctively turn to the federal government for actions which could be carried out much more effectively by private groups. It is also true, however, that in the United States, as in other countries, the federal government sometimes finds it necessary to take responsibility for certain actions because the private groups that are more competent to do so have not shown either the disposition or the initiative to assume that responsibility. In the specific case of the Alliance for Progress, there are certain functions for which the federal government is necessarily responsible. But there are others which can be handled better--or only--by various private sectors of our country. It is critical that these private sectors manifest both the disposition and the initiative to do so. U.S. universities, for example, can and should pursue the measures proposed in Chapters 7 and 8. The roles which U.S. businessmen, labor groups, and the press can and should perform are discussed in Chapters 9, 10, and 11, respectively. Measures for improving the participation of the U.S. Government, separately and in conjunction with the private sector, are discussed in Chapter 12.

And the respects in which other Free World governments and private institutions can and should contribute to the success of the Alliance is discussed in Chapter 13.

The remainder of the book--Part III and the three appendixes--is designed to meet my third objective: to provide recommendations for revision of the Alliance machinery, with special emphasis on the need of the Alliance machinery to focus on various technical matters.

CHAPTER **3** THE PATH-
BREAKING
ASPECTS

    It is important that the nature of the challenge confronting
the members of the Alliance be understood. Large amounts of
money, new laws, and intelligent men and women dedicated to
the objectives of the Alliance--all these are necessary, but
they are not enough. The Alliance calls for measures of a type
and diversity which mankind has never before undertaken--
measures with respect to which there has accordingly been no
prior experience that could serve as guidance. Deep insight
into the attitudes of the Latin American people, considerable
knowledge of the political, economic, and social problems
confronting them, and imaginative application of the knowledge
and experience acquired in different contexts--all these are
necessary for determining the measures most likely to promote
the success of the Alliance. Furthermore, effective implementation of the appropriate measures depends upon the energetic
collaboration of not only the governments but also the private
sectors of Latin America, the United States, and the rest of
the Free World. The immensity of the task before us and the
need for great patience and perseverance in the performance
of that task will become apparent, if they are not already apparent, as we examine the principal path-breaking aspects of
the Alliance and the major problems which must be resolved.

    As I see it, there are four principal respects in which the
Alliance represents a truly path-breaking venture for mankind.
The first and most important of these is that the Alliance was
designed to create--and then become identified with--a new
mystique, a new set of attitudes toward life, for the Latin
Americans as a whole.

    It was never contemplated by those who signed the Charter
of Punta del Este and the Declaration to the Peoples of America
that the aspirations of the Latin Americans will have been satisfied at the end of the ten year period covered by the Charter.

Even achievement of all of the economic and social targets set
forth in the Charter will leave the average Latin American far
short of the living standards and human dignities to which he
aspires and which we desire for him. However, the Charter
does much more than the setting forth of targets and the provision of guidelines for reaching those targets. It also encourages the average Latin American to hope, and indeed to expect,
a progressively better way of living--better than what he has
now and better than he would have under any social, political,
or economic system which would call upon him to deliver his
personal freedoms to the state.

There it is in the Charter and in the Declaration, written,
plainly for all to see: an alliance, in which the people of nineteen Latin American Republics (excluding Cuba) have undertaken to work together and with the people of the United States
to promote the economic and social progress of Latin America.
An alliance, in which the people of the United States seek
nothing for themselves and in which, on the contrary, they have
committed themselves to furnish large amounts of financial assistance to Latin America and to provide several types of additional economic and technical assistance, conditional only upon reasonable measures by the Latin Americans to help themselves. An alliance, the effective implementation of which
will leave the Latin Americans with the self-respect of knowing
that their progress has been due predominantly to their own
efforts. An alliance, which calls for the planning of social
development alongside of economic development and on the
foundation of democratic institutions, with heavy reliance on
private enterprise, foreign as well as domestic.

It is not unreasonable, therefore, to say that the intellectual ingredients of a new mystique were included in the Charter
of Punta del Este and the Declaration. Unfortunately, however,
it must be conceded--in fact, it must be stressed--that the mystique has not caught fire. I doubt that more than a tiny percentage of the people of Latin America has even heard of, let alone
read, either the Charter or the Declaration. The Alliance for
Progress continues to be understood as just another name for
U.S. financial assistance. The signatories of the Charter of
Punta del Este thought that they had produced a political, as well
as an economic and social, manifesto that would capture the imagination of the people of the continent. In practice, it has captured the imagination of no more than an insignificant percentage
of them.

Meanwhile, the people of Latin America are growing increasingly restive. Tad Szulc has very accurately described
the "winds of revolution"[1] which are blowing with ever greater force in Latin America. The proponents of Marxism are
busily cultivating the soil of the discontent in the area. They
are vigorously converting the persistent disenchantment with
private enterprise, other democratic institutions, and United
States assistance into a rationale for "socialism" and collaboration with the East.

There is no struggle in Latin America more serious than
the struggle of ideas. I share Szulc's belief that, "Despite
the disenchantments and disappointments, a great reservoir
of good will toward the United States, and what it stands for,
still exists."[2] But I also share his principal thesis, which is
to the effect that time is working against us and we must
greatly strengthen our efforts to convince the people of the
continent that the peaceful and democratic revolution embodied
in the Alliance for Progress is preferable to any alternatives.

Latin America has been seized by an intellectual and political fervor. The Alliance for Progress is a unique, path-
breaking venture in the major sense that it is not merely a
negative response to the threat of Communism. It is a highly
imaginative program for demonstrating to the people of that
area that the concepts encompassed within the word, democracy,
are vital concepts, holding drama, meaning, and great promise
for them and for their children.

A second respect in which the Alliance is breaking new
paths is in its emphasis upon planning. The United States has
always felt a certain repugnance toward the concept of planning,
at least as applied to governmental affairs, in view of our association of that concept with state management or state controls of the Russian type. This repugnance used to be shared
by many Latin Americans, but somehow the concept has been
become very popular--in fact, a shibboleth--with them in
recent years, because of its reputed qualities of order over
chaos, husbandry over waste, and foresight over improvisation.

The Charter of Punta del Este has made long-term planning
one of its central themes. It encourages each of the Latin American governments to prepare its own long-term plan for economic and social development, in the expectation that the plan is then
to be submitted to the inter-American Panel of Experts (popularly

identified as "The Nine Wise Men"). The Wise Men, after
evaluating the plan in consultation with the government concerned, are then to issue their own report which, if sufficiently favorable, is expected to serve together with the plan
as the principal basis for attracting U.S. and other foreign
financial support for the development program. No government is obligated to go through this procedure, but it has
been clearly understood that the governments that do so will
have a great advantage over those that do not in obtaining
foreign financial assistance. [3]

Consider the implications. The Latin Americans have
undertaken to maintain democratic institutions, but have at
the same time undertaken to make their central governments
responsible for planning the futures of their economies.
They are relying heavily upon private investment, foreign as
well as domestic, to make their economic plans come true,
even though businessmen everywhere are distrustful of government planners. Foreign assistance is to be geared into
the national development plans, despite the unfavorable investment climates in some of the countries and despite the
fact that the Latin American governments have had very little
experience with either the drafting or the implementation of
such plans. Countries which are suffering serious political
and social disorder are nevertheless being expected to submit to the disciplines of long-term development plans.

This venture into government planning is one of the most
portentious innovations of the Alliance for Progress. I cannot deny that it poses the serious danger of increasing governmental regimentation and dictatorship. On the other hand,
the formulation of development plans had already been started
in some of the Latin American countries before the Alliance
for Progress was undertaken, and I believe it would almost inevitably have spread to the others even had there been no Alliance. Moreover, I believe that the framework of the Alliance has put planning into a perspective it would not otherwise have had--a perspective which offers realistic prospects
for strengthening democratic institutions.

* * * *

The Alliance is breaking new paths for the United States,
and for Latin America, in a third important respect: its objective of development, rather than reconstruction.

Implementation of the Alliance can be facilitated by drawing certain lessons from the experiences of the Marshall Plan
(the European Recovery Plan). Unfortunately, however, the
lessons of the Marshall Plan are for the most part quite inap-
plicable--if not irrelevant, and even misleading--for implementation of the Alliance. For the Marshall Plan was, in my
opinion, a far less difficult task. Not that it was a simple task,
or even that it was "only" concerned with reconstruction. The
Marshall Plan also had important political objectives, though
they were for the most part very different from those of the
Alliance. Moreover, such Marshall Plan projects as the European Payments Union served not only to facilitate reconstruction
of many European industries, but also to promote the growth
of others.

Nevertheless, it must be recognized that the Marshall
Plan was essentially directed toward promoting the recovery of
Europe from the destruction and dislocations of World War II,
whereas the Alliance for Progress is directed toward creating
new industries and in fact new economies.

Let me indicate some of the principal respects in which
the economic problems of the Alliance differ from those of the
Marshall Plan, even at the cost of some oversimplification:

(1) The creation of a new factory where none has existed
before is relatively hazardous because there is no direct experience to rely upon in estimating costs of production.

(2) Skilled labor, experienced technical personnel, and
even experienced management personnel are generally very
scarce in the underdeveloped countries.

(3) Companies contemplating the manufacture of new finished products in underdeveloped countries must often be prepared to manufacture also most or all of the component parts
of those products. Accordingly, the amount of the required
investment will be higher than if the component parts could
be procured from other companies, as is generally possible
in more developed countries. Moreover, the cost of producing the component parts will often be higher than in the
more developed countries where the existence of other markets permits the economies deriving from mass production of
the components.

(4) The existing markets for industrial products are much smaller in the underdeveloped countries of Latin America than in the more developed countries of Europe.   The possibilities of trade among the Latin American countries--and even of trade within some of the larger countries of the area--are greatly handicapped by the large distances between the market centers and by the generally poor transportation facilities.   Probably even more important, moreover, effective markets can exist only where people have incomes adequate to purchase the products they want, and the per capita income in each of the Latin American countries is, of course, very low.

(5) The economies of all the Latin American countries continue to be highly dependent upon the earnings they derive from the exportation of various basic commodities.   Efforts to promote the development of those countries will be greatly impeded, therefore, if the world prices for those commodities continue to fluctuate as widely as they have in the past.

(6) A very large percentage of the population in Latin America has had no, or very little, formal education.   And various types of disease are still sapping their strength and energies.   Yet no country can be strong unless its people have certain minimum levels of education and health.

I have no desire to disparage those who contributed so much to surmount the challenge of the Marshall Plan.   The reconstruction of Europe would not have been possible without their ingenuity, their patience, and their hard work.   However, I consider it important to recognize that the challenge of the Alliance for Progress is of a very different and more complex character.   It requires even greater ingenuity, patience and hard work.

* * * *

The fourth and last of the path-breaking aspects of the Alliance for Progress lies, as I see it, in the fact that the members of the Alliance have undertaken to promote social development alongside of economic development.

It had long been held--in the United States and almost everywhere in Latin America--that the fundamental correction of social malpractices and social inequities could transpire only as a by-product of economic development, and that the Latin Americans should accordingly mobilize their resources, and whatever

foreign sources might be available to them, toward achievement
of the primary objective: economic development. Then, late in
1960, the general concurrence in that conclusion was upset at
the inter-American conference in Bogota, Colombia, where agreement was reached with the concept--championed by the U.S.
Delegation, headed by Under Secretary of State Douglas Dillon--
that social development must be promoted simultaneously with
economic development. This new concept was opposed by some
of the Latin American delegations, led by the Brazilians, but
general agreement with it was finally reached with approval of
the Act of Bogota, facilitated, perhaps, by the U.S. commitment
of $400 million for a social progress fund.

Some disagreement on this subject continued even after approval of the Act of Bogota. Nevertheless, the new concept became a basic principle of the Alliance for Progress, firmly
established in the Charter of Punta del Este. Thus, mankind
has entered upon a new task--the task of overcoming social
distress in countries which have not yet developed economically to the point where they can do so alone.

Having undertaken this task, the Alliance is confronted
by a number of difficult questions which will be discussed more
fully in Part III. I shall mention here just two of them. The
first is that, insofar as the availability of internal and external
resources is limited, there is a possibility of conflict between
the objective of economic development and that of social development: the resources put into the construction of low cost houses,
for example, might alternatively have gone into the construction
of a warehouse. The second is that it is much easier to diag-
nose a social ailment than it is to prescribe a sure cure; indeed,
the wrong medicine--such as an ill-conceived program for land
redistribution, even if labelled land "reform"--might in practice
aggravate the ailment it was designed to cure and might actually
create additional ailments.

CHAPTER **4** THE
ORGANIZATIONAL
PROBLEMS

The fact that the Alliance for Progress contains such formidable pathbreaking aspects has greatly aggravated both its
problems of organization and its problems of implementation. If
history had offered precedents furnishing practical guidelines
for successful organizations and implementations of the Alliance,
we probably would have been able, by now, to say that the Latin
American members have been moving rapidly toward economic
and social progress, arm in arm with one another and with the
United States. We would probably have been able to say that
confidence in the ultimate success of the Alliance is widespread
in Latin America and in the United States.

What do we find instead? There is still almost no recognition among the people of Latin America that the Alliance offers a new way of life, new and reasonable hopes for fulfillment of their material and spiritual aspirations without the loss
of any of their individual and national freedoms. There is very
little understanding of the fact that the success of the Alliance
depends predominantly upon the efforts made within and among
the Latin American countries and very little understanding of
the kinds of efforts required. Each country continues preoccupied with its national problems, with little concern for the
problems of its partners in the Alliance and with little collaboration in meeting common problems. This latter statement
might be qualified by reference to the important collaboration
being effected through the Inter-American Development Bank,
the International Coffee Agreement, the Latin American Free
Trade Area and the Central American Common Market, but it
must be conceded that none of these instrumentalities was con-
ceived--or is generally understood to be--an Alliance for
Progress project.

In general, the people of Latin America continue to think
of the Alliance as a United States aid program. The "self-help"
features of the Alliance are interpreted as requirements im-

posed by the U.S. Government as prerequisites to the receipt of U.S. aid. And while they generally attribute "idealistic" motivations to the United States in proffering the aid and even in requiring certain types of self-help, there are a great many Latin Americans who distrust the motivations behind the aid and, especially, many believe that the basic U.S. motive is to seduce the Latin American governments and people away from pursuit of their "true" national interests. Many believe that the United States Government is concerned primarily with protecting or strengthening the positions of the U.S. -owned firms in Latin America, or with preserving Latin American markets for U.S. exports. Many actually believe that the United States is trying to retard their economic development by inducing them to devote their limited resources to social development or by insisting on financial stability.

Many of the measures necessary to correct these and other misconceptions will be discussed in subsequent chapters. However, I wish to focus here on the special problem of Alliance leadership, because clarification of misconceptions will often depend as much on who does the clarifying as on what he says.

THE NEED FOR LATIN AMERICAN LEADERSHIP

Many of the misconceptions about the Alliance are undoubtedly attributable in large part to the pre-eminent role being played by U.S. Government officials in administering the Alliance. It is not that I have any quarrel with the way the U.S. officials have played their role; they are as intelligent and as dedicated a group of men and women as I have seen anywhere. Nor do I believe that the role of the U.S. officials can be a small one, even under the most ideal circumstances. As long as the Government of the United States continues to honor the commitments it made at Punta del Este, U.S. officials will continue to bear the responsibility for evaluating the merits of requests for U.S. Government loans; and I believe that such evaluations will necessarily pertain not only to the specific projects in question, but also to the question of whether the broader objectives of the Alliance would be furthered by the loans.

Nevertheless, I believe that the role of the Latin Americans in administering the Alliance must be greatly expanded if the Alliance is to succeed. I believe that Latin Americans must be given the responsibility for <u>publicly</u> encouraging, assisting, and, if necessary, prodding one another into improved performance, thereby relieving the United States of its taskmaster function. As soon as possible, furthermore, Latin Americans must be given <u>public</u> responsibility for making certain basic decisions concerning the performance standards which should serve as the major determinants for the division of the total available foreign loan resources among the separate countries of the area--standards which would accordingly manifest <u>their</u> judgments of how, and even where, foreign assistance can be utilized most effectively in furtherance of the Alliance. Moreover, Latin Americans must accept the responsibility of conveying the political, economic and social philosophy of the Alliance to the people of the area.

A number of important processes are already under way toward the necessary "Latinization" of the Alliance:

The Inter-American Development Bank, which was approved in 1958 and formally constituted in 1960, has proven to be an especially effective organization--so much so that it is increasingly becoming known as the "Bank of the Alliance,"[1] even though the loans granted by the Bank have not generally been identified as Alliance for Progress loans, except insofar as they emanate from the Social Progress Trust Fund, which the Bank administers on behalf of the U. S. Government. The man to whom most of the credit must be given for the success of the Bank is Dr. Felipe Herrera, a Chilean who has been the Bank's President since its inception. The Bank's Latin American Executive Directors hold about 60 per cent of the voting power, the remainder being held by the U. S. Executive Director, at present Ambassador True Davis.

Another important institution originally contributing to Latinization of the Alliance was the OAS Panel of Experts, to which reference was made above. The Panel of Experts (generally known as "<u>Los Sabios</u>" or "The Wise Men") were headed for much of the period until they resigned in April, 1966, by another outstanding Chilean, Raul Saez, and consisted of seven Latin Americans, one U. S. citizen, and an Englishman. They were highly regarded for their intelligence, industry, and forthrightness by all who were familiar with their work, and they deserve a great deal of credit for having kept the Alliance on the right track. However, they found it necessary to conduct most of their work inconspicuously, and it cannot be said that they were widely known or appreciated in Latin America.

A third important means for Latinization of the Alliance
was instituted in Mexico City in October, 1962, during the
three-week "Meeting of the Inter-American Economic and
Social Council (IA-ECOSOC) at the Expert Level" and then
the one-week "Meeting of the IA-ECOSOC at the Ministerial
Level." These meetings were devoted to the first annual appraisal of the Alliance for Progress by the various governmental representatives and were characterized by the considerable frankness--particularly during the Expert Level
meeting--of most of the Latin American representatives in
commenting upon the previous year's performance by the other
governments, as well as their own.

Most of the Latin American representatives at those meetings were very convincing in their frequently reiterated expressions of determination to improve upon their national efforts "because, after all, this is our Alliance." Only one session (a night session which continued, like many of the others,
until the small hours of the morning) was devoted to a critical
appraisal of the U.S. Government's participation, almost all of
the other sessions during those four weeks being devoted to
what the Latin American governments had--and had not--been
doing to further the objectives of the Alliance. [2]

The annual meetings of the IA-ECOSOC, the last of which
to date was held in Buenos Aires in March-April, 1966, have
all been highly useful, particularly for the full and frank discussions which they have generated among the leaders of the
various governments. It is regrettable that the most fruitful
discussions have been held behind closed doors, so that little
of what has been said has become known to the general public.
However, it is doubtful that the discussions would have been
as candid and as fruitful if the sessions had all been open to
the public.

The latest important move toward Latinization of the Alliance was made in Sao Paulo, Brazil, in November, 1963, during the IA-ECOSOC meetings at which the second annual ap-
praisals of the Alliance were made. A major topic on the
agenda of those meetings was the proposal for the creation of
a new Committee for Inter-American Development, as recommended separately by ex-President Juscelino Kubitschek of
Brazil and ex-President Alberto Lleras Camargo of Colombia
in June, 1963. There had been certain differences in the rationale offered by the two statesmen, particularly, in regard to

the standards it should follow in exercising those powers. But
they had concurred on a major conclusion: the need for a committee which would increase the extent to which Latin Americans
are responsible--and publicly known to be responsible--for the
course of the Alliance. Agreement was reached at the Sao Paulo
Meetings on the creation of such a committee, to be called the
Inter-American Committee for the Alliance for Progress (CIAP).
I believe that its creation is likely to contribute significantly to
the Latinization of the Alliance, although I also believe (as discussed in Part III) that CIAP has started off on the wrong foot.

It is encouraging to note the steps already taken and those
in process toward Latinization of the Alliance. Much to my
regret, however, I am compelled to conclude that it is unrealistic to expect anything like full Latinization of the Alliance in
the immediate future. I do not believe that the Government
and the people of the United States are prepared to delegate to
the Latin Americans a major share of the authority to determine the eligibility of the countries seeking U.S. Government
loans. And I do not believe that the governments and the people
of Latin America are ready to accept the responsibilities that
would necessarily accompany the types of authority implicit
in the Latinization of the Alliance.

It is important to note that there may be a substantial
amount of interrelationship between the U.S. and Latin
American attitudes. The U.S. might be more willing to
grant authority over U.S. loans to the Latin Americans if the
latter were manifesting a greater sense of responsibility for
the fate of the Alliance. On the other hand, the Latin Americans might have been showing a greater sense of responsibility if they had really felt that the fate of the Alliance was
in their hands; and unfortunately, they have generally felt--
very erroneously--that the fate of the Alliance rests in the
hands of those holding authority over U.S. loans.

The excessive importance still being attributed to U.S.
loans is without doubt one of the most disturbing features of
the present state of the Alliance. I cannot quarrel with the
fact that U.S. loans--plus those of the several international
financial institutions and those of the other capital-supplying
countries of the Western World--are, in fact, important.
They are important as supplements to the limited resources
which the Latin American countries themselves can reasonably be expected to mobilize for their economic and social
development. They are important as catalysts for the effec-

tive mobilization of the internal resources of Latin America. And
they are important as evidence of our desire to be helpful. Indeed, I consider it entirely possible that the time will come when
the people of the United States will want to increase their loans
to Latin America substantially, as those loans become increasingly effective. [3]

In my opinion, however, the question of whether U.S. loan
availabilities should be increased is not the major issue at this
time, though a decrease of those availabilities might well destroy the Alliance by casting serious doubt on the determination
of the United States to honor its Punta del Este commitments.
As I see it, the major issue at this time is how to increase the
effectiveness of U.S. and other international loans, inasmuch
as the measures necessary for that purpose lie at the heart of
the commitments undertaken by the Latin Americans at Punta
del Este. It is in the stimulation of these measures that Latinization of the Alliance would have its greatest impact. The
processes now under way for increasing Latin American authority over the extension of international loans should be pursued
as vigorously as possible. But even this purpose would be promoted by evidence that Latin Americans have assumed the responsibility of promoting the internal measures necessary in
their own interests, i.e., "self-help" and "reform."

I expressed the opinion above that the Latin Americans are
not yet ready to accept the full range of responsibilities that
would be implicit in Latinization of the Alliance. This is not
because I doubt their desire to do so; I am confident that the
desire exists. The problem, rather, lies in the fact that there
is little agreement among the people and governments of Latin
America--or between them, on the one hand, and the people and
Government of the United States, on the other--as to the precise
composition of the self-help and reform measures. There are
important differences of interpretation of many of the key elements
of the Charter of Punta del Este, such as "land reform" and
"tax reform." Moreover, there are even important doubts about
the desirability of some of the provisions of the Charter, such as
those pertaining to financial stability and to the need for private
foreign investments.

In my opinion, the time has come when the partners in the
Alliance must make an intensive effort to resolve the basic differences of understanding which have continued to lie under the
surface of the Alliance. I do not contemplate that the differences
can be resolved quickly or easily; the time and energy which the

U.S. Congress devoted to consideration of the "tax reform" proposed by President Kennedy in 1962 demonstrates some of the difficulties involved. However, I consider that resolution of the basic differences has become critical, not only so that the partners in the Alliance might move together along common paths and in greater harmony, but also so that the Latin Americans selected to provide the necessary leadership will have clearer guidelines of what is expected of them. Part III and the technical appendexes of this book are accordingly designed to help resolve those differences.

THE SCOPE FOR FREE WORLD PARTICIPATION

The membership of the Alliance for Progress is generally understood to comprise the governments of the Latin American Republics (excluding Cuba) plus the United States. After all, it is those governments which undertook the commitments of the Alliance when they signed the Charter of Punta del Este. Nevertheless, I believe it is extremely important that the Alliance elicit much wider participation. The governments of many of the other countries of the Free World could contribute greatly toward the success of the Alliance, particularly in the ideological struggles which are racking Latin America. A great deal could--and must-- also be contributed in this area by the universities, the business organizations, the labor unions, and the press of the United States and other Free World countries. [4]

There is much for the United States Government to do to help the Latin Americans achieve victory for democratic institutions in the war of ideologies taking place there. However, there are many ideological areas in which the U.S. Government is not competent to participate or in which its participation would not be proper. Moreover, much of what it can do will be inadequate to meet the challenge unless it receives much more effective collaboration from the governments and nongovernmental institutions of the United States.

Most of the Western World has come to accept the thesis, without much examination, that Latin America belongs to "the United States Government's sphere of influence" in a partitioned world. This is not the place to discuss all of the implications of that thesis. And I do not wish to call into question the fact that the United States has a very special set of responsibilities vis-a-vis Latin America. Nevertheless, it is important to recognize that those responsibilities are not necessarily preclusive. The entire Free World has a

great deal at stake in the fate of Latin America, and many elements of the Free World, governmental and nongovernmental,
have a great deal to offer in helping protect that stake.

U.S. Government officials conduct many types of formal
and informal relations with the officials of other governments.
This is the usual function of the government officials involved
in foreign affairs, and I believe that our representatives are
generally competent and effective in the performance of this
function, the importance of which should not be disparaged.
However, almost all conversations with the officials of other
governments are for various reasons held in private. The public welfare may be affected by the conversations, but the idea
held by the public will normally be influenced only indirectly
and only in a small degree, if at all.

To be sure, opportunities occasionally arise for U.S.
officials abroad to meet and talk with foreign businessmen,
labor leaders, journalists, professors, students, and others.
Many of our Ambassadors and other officials have made excellent use of such opportunities. Almost invariably, however,
the U.S. officials at such meetings have had to operate under
handicaps severely limiting their effectiveness.

Since it is not normally feasible to establish, and hold to,
fixed agendas for such meetings, the range of questions is generally too great to permit really intensive discussion of any of
them. Moreover, the questions which most interest the public
frequently are those bearing on their own government's policies, and our official representatives must be extremely circumspect in avoiding any statements which might be interpreted as
being critical of the government to which they are accredited. In
fact, our official representatives must be circumspect in avoiding statements which might offend other friendly governments.
For that matter, they normally feel that they must be very cautious even in discussing some issues applying to the United
States, for fear of offending any important segments of U.S
public opinion.

On the other hand, private American citizens representing
separate segments of U.S. life can speak with much greater freedom about most subjects and with much greater authority about
their own specialities. For example, U.S. professors and U.S.
students can engage in much more intensive and conclusive discussions with their Latin American counterparts. Our labor

union representatives can discuss labor practices in the United
States more convincingly than U.S. Government officials who may
be suspected of misrepresenting the facts.   U.S. businessmen
can provide authoritative and illuminating details about the conduct of the U.S.-owned firms abroad.   Our press, including our
books and magazines, capture headlines in the news media of
Latin America daily and can do a great deal to present a more
accurate picture of the United States in Latin America as well
as a more accurate picture of Latin America in the United
States.

Governmental and nongovernmental representatives of
other Free World countries, especially those of western Europe
and Japan, could play a particularly significant role.   A great
many emigrants from those countries have settled in Latin
America, and they and their descendants are often very attentive
to the views emanating from "the old country."   Moreover,
there is a widespread feeling in Latin America that the experiences of certain European countries and Japan are more rele-
vant to the problems of Latin America than are the experiences
of the United States.   Furthermore, Latin Americans will often
be much more open-minded in discussing Marxist doctrines with
representatives of those countries where "socialism" has long
been a respectable, even though controversial, belief than with
representatives of the vociferously anti-Marxist United States.

It is perhaps especially important to be aware of the fact
that many Latin Americans are highly restive under the concept that the great Western powers have sliced up the Free World
and have allocated Latin America to the U.S. Government's
sphere of influence.   Realism compels the Latin Americans to
recognize that they do not have the military strength or, as yet,
the economic strength to constitute a separate "power bloc."   On
the other hand, because of their personal and national pride
they are increasingly balking at the idea that they are pawns to
be moved by any other country or bloc.

The relations between Latin America and the United States
continue to be close, but the fundamental reason for that fact is
spiritual rather than either military or economic.   Latin America needs our military and economic support, but the people of
the area are no more disposed to grant their friendship in exchange for that support than we would be in similar circumstances.   In fact, human psychology being what it is, I consider
it unreasonable to expect any more gratitude for that support from

most Latin Americans than we received from most Europeans
during the Marshall Plan. Among other considerations, most
people believe that it is only "natural" or "right" that they receive help, in times of need, from their wealthier or stronger
friends. Or they believe that those providing the help are doing so because it is in their own interests to help make the re-
cipients stronger and healthier. In fact, it is usually necessary
(as pointed out above) that the U.S. Government make a special
effort to counter any suspicion that the U.S. assistance is somehow designed to promote U.S. interests at the expense of the
basic interests of the recipient.

    The fundamental reason for the fact that relations between
Latin America and the United States have continued to be close
has been the desire for such relations on the part of the people
on each side of the border. It is the intellectual and emotional
bonds between our peoples that have kept us close. Those bonds
in turn are largely intertwined with the intellectual and emotional
bonds which we, on the one hand, and the Latin Americans, on the
other, have maintained with the other countries of the Free World,
particularly in western Europe.

    If our ties with Latin America are to be strengthened, or even
just preserved, the people of Latin America must want those ties
emotionally and must be intellectually convinced that the ties are
in their interests as well as ours. Various focal centers of Ameri
can life must strengthen their separate, though interrelated, bonds
with Latin America. And many sectors of the Free World, other
than those of the United States, must strengthen their bonds with
Latin America. The success of the Alliance for Progress therefor
depends largely upon broader Free World participation, and Part
II will be devoted to the measures necessary to bring this about.

CHAPTER **5** THE PROBLEMS
OF IMPLEMENTATION

The people who have shared the widely prevalent feeling
of impatience with the slow progress of the Alliance have generally attributed that slowness to its defective implementation.
However, it would be at least as reasonable to attribute the
defects of implementation to the feeling of impatience which
has animated the Alliance officials as well as the public at
large. Even many of those who have appreciated the immensity of the path-breaking venture we have undertaken
have felt that progress must "somehow" be achieved rapidly
in order to "prove" the success of the venture. An important
degree of frenzy has influenced the conduct of almost everyone
connected with the Alliance. I consider it remarkable that
the Alliance officials with whom I was associated worked as
effectively as they did, in light of the great and often unreasonable expectations which have surrounded the Alliance ever
since its inception.

The Alliance started off with a loud bang. It received great
publicity when its basic philosophy was expressed in the statement
made by President Kennedy to the Latin American Ambassadors
on March 13, 1961. The publicity remained great for several
months and then was intensified following signature of the Charter
of Punta del Este. It has remained strong, though declining
somewhat both in volume and in enthusiasm.

I believe that, on net balance, the publicity was helpful. Most
importantly, it provided clear manifestation of the fact that the
Government and people of the United States were at last taking
their responsibilities toward Latin America seriously--after what
most Latin Americans consider too many years of neglect, too
many years of blithely taking it for granted that Latin America
would remain within the Free World. The publicity helped awaken
the hopes of many Latin Americans, and to strengthen the flagging
hopes of many others, that a new and better way of life was indeed
possible in the area, under democratic institutions. And it gave
a new burst of energy and some new public support to the many

Latin Americans who were trying to overcome the economic and
social troubles of their countries.

On the other hand, the publicity unquestionably had important negative effects. In emphasizing the objectives of the Alliance and in failing to emphasize the handicaps it must overcome if it is to be successful, the publicity led a great many
people--in the United States as well as in Latin America--to
expect miraculous results, and quickly. The expected mira-
cles not having transpired, it is not surprising that the build-
up has been followed by a letdown, even among some of its
principal adherents and despite some of the important achievements of the Alliance.

Moreover, the sense of urgency permeating the publicity
about the Alliance has reinforced the counter-productive tendency already present among some Latin Americans to try to
force results, even under circumstances which do not make
them feasible, or when the results would be offset by negative
effects elsewhere. Furthermore, public stress upon the need
for undefined reforms has in some cases strengthened the
hands of people who, even when well-intentioned, are promoting
policies in the name of "reform" which would actually run
counter to the objectives of the Alliance. Indeed, there is reason
to believe that many potential investors, Latin American as
well as foreign, have held back on investment precisely because of their fears about the policies which might be adopted in
the name of reform.

THE PROBLEMS DERIVING FROM URGENCY

I wish first to stress my twofold belief that (a) there is
great urgency for a vigorous attack from many directions on
the troubles infesting Latin America, but that (b) the urgency of
impressive "accomplishments" is not as great as some analysts
of the Latin American scene believe.

I consider it important to draw this distinction between the
two types of urgency because the Alliance has suffered, since
its inception, from an excessive feeling that "time is working
against us; we must show important results fast if Latin America
is to be saved." There has been an excessive preoccupation with
the need for "proof" that the Alliance is succeeding. There has

been an unwarranted tendency to despair for the fate of the Alliance every time there has been a military coup d'etat or a
news story of unabated economic or social distress. The crisis
atmosphere has to some extent been justifiable and even useful.
However, I believe that it has unnecessarily impeded concentration on the fundamental requirements for the long-run success
of the Alliance.

Much has been achieved during the years since Punta del
Este in laying the foundations for the long-run success of the
Alliance. Nevertheless, I have considered it necessary to
write this book primarily because of my conviction that much
more remains to be done before the foundations can be said
to have been laid securely. And even if my thesis is accepted
that impressive "monuments" to the success of the Alliance
are not as urgently required as some observers think, there
is little doubt that the longer those monuments are delayed,
the greater will be the jeopardy to the Alliance. Yet the laying
of a foundation is, by definition, only a preliminary step toward construction of the monument. To use one example, time
is necessary between the conception of a dam, the drawing of
plans for its construction, and finally its actual construction.
To use another, time is necessary between the conception of a
sound tax reform bill, its enactment into law, the promulgation
of sound implementory regulations, and their actual implementation.

It is clear, therefore, that there is no time to lose in preparing the way for the long-run success of the Alliance. However, it may not be so clear that the Alliance will probably survive despite some delay in the appearance of impressive accomplishments serving as "proof" that the Alliance is already
a success.

We are all impatient for the appearance of that "proof." Success no doubt feeds on success. The morale, the dedication, and
the energies of all of the partners in the Alliance (including the
U.S.) would be greatly reinforced if their doubts about its value
were eliminated. On the other hand, it does not necessarily follow that the morale, dedication, and energies of the Alliance
partners will quickly collapse in the absence of such proof.

Most Latin American leaders realize--and we too should
realize--that political instability and economic and social ailments have existed in Latin America for a long time. I doubt

that many Latin American leaders really expect that these troubles will soon disappear even under the most optimistic of assumptions. We must be no less realistic. It should be obvious, for example, that it will inevitably take many years to erase illiteracy and many more years to reach the average levels of general and technical education so necessary for a smoothly functioning democracy and for advanced stages of economic and social development. It will inevitably take many years and require immense resources to satisfy the housing requirements of the area. It will likewise inevitably take many years and immense resources to establish an industrial base to provide enough employment to absorb the continuing influx of population into the urban centers and, in fact, to absorb the rapid increase of total population.

Furthermore, even a rapid rate of economic and social progress will not, in itself, satisfy the material and spiritual aspirations of the people of Latin America. The average per capita income is so low now that achievement of the 2.5 per cent increase per annum which was established as a target in the Charter of Punta del Este, or even achievement of twice that rate of increase, would still leave the average Latin American abysmally poor for many years to come. Meanwhile, the "winds of revolution" will undoubtedly continue to blow, and the danger that they will blow in the direction of other Fidel Castros will continue to persist.

Nevertheless, I see no basis for any feeling of hopelessness or even for a feeling of desperation. On the contrary, I see much cause for hope and even for reasonable confidence, provided that we strengthen the measures necessary to assure the long-run success of the Alliance along the lines recommended in this book. The winds of revolution will continue to blow, but the prospects appear good that the winds of peaceful revolution predominate, as contemplated by the Alliance for Progress. In fact, as President Kennedy stated on several occasions, the Alliance is purposefully designed to facilitate peaceful revolution.

True enough, no one can claim that the Alliance has moved forward as well as we had hoped. On the other hand, the forces for violent revolution have also had their set-backs. Whatever sympathy still exists in the rest of Latin America for Fidel Castro's "social revolution," the initial spur which it provided to similar revolutions elsewhere has unquestionably been dimmed by the manifest deterioration of the Cuban economy, a deterioration which would clearly have turned into collapse had it not been for the huge sums of money which the Russian Government has been pouring into Cuba. The forces of violence have been substantially weakened, furthermore, by the internecine struggles among those forces which have resulted primarily from the ideological split between the Russian and the Chinese Communists. Finally. and though I have conceded that the Alliance has not moved forward as well as we had hoped, it is important to note that it has moved forward, and in some respects quite impressively. The desire of most Latin American governments to make a success of the Alliance continues strong, despite a growing sense of frustration.

Stated more succinctly, I believe that while time may be working against us, it is not working against us so rapidly as to require the urgent construction of "monuments" in a last-ditch effort to keep the hopes of the Alliance alive. It is urgent that we combat frustration with the Alliance by strengthening our efforts to build foundations which will so far as possible assure its long-run success and by helping create a general awareness that the best yardstick of the success of the Alliance in its present stage is in the soundness of its foundations.

To the extent that evidence of accomplishment is necessary, we must concentrate on accomplishments which will pay off in the long run, not on those the principal effect of which will be to create a splash in tomorrow's newspaper headlines. Likewise, we must continue to concentrate on the fundamental requirements of the Alliance despite any discouraging events reported in those headlines. Bad news finds its way into the headlines much more easily than good news, particularly when the latter is no more dramatic than the over-all maintenance of progress. It is crucial for the ultimate success of the Alliance that we and the Latin Americans and, for that matter, the entire Free World resign ourselves to the need for a long, hard struggle and to the inevitability of temporary setbacks.

The problem of maintaining a sense of perspective while pressing forward vigorously to meet the fundamental requirements of the Alliance is complicated by two principal subsidiary problems.

First, there is the problem of overcoming possible conflicts between the public's aspirations, on the one hand, and the basic requirements for long-term progress, on the other. For example, the people of a given country may believe that the large-scale construction of low-cost housing is an urgent necessity. On the other hand, Alliance authorities may believe that the resources needed for that housing could be put to better long-run advantage if allocated to the construction of roads and bridges. Since the available resources are necessarily limited, there is a clear need for the determination of relative priorities among the alternative uses of those resources, with the major emphasis on the long-run effects. There is also a clear need for public acceptance of such decisions.

Second, there may on occasion be a genuine and urgent need for emergency foreign assistance having few, or no, discernible long-run advantages. Admittedly, the arguments offered in justification of such assistance have often been much less persuasive to me than the arguments against them. Too often, countries have been confronted by balance-of-payments crises deriving primarily from their own financial mismanagement, and the extension of balance-of-payments loans to those countries would have facilitated perpetuation of that mismanagement. Too often, the extension of budgetary support loans would have helped perpetuate the poor fiscal practices which provoked the budgetary imbalance. Too often, governments have exaggerated the threats of violent revolution facing them or have contributed to the existence of such threats by their own policies or lack of policies.

However, the Alliance must function in the real world, not in the ideal world we would have preferred. Countries experiencing severe balance-of-payments or budgetary crises can rarely overcome them quickly, however much they improve upon their financial or fiscal management and however culpable they may have been for not having done so sooner. Moreover, violent revolutions have occurred in Latin America and they may be followed by the restoration of democratic processes through the holding of free elections, as in the recent examples of the Dominican Republic and Brazil, but they may instead be followed by the overturn of all democratic institutions, as in Cuba.

One of the basic objections to most emergency loans is that their beneficial consequences may not be readily discernible. A balance-of-payments loan will serve to pay for goods and services which the economy as a whole has regularly been acquiring abroad but which are not usually destined for any specific project which can be identified with the loan. A budgetary support loan will ordinarily finance the regular budgetary payments for salaries of government employees, etc. , and can rarely be identified with specific projects.

Essentially, an emergency loan to any country is designed
to keep its economy or government from collapsing, neither of
which objectives is mentioned in the Charter of Punta del Este,
so that loans for these purposes have been considered by some
observers to be improperly classified as Alliance for Progress
loans. I have some sympathy with this point of view, but I believe that this is essentially no more than a matter of definition
and therefore beside the point. The real issue is whether the
loans are necessary for the purpose of furthering the objectives
of the Alliance.

THE DIFFICULTY OF SPENDING MONEY INTELLIGENTLY

The claim is frequently made that expenditures by private
investors will almost certainly be sounder than expenditures by
government officials because private expenditures are determined
by the impersonal forces of the market place while governmental
expenditures are determined by human beings who must rely on
subjective, nonquantitative judgments. In actual fact, subjective,
nonquantitative judgments play an important role even in determining private expenditures, as when decisions are dependent upon
forecasts of consumers' tastes, the conduct of competitors, the
reactions of labor unions, the likelihood of new inventions, etc.
Furthermore, the market place itself may be greatly affected
by governmental decisions such as those calling for the nearby
construction of a dam or a highway, or the awarding of a contract
for fighter aircraft, or for a new minimum wage. And governmental decisions may be based predominantly on market place considerations, as when contracts are awarded to the lowest bidders.

If it was ever true that most expenditures, public or
private, were based on "pure" market place considerations, it
certainly is true no longer. Nevertheless, it must be conceded
that the guidelines governing private expenditures generally
leave much less room for errors of judgment than do those governing governmental expenditures. The stockholders of a profitable business firm may not always be as harsh as they should be
in evaluating the judgments exercised by the executive officers
of that firm, but the stockholders of a firm incurring substantial
losses will inevitably be extremely harsh in such evaluations.
Profit and loss statements are not infallible guidlines, but
they are certainly much simpler and more reliable than any guide-

lines I know of for evaluating the judgments of government officials.

The difficulty of arriving at guidelines for evaluation of the judgments pertaining to Alliance for Progress expenditures is exceptionally pronounced. The foundations for long-run progress must be laid on unstable economic sands and during the intense political winds of the short run. The Alliance partners must devote a great amount of their resources to the construction of those foundations in the short run even though it will take many years before we can know whether the foundations are reasonably secure. Moreover, the situation in a few of the Latin American countries is so unsatisfactory at present that "progress" there may have to be measured for some years by a decrease in the rate of decline before we can expect a turnaround, as reflected in an increase in the rate of growth. In fact, I consider it important to recognize that the statistics commonly used to measure growth are generally so unreliable in Latin America that we might be seriously misguided if we were to rely on those statistics for determining the annual rate of progress under the Alliance.

It is accordingly apparent that, even assuming a universal determination to press ahead with the Alliance, it may be several years before we will be able to speak with any confidence about the success or failure of the Alliance. This makes it all the more important that we arrive at certain agreed guidelines to determine the soundness of Alliance expenditures as rapidly as possible. The greater the uncertainties confronting a group of men as they prepare for a long trip, the more important it is that they agree in advance on the measures to be taken to overcome the problems which are considered likely to arise.

As I see it, the problem of spending Alliance money intelligently has three principal aspects:

First, there is the need to arrive at clear standards for determining whether any given Latin American country is doing what it reasonably can be expected to do by way of "self-help. " The concept that foreign economic help is justifiable only for countries which are helping themselves by mobilizing their own economic resources as fully and as effectively as they can reasonably be expected to do is one of the pillars of the Alliance for Progress. Like mother love, it would be hard to find anyone, including any Latin American, who would quarrel with

it. Unlike the problem of defining mother love, however, there
is considerable controversy about how to measure the degree of
"self-help" and about the meaning of "reasonable" self-help.
Yet, if self-help is to be a major criterion for determining the
allocation of foregin assistance among the Latin American countries, it is important that they know in advance precisely how
the existence of self-help is to be measured; the question of what
is reasonable will inevitably be troublesome, but should become
less serious as Latinization of the Alliance increases.

     Second, it is important that agreement be reached on the
definitions of various types of "reform" and on the standards
for determining whether satisfactory progress is being attained
in the implementation of those reforms. As in the case of self-
help, the Charter of Punta del Este provides that one of the major
criteria for allocating foreign assistance shall be the degree of
progress among the separate Latin American countries in recti-
fying various social and economic injustices by means of the
appropriate reforms. However, the passage of a law denom-
inated a reform law does not necessarily mean that the law is
a good one or even that its purpose should properly be designated as reform. Moreover, the enactment of a law does not, in
itself, mean much unless the necessary steps are taken for its
implementation. In fact, the specific circumstances of a given
country might be such that no new laws are required for a given
type of reform, but that improved administration of existing
laws is necessary. Furthermore, care must be taken to avoid
encouraging measures which, however well intended in and of
themselves, will actually impair achievement of other important
objectives. For example, the enactment of a law establishing
a 30-hour work week in some country might be desirable in itself, but might seriously retard that country's prospects for
economic development.

     Third, it is critical that the necessary steps be taken
quickly to promote the more rapid formulation of sound development projects. However satisfactory the self-help and
reform measures of a country, there may be little justification for foreign economic assistance to that country unless
that assistance can be allocated, directly or indirectly, to
specific projects which will further long-term economic or
social development. The objectives of the Alliance would be
greatly promoted if each eligible country were devoting all of
its own savings to sound projects and if it had the completed
blueprints for many other public and private projects the implementation of which was only awaiting the availability of foreign

assistance. It is a sad fact, however, that few of the Latin
American countries have had such a "reserve" of sound projects just waiting for financing. Indeed, there have been many
occasions when U.S. and other foreign lending institutions
were prepared, and even anxious, to extend loans to some
countries but have refrained from doing so because of the lack
of such projects.

A $10 million loan to a country of 10 million people could
easily be spent on the importation of consumer goods, for example, without improving that country's long-term prospects
for economic or social development. The same loan might
greatly promote development if utilizied for the procurement of,
say, generators for a hydroelectric plant or refrigeration equipment for warehouses or machinery for a tractor factory. But
utilization of loans for such purposes has very often been impeded by the scarcity of carefully formulated projects of these
types. Underdevelopment is usually characterized as the inadequacy of capital investments. I believe it can also be
characterized as the inadequacy even of the public and private
skills needed to determine the precise nature of the new
capital investments which would best promote the country's
development.

PART

II

THE WAR OF IDEOLOGIES

CHAPTER **6** ELEMENTS OF
AN ALLIANCE
FOR PROGRESS
MYSTIQUE

The opinion was expressed in Part I that while a number
of measures must be taken to strengthen the Alliance, "the
Alliance still is likely to be the salvation of Latin America
and of Latin America's partnership in the Free World." Yet,
the opinion was also expressed that we cannot anticipate
early eradication of the political instability and the economic
and social ailments that have long prevailed in Latin America,
even under the most optimistic of assumptions concerning the
success of the Alliance.

What may appear to be an incompatibility between these
opinions is, however, illusory. Much time will inevitably
be required for the attainment of satisfactory levels of income
and satisfactory social relationships in Latin America. But
it should not take nearly as much time to create the ingredient which has so far been most seriously lacking in the Alliance: the dedication of the people of Latin America to the
objectives and mechanisms of the Alliance.

In speaking of "dedication," however, we have moved
into the world of ideas and emotions. The people of Latin
America should be highly enthusiastic about the Alliance,
but they are not. Their minds and their hearts have not been
touched by it, and their basic attitudes have remained unaf-
fected. In a word, no Alliance for Progress "mystique" has
been created. And while the creation of that mystique should
not take a great deal of time, there can be no doubt about the
fact that its creation will depend upon strong Latin American
leadership and the energetic participation of many sectors of
the United States and the rest of the Free World. The need
for Latin American leadership was discussed in Part I and
will be further discussed in Part III. The need for broad
Free World participation was likewise discussed in Part I,
and the forms which that participation should take will be discussed in Chapters 7-13. First, however, it is important

71

that the elements which must be encompassed within the necessary mystique be clearly understood.

Webster's Seventh New Collegiate Dictionary[1]   defines
"mystique" as:

> a complex of transcendental or somewhat mystical
> beliefs and attitudes developing around an object.

Accepting this definition, an Alliance for Progress mystique may
be founded on a wealth of human knowledge, but will come to exist
only if its basic tenets are "believed" in a somewhat mystical
manner. It is highly reassuring that human knowledge and intelligence endorse the soundness of the Alliance's tenets, but an
Alliance mystique will nevertheless not exist unless and until
the people of Latin America take those tenets to their hearts, as
articles of faith as well as hope.

The Charter of Punta del Este has the right words. It has
established an alliance of the people of 20 countries, including
the United States, for promotion of the economic and social development of Latin America. It provides for governmental planning for economic and social development, with considerable
stress on the role to be played by private enterprise. Throughout, it stresses the importance of democratic institutions for
protection of the dignity and the God-given rights of the individual
from encroachment by the state.

The strength of the intellectual support for the Charter of
Punta del Este is clearly manifested by the fact that, to the
best of my knowledge, no objective Latin American has voiced
any criticism of it.

To be sure, there has been criticism of the manner in
which the Charter has been implemented. In particular, there
has been criticism that the U. S. Government has been "too
slow" or "too bureaucratic" or "too political" in processing
loan applications under the Alliance, and that the differences in
the data requirements of the different lending agencies have
caused unnecessary burdens to loan applicants. There has
been criticism that the role of U. S. Government officials in
the Alliance has been too great, especially in the determination
of eligibility for Alliance loans. The judgments of U. S. officials concerning the "self-help" and "reform" measures of
certain Latin American countries have been criticized, as has
been the requirement that the proceeds of U. S. loans be spent
in the United States. And especially severe criticism has

been directed at the requirement established unilaterally by
U.S. law that AID loans be withheld from countries in which
U.S. private investments have been expropriated without satis-
factory provision for compensation and from countries the gov-
ernments of which have broken service or other contracts with
U.S. firms.

The nature and vehemence of some of the criticisms which
have been directed at the implementation of the Charter of
Punta del Este clearly reflect more than differences of opinion
over administrative procedures. They reflect also differences
of emphasis upon, and interpretation of, various provisions of
the Charter itself. If these differences are allowed to persist
unmitigated, they might ultimately have the effect of destroy-
ing support for the Charter itself. Indeed, one of the objectives
of this book is to help bring about as much resolution of those
differences as is possible. However, the fact that there are
differences of interpretation or emphasis should not provoke
despair. Differences of opinion are endemic among humans,
and we cannot expect unanimity of opinion about the Alliance,
any more than about any other great ideology.

What is really remarkable is the fact that the basic soundness of the Charter itself has not yet come into question, except
on the part of the Communists and on the part of those whose
feelings of nationalism and anti-Yanquismo have led them to
oppose any form of collaboration with the United States. The intellectual endorsement of the Charter continues strong among
all of the others who have read it.

However, this is far from stating that there is general endorsement for the Alliance for Progress in Latin America.
Though all objective Latin Americans who have read the Charter
of Punta del Este endorse it, we must recognize that the number
who have read it is very small. Moreover, of those who have
read and endorsed it, only a handful have made any effort to
bring its message to the people of Latin America for whose
benefit the Charter was drafted. A few statesmen, such as ex-
President of Colombia Alberto Lleras Camargo, have tried to
popularize the Charter and the Alliance for Progress. But the
few such efforts that have been made in Latin America as a
whole have been both spasmodic and weak. The Alliance continues to be viewed by almost everyone as the U.S. Government's aid program. The "message" of the Charter of Punta
del Este and the Alliance for Progress has not yet been put

into words which the people of Latin America would even understand, let alone take to their hearts.

Title I of the Charter of Punta del Este begins with the following paragraph:

> It is the purpose of the Alliance for Progress to enlist
> the full energies of the peoples and governments of the
> American republics in a great cooperative effort to ac-
> celerate the economic and social development of the
> participating countries of Latin America, so that they
> may achieve maximum levels of well-being, with equal
> desires.

The United States Assistant Secretary of State for Inter-
American Affairs, Professor Lincoln Gordon, quoted this
paragraph in his recent book,[2] and then stated,

> Yet it is clear that the "full energies of the peoples
> and governments" have not yet been enlisted in this
> effort. There is not yet a sense of a great cooper-
> ative effort as the highest priority of the inter-
> American community, securing the devoted efforts
> of the most talented leaders in public and private
> life throughout the hemisphere. Democratic in-
> stitutions remain under very great pressure, and
> in some cases they are once again temporarily in
> eclipse, although not irrecoverably.[3]

The authoritativeness with which Assistant Secretary
Gordon can speak on this subject is such that special attention should be paid to his views concerning the shortcomings
of the Alliance.[4]

> In my opinion ... the basic shortcoming has been
> squarely identified by Roberto Campos, the Brazil-
> ian Minister of Planning and Economic Coordination,
> when he speaks of the need for a political mystique.
> Unless the pursuit of economic and social progress,
> in the terms of the Charter of Punta del Este, be-
> comes a major part of the national political life of
> each participating country, and unless the great
> majority of people and organized groups and leaders
> of influence feel themselves involved and committed
> to these goals, the Alliance for Progress will not
> succeed regardless of the technical soundness of in-

dividual projects and the amounts of foreign financial
support made available to Latin America. . . . The
problem is to find and encourage articulate and effective leadership for the aspirations of the vast majority,
and to relate a political mystique to the technical
problems that must be objectively diagnosed and
solved. That sort of leadership clearly must be
Latin American; it cannot come from outside. [5]

Later, Assistant Secretary Gordon states that while the
differences between the Alliance for Progress and the Marshall
Plan are greater than the similarities,

the European experience does contain some useful
pointers. As a certain point in the development of
the Marshall Plan, there became evident a com-
pelling need for European political leadership at a
high level as part of the cooperative machinery.
And when the idea of European integration was conceived as the basis for a great new move forward
on the foundation of postwar recovery, it was given
vital political leadership by Jean Monnet and his
Action Committee for the United States of Europe,
a necessary informal prerequisite to the later establishment of formal institutions for economic and
political unification. Nor were these movements
limited to cabinet ministers and public officials.
They sank their roots into the national communities,
enlisting members of parliament, political parties,
organizations of businessmen, labor unions, and
the liberal professions, universities, the press,
and other organs of mass communication. Is there
not in this experience something to be drawn on
for guidance in the contemporary Latin American
scene?[6]

I could hardly agree more enthusiastically with Assistant
Secretary Gordon's conclusion that "the problem is to find and
encourage articulate and effective leadership for the aspirations
of the vast majority" and his implied conclusion that the leadership must come not only from government officials and politicians,
but also from organizations of businessmen, labor unions, universities, and the press. I am very distressed, therefore, that the
necessary leadership has not yet appeared. I know too many outstanding Latin Americans to have any doubts about the fact that
the human material and the will for such leadership already exist.

But I believe that the pathbreaking aspects of the Alliance as well as its organizational and implementory problems are such that the rest of the Free World can and must do a great deal to provide the necessary encouragement and assistance to that leadership.

The war of ideologies in which the Alliance for Progress is engaged is taking place on many fronts. Victory in that war will require the utilization of all available forces on each of those fronts. Perhaps even more important, victory will depend upon a fairly high degree of communication and coordination among the forces employed on the various fronts. For I am convinced that no ideology can be a living and potent instrument in guiding the destiny of Latin America unless it holds together as an integral unit.

Such unity is, in fact, a major element in the strength of the Marxist ideology. The labor theory of value; the promised achievement of social justice through replacement of the "system of exploitation" by the "system of common ownership of the means of production"; the promised elimination of wars "when capitalistic countries seeking markets for their surplus production" no longer exist; the elimination of internal strife as a "classless" society is created; the elimination of the depressions and the "waste," "greed," "materialism" and "vulgarity" provoked by competition; and the "inevitable" triumph of socialism, as "proven" by Marx's theory of dialectical materialism--all of these concepts and many others mesh smoothly with one another into an integrated philosophical and political mystique. A mystique which has elements of strong appeal for the intelligent and unintelligent, the educated and uneducated, alike.

Very little, if anything, has been accomplished over the years by the many efforts on the part of the U.S. Government to demonstrate the weaknesses and deceptions of the Marxist doctrine or even the Marxist ideology as a whole. Undoubtedly, some people have been impressed by our arguments. Undoubtedly, too, however, some people have interpreted our efforts as evidence that the United States is trying to preserve its foreign markets and the foreign investments of its private firms by seducing the poorer countries of the world away from adoption of the "only" path which will lead them toward the fastest possible economic and social progress.

What is needed in Latin America is a Free World ideology which provides inspiring and convincing answers to all of the major questions troubling the people of that area. It must provide satisfactory responses to the questions posed by the educated, patriotic, and honest intellectuals of Latin America--responses which can also be phrased in terms which will have meaning to the uneducated. There can be no Alliance for Progress mystique until the philosophy lying behind the provisions of the Charter of Punta del Este has been conveyed to the people in words, as well as actions, which strike directly at the roots of the important questions which are troubling them--however unreasonably, however unfairly, however much inspired by Marxists. Until the democratic leaders of Latin America are able, with or without the support of the rest of the Free World, to provide inspiring and convincing answers to questions such as the following, we cannot expect an Alliance for Progress mystique or any other mystique capable of guiding the area's winds of revolution westward:

My country has always depended upon private enterprise, and look where it has gotten us. Why should I contine to depend on this system when it has left me just as poor, ignorant, and down-trodden as my parents and their parents? Why should I assume that my children will be any better off than I am?

The United States and other industrialized countries have always profited by selling us their manufactured products at high prices while buying our agricultural commodities and other raw materials at low prices. Isn't it obvious that we must change this by becoming industrialized ourselves, whatever the cost?

It is easy enough to say that private businessmen will invest in public utilities and other basic industries if those industries are economically sound for the country. In fact, however, they have not done so. Private enterprise may be fine in theory, but when it doesn't do its job in practice why shouldn't the government do that job? When investments in basic industries are necessary, yet private businessmen refuse to make those investments, isn't it the duty of the government to do so?

Everyone knows that our government officials have always been controlled by the oligarchs who put them into office. In fact, one of the principal objectives of the Alliance for Progress is to break the grip of those oligarchs through basic social and economic reforms. This is a fine objective, but how can we hope to accomplish it without undermining some of what you Americans call the basic principles of private enterprise? Take land re-

form, for example. How can we hope to break up our huge land-
ed estates and distribute them among our peasants unless we ex-
propriate those estates? We certainly can't afford to buy them
from the oligarchs. Even if we had all that money, wouldn't we
be morally justified in using it to improve the welfare of our
people instead of giving it to the oligarchs who acquired the estates improperly in the first place?

The corrupt and selfish oligarchs who used to run our country concluded contracts with certain foreign trusts whereby both
the oligarchs and the foreign trusts enriched themselves at the
expense of our people. Now that the people have finally succeeded in getting a government which truly represents us, why
should the United States Government object if our government
cancels those contracts? Isn't it because the trusts in the United
States are so strong that they really control the U. S. Government despite all the high-sounding words the Government officials
use?

We are told that the system of private enterprise is necessarily more productive than any other system because competition promotes efficiency. If this is true, why is it that the
gross national products of the socialist countries have not only
been increasing more rapidly than those of the Latin American
countries, but have even been increasing more rapidly than those
of the industrialized countries of the West, including the United
States?

We are told that the socialist countries are dictatorships,
that they are cruel, stifle individual initiative and destroy the
human spirit. Yet, isn't it true that the Russian Government
spends more on education and on promotion of the arts than any
other government in the world? Isn't it true that the American
people are very materialistic, their so-called culture consisting
primarily of rock-and-roll and the twist, trashy movies, and
comic books?

Everybody knows how the Negro is discriminated against
in the United States. Americans say that their Government
cannot prevent this because their country is a democracy and
the rights of every individual in a democracy include the right
to associate, or refuse to associate, with any other individual.
On the other hand, the Russians also say that their country is
a democracy and they have eliminated racial discrimination by
making it illegal. Isn't the Russian form of democracy better
than the American form?

There has been considerable intermarriage among whites, Negroes, and Indians in most of the Latin American countries. In view of the attitude of the dominant whites of the United States toward their own Negro population, how can we believe the Americans when they speak of friendship for us and even an "alliance" with us? Isn't it true that the Americans are only pretending friendship with us in an effort to deter us from following Castro's example? Isn't the Alliance for Progress just an American scheme to tie Latin America into the cold war on the U.S. side? Wouldn't Latin America be better off to stay free of the cold war which, after all, is none of its business and which might later turn into a hot war?

Many of the foregoing questions are predicated upon erroneous impressions of fact about the United States and other countries of the Free World, about the Communist world, and even about Latin America itself. Many of them reflect an inadequate understanding of economics, sociology, and political science. But all of them represent issues which are seriously troubling the people of Latin America. And none of them is so simple that it can be answered satisfactorily by a few well chosen statements.

The questions (and many others which are closely related to them) are disturbing the minds and emotions of a great many people whose basic predilections still call for alignment with the other countries of the Free World, but who are increasingly being torn by doubts as to whether the institutions of the Free World are in fact the right ones for Latin America. A concerted and sustained effort must be made by various segments of the Free World to resolve these doubts if an Alliance for Progress mystique is to prevail. For reasons discussed in Part I, the U.S. Government cannot make an adequate contribution to this area of the war of ideologies. Furthermore, the Latin American leaders who must carry the major responsibility in this area will be able to do so effectively only if they are adequately buttressed by the necessary facts and argumentation. The role which U.S. universities can play in this process is especially important, and I shall turn to them first.

CHAPTER **7** THE ROLE OF
U. S. UNIVERSITIES
IN STRENGTHENING
EDUCATION

The principal measures which U. S. universities* should
pursue in support of the Alliance for Progress are of three
different types: (1) those designed to help strengthen Latin
America's universities and to improve the educational background of Latin America's intellectual leaders by encouraging
a great expansion in the enrollment of students from that
area in U. S. universities, (2) those designed to promote a
great increase in direct communication between U. S. professors and those of Latin America, and (3) those designed to
increase the authorship of books and articles to clarify some
of the issues involved in the war of ideologies taking place in
Latin America. Measures of the first type will be discussed
in this chapter and the others in Chapter 8. First, however,
it is necessary to understand the importance of the Latin
American universities to the success of the Alliance for Progress.

Universities everywhere can exercise enormous influence
by disseminating the world's great ideologies and by transform-
ing them into political movements. As stated by Clark Kerr, whe
President of the University of California, "The intellect, and
the university as its most happy home, can have great potential
roles to play in the reconciliation of the war between the future
and the past, and the solution--one way or the other--of the war
between the ideological giants who now rend the world with their
struggles."[1] There is no region of the world where the "potential roles" of the intellect and the university have been trans-
formed into active roles as fully as in Latin America. The war
of ideologies is being waged on many battlegrounds, but I am
convinced that the university campuses of that region will ultimately prove to have been the most decisive of them all. It is

---

*As used here, the term "universities" will ordinarily embrace
all institutions of higher education, including colleges.

a matter of great concern, therefore, that the ideologies of the Free World are faring very badly on those campuses.

Let us examine some of the principal attributes of most of Latin America's universities:[2]

> There are only about 120 universities--the exact number depends on how one classifies universities--in the twenty republics of Latin America; of these, more than 100 are national universities. Their enrollment totals approximately 430,000. A great majority of these institutions, many of them of most ancient lineage, have wholly failed to keep pace with today's world standards.[3]

As to the national universities,

> There is ... one organic similarity among them all. They share a system of academic organization and control which resembles that which developed in Bologna in Italy around the beginning of the 13th Century .... There the students engaged the professors, set the terms of their contracts and reminded them in various ways that they were the hired men.[4]

Student representatives actually sit on the governing councils of all Latin America's national universities, except in Brazil, and formally exercise a dominating--and usually controlling-- voice in those councils. Informally, their influence is often even greater, in view of the tremendous influence they are able to apply directly on governmental leaders, and indirectly through students' "demonstrations" and "strikes," including violence.

Professors' salaries are very low in all of the national universities and in most of the private universities. As a result, few professors are able to devote full time to their university responsibilities. Commonly, they have additional occupations elsewhere, very often as government officials. By virtue of these additional occupations, many professors have an important direct, as well as an indirect, impact on governmental policies and public opinion. On the other hand, the quality of their professorship suffers.

Moreover, the low salaries discourage all but the most dedicated from devoting their lives to university instruction, particu-

larly in view of the many disheartening consequences deriving
from student control of the universities. Certainly, there is
little inducement for the young men and women of Latin America to invest the several years and the substantial amount of
money necessary to acquire Ph. D. 's in their specialized
fields of knowledge. Very few of the universities of the area
have facilities for postgraduate work, and the young man or
woman seeking advanced degrees usually must go abroad to
get them. The expense is such that few do so.

"The universities today are largely geared to students
who seek to specialize in law, medicine or government service.
They have not adjusted themselves to the emerging industrial
societies."[5] This means, first, that the universities are
failing to perform adequately one of the most critically important tasks in Latin America--the highest possible development
of its human beings; and no prerequisite for the economic and
social development is more important than education at all
levels. It means, second, that many students become frustrated and embittered because graduation does not automatically lead to jobs, particularly in such overcrowded fields as
law. As Benton puts it,

> Many students feel that the fact that they have a col-
> lege education means that society thereafter owes
> them a permanent special status. But because they
> often receive no real or significant training, there
> develops a group of displaced (or better, never-placed)
> persons who are theoretically schooled, but not
> trained, and who find society unable to absorb them.
> They are picturesquely called the "intellectual pro-
> letariat." They are a politically dangerous and often
> highly irresponsible group.[6]

Communist and other Marxist elements are strong in the
faculties and in the student organizations of almost all the universities. The pernicious effects are especially serious
among the economists in view of the important role which they
play in determining and implementing government policy in
Latin America. It would be a gross distortion to say that Communist or other Marxist-oriented economists control most of
the governments, but there is absolutely no question about the
fact that their influence is immense. According to Benton,

> One observer reported to us that a grave problem in
> Chile has been posed by the Marxist, left-wing-
> oriented economists who have come from the university

economic departments and who have infiltrated into
the Chilean government and economy; we had exactly
the same report on the impact of the economics
department at the National University of Mexico on
the government and attitudes in Mexico. [7]

I can testify from my own experience that the same situation
prevails in several other countries.

The library facilities are generally deplorable.   There
are few foreign books, most of them quite old, and few of them--
except for those which are Marxist-oriented--translated into
the appropriate national language.   There are far too few
copies even of those books which are printed in the appropriate
language and which are considered even by their own faculties
to be standard reference works.   Students wishing to delve
into source materials other than those prescribed by their
professors are severely handicapped by the scarcity of those
source materials.

On the other hand, there are many encouraging features
about the situation prevailing in Latin America's universities.
There are many dedicated and competent professors who have
been recognized around the world for their outstanding qualifications in their respective fields.   And there are many non-
Marxist as well as anti-Marxist elements among all the faculties and student bodies.   Indeed, pro-democratic students have
recently succeeded in wresting control of certain student organizations away from the Marxist elements previously controlling them.

Perhaps most encouraging of all is the deep respect for
ideas which permeates all of Latin America's principal communities.   No doubt, there is an undue receptivity to oratori-
cal bombast and political demagoguery, and the standards
by which ideas are evaluated are not as sophisticated as they
are in countries with higher average levels of education.   But
the man considered to be an "intellectual" is honored in Latin
America as he is in few other areas of the world.   Even the
university students derive much of their power from their
claim to intellectualism in communities where the general populace is only too painfully aware of its educational limitations.

I have met with different student groups in Latin America
on several occasions and have almost always been distressed
by the evidence of the extent to which they generally (but by no

means universally) have swallowed Marxist doctrines as well as erroneous "facts" about the rest of the Free World, the Communist countries, and even their own countries. At the same time, I have uniformly been impressed by their willingness and even anxiety to hear "the other side." Prejudiced, yes. But also intellectually honest. The market place for ideas contains a great deal of shoddy merchandise, but it is wide open for the introduction of better merchandise.

The average student is not getting the education which he and his country require, particularly with respect to certain fundamental matters affecting the destiny of his country. There is much that the rest of the Free World can and must do to help him get a better education. I believe that the most important single objective which U.S. colleges and universities must pursue if they are to fulfill their responsibilities in this regard is to widen their gates so as to facilitate the greatly increased entry of Latin American students, especially graduate students, and especially graduate students majoring in economics.

As John Maynard Keynes pointed out,

> ... the ideas of economists and political philosophers, both when they are right and when they are wrong, are more powerful than is commonly understood. Indeed, the world is ruled by little else. Practical men, who believe themselves to be quite exempt from any intellectual influences, are usually the slaves of some defunct economist. Madmen in authority, who hear voices in the air, are distilling their frenzy from some academic scribbler of a few years back. I am sure that the power of vested interests is vastly exaggerated compared with the gradual encroachment of ideas. [8]

The immense political impact--direct and indirect--of men such as Adam Smith, Karl Marx, and Keynes himself, can be offered in illustration. I can personally testify to the tremendous influence which their followers exercise in the governments and in the public opinion of Latin America. They may be conscious or unconscious followers. They may accurately understand what their intellectual masters taught, or their understanding may be badly distorted. They may follow those teachings blindly, or may try to adjust them to the realities of the present world. Their devotion to their intellectual masters may be passionate and irreversible, or open-minded and subject to dissuasion. However, one thing is certain: the prospects for success of the Alliance for Progress will be greatly impeded until the bulk of Latin America's economists and pseudo-economists have acquired greater regard for some of the basic principles underlying the Alliance.

One other thing is certain: the Marxist-oriented economists and Keynesian economists with seriously defective understandings of Keynes have been having a field day in Latin America. Many badly educated professors of economics have been passing their misconceptions to their students. And many badly oriented professors have been encouraging and actually instructing their students toward the same orientation. The students have then been entering their governments or private life, where they have been propagating the same theses. Perhaps even worse, some of the students have become professors, influencing new groups of students in the same way.

The circle is indeed vicious, and several measures for breaking it will be proposed in this chapter. First among my objectives is that of facilitating the intensive training in U.S. graduate schools of large numbers of Latin American students of economics, preferably toward the goal of Ph.D.'s. The Latin American students would thereby be enabled, if they so desired, to obtain a really good education in "pure" economics--economics which is as free as humanly possible of political bias; economics which not only puts Keynesian "macro-economics" into its proper perspective but which also, by its attention to "micro-economics," places proper emphasis upon the pricing mechanism which is as important to the optimum allocation of resources in "socialist" as in "capitalist" societies; economics which is as applicable to the progress of the underdeveloped countries as it is to that of the developed countries.

Upon returning home, the students would then be able, as government officials or in private life, to enter the market place of ideas intellectually equipped to counteract and quite possibly to turn around many of the noxious concepts which are now retarding the economic and social progress of their countries. Those who are willing to dedicate themselves to university instruction--and there would undoubtedly be some-- would be able not only to enter the same market place of ideas but also to start a new circle: good instruction leading to educated students leading to good instruction, etc.

It might be argued that the same objective could be accomplished more efficiently and less expensively by sending larger numbers of economics professors to the Latin American universities where one professor can teach many students. I would not agree. Among other considerations, we should not underestimate the expense of a professor's salary plus allowances, and the cost of transporting him, his family and his household effects to a Latin American post and back. More important, we should not overlook the experience gained during the last several years concerning the problems confronting U.S. professors in Latin America. The experience has not been entirely negative, and it would be desirable that we increase the number and quality of our professors in that area. However, this could not be considered an adequate alternative to training Latin American economists in the United States.

The campuses of most Latin American universities simply do not provide environments conducive to scholarship, and the U.S. professors share most of the handicaps of the Latin American professors. In addition, they generally have the extremely serious handicap of trying to teach in a foreign language. It is the very rare professor who is able to transmit his ideas accurately and effectively in a foreign language, particularly in a subject as abstruse as economics. It is difficult enough for the Latin American student in the United States to understand the subtleties of economics in English; it is much more difficult for the U.S. professors to convey those subtleties (and to resolve the normal uncertainties which they arouse) in Spanish, Portuguese, or French.

Moreover, it would be as unreasonable to expect a small number of U.S. professors to teach "economics" at a Latin American university as it would be to expect a small number of U.S. professors to teach "medicine" or "engineering." The study of economics requires intensive work in such separate, but interdependant, disciplines as money and banking, the history of economic thought, international finance, agricultural economics, labor, econometrics, business cycles, national accounts, statistics, and various aspects of "economic theory." In my opinion, no one can properly be considered an economist until he has received adequate training in each of these disciplines and at least a rudimentary exposure to others, such as sociology, psychology, accounting, history, and anthropology. The satisfactory training of an economist requires a large professorial staff as well as excellent library facilities.

Under present circumstances we cannot reasonably expect such training at most Latin American universities.

It seems evident, therefore, that U.S. universities would make a contribution of inestimable value to the Alliance for Progress if they were to accept responsibility for giving maximum feasible facilities for the training of Latin American economists in the United States until the Latin Americans themselves are able to take over that responsibility more satisfactorily. This applies particularly to graduate, but also to undergraduate, training. Moreover, the U.S. universities could greatly improve upon the facilities they have been providing for the training of Latin Americans in many fields other than economics, such as agriculture, the physical sciences, other social sciences, business administration, engineering, and the humanities. I am convinced that priority must be given to economics, but the problems of economic and social development are too manifold to permit neglect of any of these other fields.

The statistics pertaining to foreign students in U.S. universities supply clear evidence of the thoroughly inadequate contribution which these universities are making to the education of Latin Americans. Thus, although a large expansion in the enrollment of Latin Americans could reasonably have been anticipated following the Act of Bogota and inception of the Alliance for Progress, that enrollment actually increased by only about 36 per cent between 1959 and 1966, while the enrollment of other foreign students increased 86 per cent! Latin American students accounted for only about 17 per cent of all foreign students in 1966, and only 40 per cent of the Latin American students were doing graduate work as compared with 56 per cent of the other foreign students. In fact, it is estimated that less than fifty Latin Americans were working for Ph.D.'s in Economics!*

---

* The following breakdowns of the available statistics will be of some interest:

During the academic year, 1965-66, there were 82,709 foreign students in U.S. colleges and universities. Of these, 13,998 (17 per cent) were from Latin America. As compared with the academic year, 1958-59, the number of Latin American students had increased by about 3,700 (36 per cent) whereas the number of all other foreign students had increased by about 31,700 (86 per cent).

Of the Latin American students enrolled during 1965-66, only 40 per cent were graduate students as compared with

There are undoubtedly many factors responsible for the
deplorable situation, and I would not claim that the U.S. colleges and universities could rectify it alone. In fact, I see a
clear need for assistance by the U.S. Government, as recommended in Chapter 12. Furthermore, it is evident that the
Latin American students themselves will make the decisions as
to where they study, what they study, and how deeply they study.
Nevertheless, I believe that U.S. colleges and universities could
do a great deal to promote the more satisfactory inflow of Latin
American students if they would pursue measures of the following
principal types, which will be discussed more fully below:

---

56 per cent of those from other areas.   Graduate students working
for Ph. D. 's accounted for 779 (6 per cent) of the Latin Americans,
as compared with 10,425 (15 per cent) of the other foreign students.
A more detailed breakdown of other doctoral candidates, by area,
may be of interest.   They accounted for 887 (13 per cent) of the
African students; 1,372 (13 per cent) of the Europeans; 5,147
(18 per cent) of those from the Far East; 1,327 (12 per cent) of
those from the Near and Middle East; 1,413 (14 per cent) of those
from Canada and Bermuda; 266 (20 per cent) from Oceania; and
13 (10 per cent) stateless.
    Of all of the Latin American students (graduate, undergrad-
uate, and special) enrolled during 1965-66, only 780 (6 per cent)
were majoring in Economics.   Unfortunately, the Institute of International Education, which compiled these data, does not publish
a statistical breakdown which would indicate the number of doctoral
students in each field of study.   However, if we were to make the
assumption (lacking any more scientific basis) that the 6 per cent
ratio of Latin American Economics students to the total number of
Latin American students prevailed equally in the case of undergraduate students and all classes of graduate students, we would
arrive at the estimate that only 43 Latin Americans were seeking
Ph. D. 's in Economics that year.   The fact that this is a miniscule
number is underscored by recognition that it applies not only to
the 19 Latin American countries which are members of the Alliance for Progress, but also to Cuba and the other independent countries and dependent territories of the area.   Of the 779 doctoral
candidates from "Latin America," 29 were from Cuba, and an
additional 172 were from Jamaica, Trinidad and Tobago, Guyana,
and others.   Source for 1965-66 data: Institute of International
Education, Open Doors--1966 (New York: Institute of International
Education, September, 1966). Source for 1958-59 data: American
Universities and Colleges (8th ed. ; Washington, D. C. : The
American Council on Education, 1960), ch. 8.

1. They should revise their admission standards, and particularly their standards for admission into graduate schools, so as to reduce the present obstacles to enrollment of Latin Americans.

2. Special instruction should be made available in greatly expanded amounts to help the Latin American students overcome the handicap they face in their inadequate mastery of the English language.

3. Latin American students should be granted a much larger percentage than they now receive of the financial support extended by U.S. colleges and universities to foreign students.

Each U.S. university is free to fix its own admission standards for the enrollment of foreign students in either undergraduate or graduate courses. Nevertheless, a number of studies made of this subject demonstrate the reliability of the following three generalizations:

First, the general rule that admission will be denied to applicants who are not proficient in the English language has been a much more serious barrier to the entry of Latin American students than other foreign students. This has been true at both the undergraduate and graduate levels, but especially at the latter. A very large percentage of the students from other parts of the world comes from countries where English is widely spoken. Even apart from the very sizable number of students from the British Commonwealth, there are a large number of students from countries where English for one reason or another is a major language--e.g., the Philippines, Japan, Thailand; most of western Europe; Israel and Jordan; the U.A.R., South Africa, Kenya, and other African countries. In many of those countries, English is actually used as a common (sometimes even the "official") means of communication among the educated, and even much of the uneducated, populace. In contrast, English is not a common means of communication among even the educated populace of any of the Latin American members of the Alliance for Progress. English is a major subject in the schools throughout the area, but only a tiny percentage of even the educated Latin Americans can be said to be masters of the language.

Second, the universities have been far less generous in granting financial support to their Latin American students than they have been with their other foreign students. In 1966, the universities provided full financial support for 17 per cent of their foreign

students. However, only 9 per cent of the Latin Americans
were supported in this way, as compared with 19 per cent of
the students from other areas.

Third, the admission of Latin American students for graduate study has been seriously impeded by doubts as to their academic qualifications. It is the general rule that unless a foreign
student has done his undergraduate work at an "accredited"
university, he will be required to complete additional undergra-
uate work in the United States, with no commitment that he will be
accepted for graduate study even then. It is accordingly important
to realize that relatively few Latin American universities are
considered accredited by the U.S. universities. Under these circumstances, few Latin Americans are disposed to make the necess
effort to gain admission into U.S. graduate schools. It would
be the rare Latin American who would not feel resentful on
being advised by a U.S. graduate school that it does not accredit
the university at which he did his undergraduate work in his
country, and that he will have to complete additional undergraduate work in the United States. The fact that he would not be assured of admission even after completing the additional work in
the United States would normally kill any interest he might still
have in pursuing the matter.

I do not wish to appear unconcerned with the quandary in
which the U.S. educators who would like to expand the enrollment
of Latin American students find themselves. The administrators
and the faculties of U.S. universities believe that their primary
function is to provide the highest possible level of instruction.
They are accordingly reluctant to accept the enrollment of students of any nationality, including Americans, whenever they feel
that the educational standards which the universities are trying
to maintain would be jeopardized by such enrollment. The
fact that the English proficiency of the Latin American applicants
or the educational background of the graduate school applicants
among them has very often been considered inadequate has mili-
tated against their enrollment, no matter how sympathetic the
universities have been to the predicament of those applicants. *

* It is interesting to note, in this regard, that there is some objective evidence of the inadequate qualifications of many of the
Latin Americans who have actually been enrolled in U.S. graduate schools. In 1953, the Association of Graduate Schools made
an analysis of the academic performance records of 1,829
foreign students. This revealed that 37 per cent of the 182 Latin
Americans had "below average" records and 22 per cent had

The desire of the U.S. universities to maintain, and even improve upon, their educational standards is thoroughly justifiable, if only as an indispensable requirement for satisfying the material and spiritual needs of our own people. In fact, it is thoroughly justifiable also as an important adjunct of U.S. foreign policy. As has been persuasively pointed out in The Overseas Americans, [9] there is much that U.S. universities can and should do to improve the educational backgrounds of the many thousands of Americans who represent the U.S. government and U.S. business abroad. Furthermore, even the objective of educating Latin American and other foreign students in the United States will be impaired unless those who study here get the benefits of the highest possible standards of education.

However, I am convinced that maintenance of the desireable educational standards in U.S. universities need not be impaired, and may very well be promoted, by the measures which were recommended above for facilitating the enrollment of Latin Americans.

It is important to recognize that, even under the circumstances which have prevailed up to now, the American students have received at least some educational benefits from such opportunities as they have had to get to know, and to study with, students from Latin America. The value of knowledge about our neighbors and a better understanding of their different points of view on many subjects should not be underestimated as part of the education of any American. There may be some legitimate concern over the fact that many of the Latin American students belong in the category of "angry young men" (though their behavior on U.S. campuses has generally been irreproachable), but the qualities of the intellectual gadfly are useful at every university. Moreover, the fact that the educational standards at most Latin American universities are unsatisfactory most certainly does not warrant the conclusion that the educational standards at most Latin American secondary schools are unsatisfactory.

"above average" records, whereas 23 per cent of the other foreign students had "below average," and 36 per cent had "above average" records. Cited in Cora du Bois, Foreign Students and Higher Education in the United States (New York: Carnegie Endowment for International Peace, 1956), p. 185.

On the contrary, the standards of those secondary schools are in general highly regarded by U. S. educators.

There is little doubt but that the major problem of the Latin American students at the undergraduate level in U. S. universities is their English proficiency, not their educational background. The deficiency in the educational backgrounds of the Latin American students is an important problem at the graduate level, but the seriousness of the problem even at that level should not be overstated. To be sure, Latin American graduate students have not performed as well as other foreign students, as reflected in the note on page 90. On the other hand, we should not lose sight of the fact that while 37 per cent of the Latin Americans had "below average" records, 22 per cent had "above average" records.

My recommendation that U. S. universities "revise their admission standards, and particularly their standards for admission into graduate schools, so as to reduce the present obstacles to enrollment of Latin Americans" does not call for any lowering of the academic requirements now applicable to admission for undergraduate studies, but does call for a lowering of the English proficiency requirements. As for graduate work, my recommendation calls for a lowering of the admission standards with regard to both academic background and English proficiency. However, I am convinced that adoption of my recommendation would not lead to any deterioration of the educational standards of either the undergraduate or the graduate schools. What I have in mind more specifically may be summarized as follows:

So far as undergraduate work is concerned, the U. S. institutions would maintain the requirements for academic background at their present standards. However, they would give no weight to the question of the applicant's proficiency in English. Instead, they would advise each applicant that (a) acceptance of his application will not in itself make him eligible for enrollment for regular course work, that (b) he will be made eligible for regular course work as soon as he provides evidence satisfactory to the university of his adequate mastery of the English language, and that (c) until he has provided satisfactory evidence of his mastery of English, he will be expected to concentrate his work at the university in the special no-credit English courses which the university has established for the benefit of its foreign students.

The applicant would be free to choose the method he prefers for studying English. However, he would be encouraged to

attend the summer session of the university's special English
course prior to the usual beginning of the academic year. The
speed with which he would become eligible for regular course
work would, of course, depend upon his speed in mastering
English, but I believe that one semester of really intensive
training would ordinarily be sufficient even for the student with
little previous knowledge of the language. In any event, the
reasonably bright, and reasonably hard-working, student who
has completed his English training should then be able to
carry a sufficient load of credit courses (perhaps using other
summer sessions) to enable him to complete his undergraduate
work in the usual four years. Having concentrated first on
English, he would certainly get more out of--and contribute
more to--his regular courses than is the case with those who
are at present following a regular schedule of courses even
though their ability to understand the subject matter is limited
by their minimum comprehension of English.

So far as admission into U.S. graduate schools is concerned, the only academic requirement for graduates of Latin
American universities would be that they shall have graduated
in the top brackets of their class (e.g., the top 10 per cent-
15 per cent). Again, no weight would be given to the question
of the applicant's proficiency in English, but his initiation of
regular course work would be subject to the same understandings as those with regard to undergraduates. Furthermore, the pertinent graduate school would advise each appli-
cant--as and when the school authorities consider it appropriate
to do so--that he must take certain specific courses at the undergraduate level prior to, or concurrently with, the more advanced courses at the graduate level, and even though this would
delay his eligibility for receipt of a master's or doctoral degree.

In my opinion, these measures will help, not hurt, the
maintenance of U.S. educational standards. The requirement
that Latin American students meet minimum, high, standards
of English proficiency before undertaking regular course work at
either the undergraduate or the graduate level can only be helpful to the students, their classmates, and their professors.
And U.S. graduate schools have long followed the practice of
encouraging their students, American and foreign, to take specific
undergraduate courses together with their graduate courses. My
proposals would facilitate formal enrollment in the graduate
schools, per se, but would not reduce the academic requirements
for registering in any particular class. Furthermore, the fact
that only the top brackets of the graduates from Latin American

universities would be eligible for enrollment in the U.S. universities would provide adequate assurance of the intellectual capacity of those students; we could be reasonably confident that their deficient academic qualifications would be rectified by the undergraduate courses they would be required to take.

The problem of improving facilities for teaching English to Latin American (and other foreign) students is likely to be troublesome to the U.S. universities. However, much has already been done in this regard. It was estimated in 1955 that approximately 60 per cent of U.S. universities were making special provision for the instruction of English to their foreign students. The fourteen English Language Institutes which were in operation at that time and which were exclusively available to foreign students have been particularly successful. What is needed is an increase in the number of the Institutes and in many of the special courses offered at other universities. Furthermore, when scholarships are granted to Latin American students, provision should be made, so far as possible, for support of the students during the time they need for intensive training in English.

As suggested above, I believe that the universities granting scholarships to foreign students should give Latin Americans a much larger percentage of those scholarships than they are now getting. Approval of scholarships and admission into the U.S. universities on the principal criterion of competence, without regard for English proficiency, would undoubtedly be very helpful. * Furthermore, I believe that the universities can and should

---

*Benton points out,"The head of our student-exchange program in Lima told me that the brightest young men in the University of San Marcos--the oldest university in the hemisphere--often fail to get into U.S. colleges and universities, even when scholarships are available to them, because they cannot pass the English entrance examination. Yet they may have been studying English for years--with inadequate instructors and techniques. Thus, too high a proportion of the students who are admitted to United States colleges and universities come from the rich homes which can afford private school training in English." The Voice of Latin America (New York: Harper & Brothers, 1961), pp. 173-74.

take the measures necessary to make this policy effective a-
lone, without any need for support from, or collaboration with,
the U.S. Government. On the other hand, I believe that the
Government should revise its own program for scholarships to
Latin American students. My recommendations in this regard
are presented in Chapter 12.

CHAPTER **8** THE ROLE OF
THE U.S. UNIVERSITIES
IN INCREASING COMMUN-
ICATIONS AND UNDER-
STANDING

For the reasons discussed in Chapter 5, I believe that the most important measures which U.S. universities can take on their own to promote the Alliance for Progress are those which I recommended for facilitating the enrollment of Latin American students here. However, the full value of these measures will be reaped only in the long run. Meanwhile, the war of ideologies continues. The Free World must pursue measures which will be effective in the short run, as well as the long run. The contributions which U.S. universities can and should make to this objective consist, in my opinion, of two principal types: (1) an increase of direct contacts with the administrators and faculties of the Latin American universities and (2) encouragement to the increased authorship of books and articles which are pertinent to the problems of stimulating the economic and social growth of Latin America and which will help clarify some of the issues involved in the war of ideologies in the area.

THE CREATION OF A PAN-AMERICAN COMMUNITY OF INTELLECTUALS

Empathy among human beings has its origin in many different types of situations. It exists to a greater or lesser degree among people who share a nation in common, or a religion, or a race, or a language. It exists even among those who share a hobby in common, as among the world's philatelists, its radio "hams," and its athletes. It exists also in an important degree among those who share a common profession, as among the world's military officers, its engineers, its musicians, and its physicians. And it exists in a particularly significant way among those who live in the same mental spheres, especially the world's professors of a common subject, such as economics, sociology, history, political science, literature, etc.

Yet, very little has happened to promote the growth of the nascent empathy which exists among the Western Hemisphere's professors of economics, or its professors of political science, sociology, etc. No inter-American mechanism has been established to strengthen the intellectual bonds among the professors of any given subject. U.S. professors rarely see or talk with their Latin American colleagues. They rarely even exchange written correspondence. The natural affinity of interests which lies in the fact that they are teaching, doing research in, and writing about, the same subject has been allowed to lie fallow.

No one can properly assert that the misunderstandings and the animosities which have arisen between the United States and much of Latin America would have been averted if there had been many years of close contact among our intellectuals. No one can even be certain that those misunderstandings and animosities would have been significantly mitigated. And no one can be certain that the forces for democracy and individual initiative would already have won the ideological war which is rending Latin America. But my faith in the efficacy of truth and reason leads me to believe that many of the difficulties which are now impeding the success of the Alliance for Progress would, indeed, have been less serious if close contacts had long been maintained among the intellectuals of the hemisphere.

There is little to be gained, however, by discussion of what might have been. It may be late, but it is almost certainly not too late, to begin creating a Pan-American community of intellectuals. I am convinced that the Alliance for Progress requires it, and I believe that it is the responsibility of the U.S. universities to take the necessary initiatives.

The measures appropriate to one subject may differ from those appropriate to another subject, and there is considerable room for differences of preference among the various people concerned. However, the kinds of measures which I consider necessary would, in general, be along the following lines:[1]

1. The economics department of a U.S. university would take the initiative--separately or, preferably, in conjunction with the economics departments of other U.S. universities-- of inviting the economics departments of the more important Latin American universities to send representatives to an early conference in the United States. If possible, the host university or universities should undertake to finance the trips of a

limited number of the Latin Americans to this first conference.
Simultaneous translation facilities should be provided for the
conference.

2. The proposed agenda for the conference should be
drafted so as to emphasize its Alliance for Progress orientation and should include discussion of a charter for an Inter-
American Association of Economics Professors plus discussion
of the arrangements to be followed for the regular convocation
of subsequent (presumably, annual) conferences. In addition
the agenda should call for discussion of a limited number of
technical economic subjects especially pertinent to the Alliance,
such as (for example) the relationship between competition and
governmental development planning.

3. While the U.S. representatives would necessarily have
to bear the principal burden for organizing the first conference,
they should make every effort to pass major responsibility for
the conduct of that conference and all future conferences to the
Latin Americans. They should support election of a Latin
American economics professor as President of the Inter-
American Association of Economics Professors, and should
propose that future meetings be held under the auspices of the
Association, the sites of those meetings to be rotated among
the member countries of the Alliance.

4. The U.S. representatives should recommend also that
the Association publish the texts of the technical papers delivered
at each meeting, together with summaries of the discussions
of those papers. The Association might also provide for the is-
suance of a technical quarterly journal.

I have no doubt that many sharp differences of opinion will
arise at the meetings of the Inter-American Association of Economics Professors--as well as at the meetings of the Inter-American Association of Sociology Professors, the Inter-American
Association of Political Science Professors, the Inter-American
Association of History Professors, the Inter-American Association
of Literature Professors, etc. The nature of the conflicts may
be disturbing. But the fact that frank and full discussions are at
last taking place should contribute greatly toward the clarification
of misunderstandings and might very well lead to a general consensus on the fundamental issues of, and behind, the Alliance for
Progress. Creation of a Pan-American community of intellectuals
is a necessary--though not a sufficient--condition for the growth
of an Alliance for Progress mystique, if only because of the

tremendous influence which the Latin American intellectuals have over the public opinion and public policies of their countries.

THE ENCOURAGEMENT OF INCREASED AUTHORSHIP

Many thousands of books and articles are written each year under the auspices of U.S. universities. Many professors, instructors, and research assistants write up the results of their research activities annually. Many students write dissertations annually as partial qualifications for master's or doctoral degrees. It is therefore amazing that only a handful of the resulting publications over the past two or three years has had a direct bearing on the problems of the Alliance for Progress.

The increased authorship and publication of books and articles pertaining to the Alliance may very well transpire as an important by-product of the meetings convened by the proposed inter-American associations of professors. Whatever the stimulus, however, it is important that such books and articles be written and published, and the universities should take all appropriate measures to assure that this happens.

As has been frequently reiterated in these pages, the Alliance for Progress cannot be successful unless the people of Latin America truly believe in its basic precepts. Exhortation to belief by the respected leaders of Latin America and other parts of the Free World can no doubt be very helpful. However, a people's response to the exhortations of its leaders is bound to be ephemeral. Even the continuous repetition of a chorus of exhortations will have little enduring effect (except perhaps that of disillusionment) if they run counter to the people's deeply held convictions, whether right or wrong, or if the people are led to anticipate results which do not come to pass. Moreover, we cannot expect the leaders themselves to work vigorously for the success of the Alliance unless they too are intellectually committed to its basic precepts.

The problem is not simply one of attitudes or of broad philosophy. It may be a regrettable fact--but it is a fact that we must face squarely--that the principal questions troubling the Latin Americans are basically technical in nature, however nontechnically the questions may be phrased.

71962

It is not only the technicians who ask, "Why should we let foreign investors exploit us?" And "Why shouldn't we build a steel mill, since every country must have one if it wants to become industrialized?" And "Why shouldn't our Government build homes for us so that we can all live decently?" And "Why should we accept dictation from the International Monetary Fund, which is trying to keep us underdeveloped?" And "Everybody knows how much better off the Russians and Chinese are under socialism than they were under capitalism. Why shouldn't we follow their example?"

Broad social, political, and philosophical considerations must receive their due emphasis in the replies given to these and the many similar questions discussed elsewhere in this book. Indeed, there are many people to whom no other considerations would be convincing or even pertinent. On the other hand, there are many people whose doubts can be satisfied by nothing less than the most conclusive of technical analyses. The number of people in the latter group is especially large in Latin America, where Marxists and Marxist concepts have had a widening foothold for many years in the universities as well as in the public at large.

The U.S. universities can accordingly provide an important service for the Alliance for Progress by encouraging their economists, political scientists, historians, sociologists and other "technicians" to redirect their energies toward writing a great deal more about the basic questions troubling Latin Americans. Their analyses may not all be equally convincing. Indeed, there may prove to be need for collaboration among groups of technicians from the same and/or different disciplines, if analyses are to be forthcoming which will satisfy the doubts of Latin Americans as a whole, or the special doubts prevalent in the specific countries of the area, concerning any question. In any event, there can be no doubt about the potential usefulness of such analyses. The questions disturbing Latin Americans about the philosophy behind the Alliance for Progress can rarely be dismissed as being frivolous or superficial. They require careful and precise answers, and the Latin Americans who believe in the doctrines of the Free World deserve help in providing those answers. Our universities must accept a major share of the responsibility for providing that help.

Our universities can do more, however, than just helping answer the questions troubling the Latin Americans. They can

also make an important contribution toward resolving some of
the implementory problems of the Alliance. I am especially concerned about the need of Alliance officials to arrive, first, at
more precise understandings concerning the general objectives
to be sought by the various types of "reform" contemplated in
the Charter of Punta del Este, and to arrive, second, at more
precise standards for determining the specific reform measures
appropriate to the special circumstances of each Latin American country.

To be sure, the decisions on these matters must be made
by the Alliance officials themselves. However, as will be perceived from my discussion of "fiscal reform" in Appendix B,
the ramifications of any basic reform are likely to impinge
upon many different aspects of a country's economic, social,
and political structure. The complexities of a basic reform
effort will inevitably be great, and the scope for academic
analysis will be great commensurately. I am accordingly
confident that the Alliance officials would deeply welcome
any contributions which U.S. university technicians choose to
make.

Finally, the U.S. universities could do much to help the
Alliance by encouraging the authorship of more books and
articles which accurately depict the United States itself. If
the Latin Americans are to welcome the United States as a
partner in the Alliance, it is important that they do so for
reasons which go far beyond the economic assistance they hope
to derive from such partnership. It is important that they
respect, and even admire, our motives in participating in the
partnership. It is important that they find certain aspects of
our country worthy of emulation, or at least worthy of adaptation
to the special circumstances of their own countries. I am
greatly disturbed, therefore, by the wildly inaccurate and highly
unflattering picture which many Latin Americans have of the
United States.

To be sure, there are many other Latin Americans whose
picture of the United States is accurate, if not always flattering.
Nevertheless, it must be recognized that the misrepresentations--
including the deliberate falsehoods--which are widely circulating
in Latin America about the United States are seriously jeopardizing
the prospects for a genuine U.S.-Latin American alliance. It
must be recognized also that despite the strong efforts being made
by the U.S. Government to set the record straight (through the U.S.
Information Agency and otherwise), the Government cannot do the

job alone. Among other things, many Latin Americans believe
that the U.S. Government will inevitably be biased and that it
accordingly cannot be relied upon to tell the truth about the United
States. If the truth is to be credited, it must be told by persons
with a reputation for scholarship and objectivity. The scope for
useful work by our universities is clear.

Anyone browsing through the bookstores of Latin America
will quickly note the large number of books on display which were
written by Americans and/or which were written about the United
States. However, he will be hard put to find among those books
any which portray the United States in a favorable light. On the
contrary, he will find large numbers of books stressing, for example, the worst aspects of U.S. racial relations, the ubiquity
of power-hungry corporations and the alleged control of Wall
Street over almost all aspects of U.S. public and private life.
He will even find prominently displayed copies of books written
many years ago about U.S. "robber barons" and "international
trusts."

It would be both inaccurate and unwise to deny the failings
which continue to persist in the United States. Indeed, I greatly
treasure that aspect of the American "open society" which
encourages all forms of publicity about, and discussion of, every
questionable feature of our country. Freedom of the press and
freedom of speech are not only inalienable American rights; they
also are indispensable for the correction of our deficiencies.
Moreover, I believe that we must make no effort to conceal our
failings from Latin American and other foreign eyes, however irritating those failings may be to us and to them. Genuine friendship
can exist only when there is genuine understanding. The foundations of the Alliance for Progress must be built on the rocks of
truth, not the sands of deception.

I think it is high time, however, that we begin telling the full
truth about ourselves. We can confidently expect a continuing
flood of books and articles pointing to, and discussing, every questionable aspect of U.S. life. What we need now is to encourage the
authorship and publication of books and articles which will encompas
our failing within the whole picture of what is taking place in our
country. I do not know that this is necessary for the greater enlightenment of Americans themselves, but I am convinced that it
is necessary for the enlightenment of the Latin Americans and
other foreigners. And I believe that our universities can and
should do a great deal to assure that it gets done. 2

The kinds of books and articles that I believe should be written in greater quantity (and with greater objectivity, but as nontechnically as possible) include the following:

- Descriptions of how the American capitalism of today differs from the American capitalism of the nineteenth century and even from the American capitalism of the 1920's. (To a large extent, the Marxists and other anti-Americans are kicking a dead horse. It is time we buried that horse. Private enterprise continues to be the driving force of our economy. But if "powerful, uncontrollable monopolies" and "indifference to the public welfare" were ever characteristics of our private enterprise system, they most certainly are no longer.)

- Descriptions of working conditions today and management-union relations today, as compared with what they used to be.

- Descriptions of the social security benefits which most Americans are now receiving as a result of both governmental legislation and privately sponsored "group" plans.

- Descriptions of the forward-looking thrust of the American economy, with the allocation of huge sums, by the government and by private enterprise, to research and development for the production of new and better products.

- Descriptions of the steady and pronounced improvement in race relations during the past 10-20 years, with reports about the efforts being made in all parts of the United States, and by large numbers of whites as well as Negroes, to arrive at full equality of treatment between the races.

- Descriptions of the extent to which culture in its various forms has become a prominent feature in the lives of all sectors of the American people and in all parts of the United States.

- Descriptions of the "new breed" of serious-minded, imaginative, and socially conscious American business executive.

- Descriptions of the tremendous vitality,
  the revolutionary spirit of "let's do better,"
  that permeates almost every aspect of
  American life.

The caricature of Americans that is widely accepted in
Latin America depicts us as being smug and even boastful
about our material wealth, while being uncultured and insen-
sitive to injustice; and as being overly aggressive in the defense
of private enterprise, while feeling very insecure because of
"the triumphant march of socialism" in other parts of the
world. The American economy and American psyche are
depicted as essentially static, if not reactionary; and its role
as a world power is represented as emanating from its military, not its spiritual, strength. The fact that the bulk of our
own literature is so highly self-critical; the fact that so many
of our public pronouncements focus on the threat of Communism
and Castroism; the emphasis we place on our overseas military
bases and on our military alignments; our legislation cutting off
economic aid to countries mistreating American-owned firms--
all of these are offered as evidence of the accuracy of the caricature.

Those who really know the United States know that, in fact,
we are in general far from smug or boastful; we are indeed
proud of our country, but we are also deeply conscious of the
need to do better. We are vigorous exponents of private enterprise, but only because of the great benefits it has brought to us
and to many other countries of the Free World and because we
are genuinely convinced that the underdeveloped countries of the
Free World will make greater national and personal progress
if they rely predominantly on private enterprise, foreign and
domestic, than if they rely predominantly on governmental management. We do not fear the economic, social, or spiritual competition of the Communist countries, but we maintain our overseas
military bases and our military alignments because we know that
the Communist countries would otherwise impose their military
power over the rest of the world. Above all, our country is
intensely dynamic in every important sense. The spirit of peaceful
revolution is very much alive in the United States--much more
alive than it is in any of the Communist countries.

We know these facts about the United States. It is necessary
that our literature communicate this knowledge to the Latin Americans.

CHAPTER 9   THE ROLE OF U.S. BUSINESS

The success of the Alliance for Progress depends very largely upon strengthening the contribution of private enterprise toward the economic and social growth of Latin America. Private enterprise will not flourish, however, just because the Charter of Punta del Este stresses its importance. Nor will it flourish just because governments put a great deal of money into the roads, ports, hydroelectric power facilties, and other "infrastructure" projects which will help broaden the markets and lower the costs of production of private firms. Private investment depends also--and primarily--upon the existence of reasonable confidence that the firms will be allowed to seek a profit on their investment without excessive harassment and interference from the government and without the threat of some form of expropriation. The success of the Alliance accordingly depends very largely upon creating more favorable attitudes among Latin American professors, students, laborers, newspapermen--and, indeed, the public at large--toward private enterprise.

Energetic pursuit by U.S. universities of the measures recommended in the preceding chapters would contribute greatly toward clarifying many of the doubts which prevail in Latin America concerning the desirability of private enterprise. In addition, U.S. labor, the U.S. press (including the producers of books, magazines, and other information media), and other Free World institutions could make important contributions toward this objective, as discussed later. However, I believe that U.S. businessmen could play an especially important role, quite apart from the impressive role they have already been playing through the impetus which their investments have been giving to the economic and social growth of Latin America. In particular, they should greatly intensify their participation in the war of ideologies taking place in that area.

The primary function of the U.S. business representative in any foreign country is, of course, to help earn a satisfactory profit for his firm, while helping protect the realizable value of the firm's investment in that country. I will not attempt to describe here the various types of considerations which competent businessmen ordinarily and necessarily take into account

when seeking to fulfill this function. Instead, I shall concentrate
on three subsidiary functions which I believe our business representatives should--but do not always--seek to perform if they
are to serve their primary function well, particularly for the
long-run and particularly where the businessman manages some
sort of firm in the host country (rather than serving only as a
sales representative).

The first of the subsidiary functions is that of seeking to identi
fy the interests of his firm with those of the host country. It is
certainly not necessarily true that what is good for a firm must
be good for the country. In practice, however, it very often
works out that way. Moreover, the reverse is usually true,
namely, that what is good for the country is going to be good for
the firm, particularly in the long run. Certainly, the community
of interests is great, and it is important, in my opinion, that the
U.S. businessmen devote a substantial part of their energies
to demonstration of that fact. The detractors of American firms
are increasingly busy almost everywhere, and few of these firms
can be confident of a long-term welcome and nondiscriminatory
treatment abroad unless they devote much more attention to refut-
ing the unfounded allegations of their detractors. It is not enough
to demonstrate the worth of their products to their consumers.
They must also demonstrate the worth of their firms to the entire
country.

A second subsidiary function is that of helping promote an
accurate image of foreign investment in general, in terms of its
contribution to the over-all interests of the host country. Whatever advantage any firm might derive from a successful effort
to improve its own image is likely to be dissipated if foreign investments as a whole are generally considered in any country to
have little or no-- or even negative--value to that country. Yet
it is a fact, albeit a ludicrous fact, that there is a widespread and
growing belief in many countries that in one respect or another
foreign investments are impeding the growth of those countries or
unduly limiting their political or economic sovereignty. It rarely
does much good to point out that such theses are Communist inspir
since they are widely held even by people who are strongly anti-
Communist. It is necessary to meet the attacks on foreign investments head-on, and our businessmen should be prepared to partici
pate to a greater extent in that confrontation.

A third subsidiary function is that of helping demonstrate the
value of private enterprise, per se, and whether of national or
foreign origin. I consider this to be in many ways the most critica

function of all, especially in Latin America. For while I am not
ready to toll the death knell of private enterprise in any of the
member countries of the Alliance for Progress, I believe that
one would have to be very ill-informed or very prone to self-
delusion if he were to deny the growing strength of Marxism in
many of those countries. The threat which this poses for foreign
investments needs no stressing. However, much more is at
stake than the security of foreign investments. The triumph of
Marxism in any of those countries would also jeopardize their
achievement and maintenance of maximum economic and social
growth, their preservation of individual liberties, and their relationships with the Free World.

It is of some consolation that many of those who have been
persuaded of the validity of Marxist doctrines are genuinely non-
Communist or even strongly anti-Communist. As long as they
adhere to Marxist doctrines because of honest intellectual conviction, rather than because of the quasi-religious fanaticism
which characterizes most Communists, the opportunity persists
to convince them of the inherent advantages which private enterprise has over public enterprise in most fields of human endeavor.
And of course we have an even better opportunity to obtain the
support of those who are not yet committed intellectually, and to
strengthen the intellectual support of those who are still with us.
But a campaign in the field of ideology must be waged with a full
complement of ideological weapons. I believe that our businessmen in Latin America could contribute a much more effective
set of such weapons than they have so far contributed.

****

Fortunately, the subsidiary functions outlined above are, in
my opinion, consistent with one another, so that the measure taken
to perform any one of them will either not affect, or will actually
facilitate, performance of the others. On the other hand, I have
frequently heard the argument that the measures necessary to perform any or all of those functions would tend to involve the firm
or its American staff in public controversies. The argument continues that since Americans cannot expect to win in public controversies with citizens of the host country, prudence requires that
great care be taken to avoid such controversies, lest they jeopardize the market for the firm's products and thereby impede performance of the firm's "normal" function of maximizing sales and
the profit on sales.

I do not deny that such jeopardy may exist in certain situations. However, I believe, for reasons to be mentioned below, that where the jeopardy might exist, it would have existed even if the firm had not taken the initiative in calling attention to itself. I am convinced that if the recommended measures are well implemented by any firm their effect will be to reduce the jeopardy which already exists not only to the firm's markets but even to the firm's very existence. To be sure, there is an element of question-begging in the caution that the recommended measures must be well implemented. The measures are largely concerned with public relations, and therefore require delicate handling. Explosives normally can serve constructive purposes, but they can be destructive as well. It should be evident, for example, that however honest a firm might be in publicizing the facts regarding its activities, it could hurt its public relations if it were to sound paternalistic or if it were to draw unnecessary and invidious comparisons with nationally owned companies. Adroit implementation of the recommended measures is essential, but I am confident that our businessmen abroad can be relied upon in this regard.

In any event, I believe that if we are to expect U.S. businessmen abroad to implement the measures necessary for effective performance of the subsidiary functions described above, it is of crucial importance that they be instructed to do so by their superiors in the U.S. headquarters of their firms. [1] The U.S. businessmen abroad normally believe that their headquarters staff wants just one thing from them: attractive profit and loss statements. They usually believe that their sole job is to sell soap or tires or refrigerators, etc., and that their headquarters staff will accordingly be irritated if word gets back that they have involved themselves in unpleasant public controversies.

Our businessmen abroad generally believe they are expected by headquarters to follow the dictum: Tend to your knitting and stay out of trouble. The dictum may be a wise one at home, but I consider it meaningless, or at least unenforceable, abroad. For I believe that trouble is an inextricable part of any foreign investment.

Foreign-owned companies will inevitably be a special center of interest in any country. Rumors of many types--including those provoking suspicion, distrust, anger, and even hatred--are bound to be circulated about them, and troubles are bound to ensue Campaigns are under way almost everywhere in Latin America cal

ing for expropriation of some American companies or calling upon
the public to refrain from buying their products on the basis of the
allegation, for example, that the companies are making huge profits by charging exorbitant prices or by exploiting their labor
force; or that their products cause sterility; or that the companies
do not like or respect the country as proven by the small number
of the country's citizens among their management or engineering
staffs; or that foreign companies are collectively bleeding the
country by remitting excessive profits abroad; or that the companies belong to international monopolies which have succeeded
in preventing local businessmen from producing or selling similar
products; or that the companies are interfering in the country's
internal affairs by financing one of the political parties.

It is a vain hope, in my opinion, to rely upon the ingrained
American belief that the truth will out and justice triumph, or
upon the belief that the public everywhere recognizes the high
ethical standards of American businessmen, or that the public
will see through the unfounded rumors, recognizing the Com-
munistic or otherwise malevolent motivations of those who are
propagating them.   Too often, the public abroad is unsophisticated or ill-informed.   Failure to refute an allegation is too often
interpreted as proof that the allegation is true.

Our opponents know the value of the big lie.   Their charges
against U.S. business firms are gaining increasing acceptance
almost everywhere.   Accordingly, I believe that the dictum to
the U.S. businessmen abroad should be revised so as to state:
Tend to your knitting and get into trouble, intelligently but firmly.
The trouble is there already, whether in a virulent or latent form,
and our business representatives abroad will not long be able to
show the profit and loss statements desired by their headquarters
unless they take the necessary steps to help overcome that trouble.
It is no longer prudent, if it ever was, to entrust their public relations to the tender mercies of their opponents.   They are engaged
in a life and death struggle; and if truth and justice are to triumph,
it will only happen because an effective campaign is mounted to let
the truth be known.   I believe that most of our business representatives abroad recognize the problem and will be happy to undertake
the necessary measures to help overcome it.   But I believe also
that they will continue to be reluctant to do so unless those measures
are welcomed and encouraged by their headquarters.

Let me now outline five measures which I believe our business
representatives in Latin America should be encouraged or instructed
to undertake on a much greater scale than heretofore:

<u>One.</u> In addition to the "normal" advertising of its products, each firm should mount a publicity campaign to reveal the contribution which the firm, per se, is making to the welfare of the community. While the contents and extent of such publicity will obviously have to vary in accordance with the special circumstances of each firm and each country, some or all of the following ingredients should be contained:

- The number of people whose livelihoods are directly derived from employment by the firm, with a breakdown of employees as between national citizens and foreigners.

- The number of people, listed by the specific localities of their places of work, who indirectly derive a significant part of their livelihood from the raw materials or components or services which the U.S. firm procures from them.

- The contribution of the firm's activities toward resolution of the country's balance-of-payments problem. Where appropriate, this would include the annual value of the company's exports. Alternatively, it might include an estimate of the foreign exchange payments which the country would have had to make if it had had to import the products which were, in fact, produced domestically by the firm (after allowing for any raw materials or components imported by the firm for incorporation into its finished products).

- The benefits which the economy as a whole derives from the firm's affiliation with parent and sister companies in the United States and other parts of the world. Where appropriate, this should include emphasis upon the specific product and cost reduction improvements which the firm has been enabled to accomplish by having had the benefit of the research and development programs of affiliated companies. Attention might also be paid to the special trade advantages deriving from sales to, or purchases from, affiliated companies.

- The amount of taxes paid by the firm and deriving from sale of the firm's products.

- Employee wage scales, as compared with national or local averages.

- The fringe benefits available to the firm's employees, including detailed information about
  the firm's health clinics and schools for the
  employees and their families. Also, the firm's
  pension plans and its contributions to employees'
  health and life insurance policies.

- The firm's program for training its employees
  in more advanced skills, including reports of the
  number of employees who have in fact been promoted
  to more responsible and more remunerative
  positions in consequence of such training.

- Reports concerning the profits earned by the
  firm, especially where such reports are released in the United States anyhow. Emphasis
  should be placed upon the extent to which the
  profits have been reinvested in the host country
  and upon the rate of return received by the
  U.S. investors from that portion of the firm's
  profits which has been remitted to the United
  States.

- Evidence concerning the firm's readiness to
  accept local partners, including its readiness
  to sell stock on local stock exchanges.

- Evidence concerning any special contributions
  which the firm is making toward promoting the
  country's economic or social development. For
  example, I know of certain U.S.-owned firms
  dealing in agricultural products which, as a regular part of their business conduct, have long
  been providing both low-interest loans and technical assistance to small farmers in several of
  the Latin American countries. In so doing, they
  have helped strengthen the ability of those farmers to own their own plots of land and to increase
  the output and the income derived from their land.
  It would be completely justifiable for the American
  firms to say that they have accordingly helped
  bring about the "land reform" which is called for
  in the Charter of Punta del Este, and have done so
  in a manner thoroughly consistent with the basic
  principles of private enterprise.

The manager of a U.S. firm abroad once told me that, while the public image of his firm would undoubtedly benefit from wider awareness of the contribution it was making to the welfare of the country and while he would accordingly be happy to compile the necessary information, he would prefer that such information be disseminated by some agency other than the firm itself, because he was afraid of becoming embroiled in any public disputes. I have already expressed my views, above, concerning the hazards of becoming involved in public disputes, but I wish to point to one additional aspect of this subject, namely, the need to avoid putting too heavy a load on our friends. The following conversation, which I had in one of the Latin American countries and the substance of which has remained vivid in my recollection for several years, will illustrate my point:

"Yuan," I said, "you deserve a great deal of credit for the statements you made on TV a few nights ago in defense of the X Power Company. You were very fair in your comments, and I congratulate you."

To my astonishment, Yuan--who was president of one of the large power complexes owned by his government--did not appear at all pleased by my statement. On the contrary, he seemed to be distinctly irritated. He said,

> That's the trouble with you Americans. You
> rely on people like me to pull your irons out of the
> fire. The X Power Company is under serious attack
> as a foreign exploiter. And who has to defend it?
> People like me. The company never says a word
> in its own defense except behind closed doors. I
> once worked for the company, and I know the excellent job it has been doing for my country and the
> very small profits it has been earning. Among
> other things, I and literally hundreds of my
> countrymen owe our present positions in other
> enterprises very largely to what we learned as
> a result of the opportunities for personal advancement that were given to us by the company. I
> want to tell the truth about the company, and I
> know many others who would like to do so. But
> do you know what is said about us when we defend
> the company while the company itself remains silent? Do you know what people have been saying
> about me because of that blankety blank TV program? I am being accused of being a paid agent

of the company. I am being accused of having
sold out to the enemies of my country. People
are saying that the reason the company is keeping silent is that they've hired me to do their
dirty work for them. Why should I expose myself to such abuse if the company doesn't consider the attacks against it important?

Two. Each U.S. business representative abroad should
be encouraged to offer whatever technical assistance he can
appropriately offer toward implementation of the host country's development program. Of course, they must all be careful, as foreigners, to avoid the appearance of seeking through
such offers to obtain preferential positions for their firms or
the appearance of taking sides in any of the many types of political disputes which prevail in every country. It is possible
that their motives in offering to be helpful will be distorted,
however cautious they may be in expressing their willingness
to respond to requests for assistance. However, I believe
that this is a risk which must be taken.

Our business representatives in Latin America have often
been sent there precisely because they possess technical skills
and know-how of the various types which are most appropriate
to the needs of the countries of that region. I consider it proper
and desirable that the government officials of those countries
be given the opportunity to draw upon such skills and know-how
to help them implement their objectives of economic and social
progress.

To be sure, our representatives are already contributing
to such progress through the firms in which they are employed.
However, most governments aspire to more rapid rates of
growth, and many of them are severely handicapped by the inadequacy of personnel needed for the formulation and effectuation
of the specific projects which they consider to be the keys to
overcoming their critical economic or social bottlenecks. Our
representatives might accordingly be able to provide indispensable assistance to them. Moreover, the technical assistance
they could provide might well be sounder than that which the host
government could obtain if it were to seek assistance from
abroad. The technicians who have been living and working in a
country normally can foresee problems and find solutions which
are not so evident to others.

The very manifestation of a readiness on the part of our business representatives to provide technical assistance would be a gracious and proper gesture, as incumbent upon the foreign guests in any country. Even more important, I believe that such manifestation is necessary as evidence of what I believe has long been the case, but has never been adequately demonstrated in most countries--namely, the fact that the U.S. business representatives have brought to those countries the same spirit of public service, the same dedication to the public welfare as characterizes the American citizen in his own country.

During the course of my twenty-one years as a U.S. Government official, and especially during my eleven years as a U.S. Embassy official in the Far East and in Latin America, I had many conversations with American businessmen in which the latter showed a great desire to help promote the welfare of the people of the host country, but where they also showed a great fear of "getting involved," to the possible detriment of their firms. I believe that the time for them to get involved has arrived, if only because the world has become increasingly troubled, and their firms are critical elements in the troubled world. The welcome beacon for private investment in general, and foreign private investment in particular, may be dimmed in Latin America and elsewhere unless the businessmen who epitomize such investment do a better job of showing their genuine interest in the public welfare.

Three. Our businessmen should play a much more prominent role in sponsoring cultural affairs in their host countries. It is in a nation's culture--in its literature, its painting and sculpture, and its music--that its soul is most deeply embedded. Yet, there are few countries where the budding artists or even the artistic leaders are able to earn tolerable incomes from their spiritual or intellectual efforts. And in many countries, concert halls, orchestras, operatic and ballet groups, and even good publishing houses can survive only on the basis of philanthropic support--support which is not always forthcoming. It has accordingly been traditional for business leaders everywhere, and particularly in the United States, to sponsor artistic activities and, on occasion, to help support the artists themselves. The U.S. businessmen who are willing to help cultivate the arts in their own country should be willing also to do so in the country which has given them hospitality.

I consider it all the more important that they do so because of the need to refute as thoroughly as possible that particular big lie which depicts Americans as uncultured materialists.
That lie is more than just insulting. It is a highly useful
weapon in the arsenal of the Marxists, who use it as "demonstration" of their claim that whatever may be the material advantages deriving from private enterprise, the strains of competition for profit and even for mere survival are so severe
that no room is left for the more noble human sentiments. It
is only by following the path of socialism, they say, that high
cultural levels can be achieved alongside of high material
achievements.

It would be foolish to deny that Americans are interested in
material things. In the first place, it is true that we are interested in them, though I very much doubt that we are more so than
the people of every other country. In the second place, we can be
very proud of our success in satisfying the material wants of our
people, for the reason, among others, that this success has itself facilitated a deeper and more widespread dispersion of
culture through all segments of the American populace than has
transpired in any other country. The fact that violence and sen-
sationalism of various types are principal ingredients of much
of our popular entertainment cannot be denied. There continues
to be much room for cultural growth in the United States. However, this fact should not be allowed to obscure the additional
fact that there are many excellent orchestras, ballet groups,
theaters, libraries, and museums throughout our country. Nor
can anyone fail to be impressed by the extraordinarily high
annual sales of classical records, good books, and paintings
(both originals and reproductions).

Our businessmen abroad can do much to dispel the misunderstandings in Latin America on this subject, and I believe it is important that they do so.

Four.   Each American-owned firm in a Latin American country should be encouraged to participate in a campaign to demonstrate the contributions which the foreign-owned firms are
collectively making to the economic and social progress of that
country. This requires collaboration not only with the other American-owned firms, but also, so far as possible, with the firms
owned by nationals of other foreign countries.

It was pointed out above that there is a widespread and growing
belief, even among people who are strongly anti-Communist, that

in one respect or another foreign investments are impeding the growth of their countries or unduly limiting their political or economic sovereignty. Vigorous efforts to publicize the separate contributions of each of the foreign-owned firms can do much to help clarify this subject, but full clarification can only be accomplished, in my opinion, by treatment of foreign investments as a whole.

Let me summarize some of the principal charges which have been leveled, even by honest though misguided critics, against foreign investments in general:

- That the total withdrawals of profits and capital by the foreign investors in certain countries are exceeding the total entry of new capital, thereby providing a net burden for their balance of payments or--as sometimes stated--"bleeding the economy."

- That the foreign investments in certain countries are "exploitative" in the sense that they extract and export the country's natural resources in such fashion as to yield huge profits which the investors retain abroad, "leaving nothing but holes in the ground."

- That foreign investors control segments of the economy of such great importance as to constitute foreign usurpation of the country's economic sovereignty. Investments in such diverse areas as hydroelectric power facilities, petroleum exploration or refining, meat packing, railroads and telephone service have all been subjected to this charge. So have investments in such areas as bananas, sugar and copper, when the production of these commodities has constituted a large part of the national income of a large part of the country's foreign exchange receipts.

- That the foreign investments actually impede the country's economic growth because they have diverted the country's resources away from production of "essentials" such as roads, steel and tractors and into the production of "nonessentials," such as soft drinks, cosmetics, and luxurious hotels.

- That the rich foreign-owned firms have taken improper advantage of the country's generosity or laxness by borrowing from the local banks to meet working capital requirements, thereby sharply reducing the amount of credit available for financing the working capital needs of the nationally owned firms.

- That the economy is suffering, or may later suffer, several special types of injury because of the international affiliations of the foreign-owned exporting firms. It is sometimes charged, for example, that the headquarters companies of these firms allocate total import markets among their separate exporting subsidiaries around the world in such fashion as to maximize the profits of the headquarters companies without regard for the effect of such allocations upon the balance-of-payments positions of the separate exporting countries. Likewise, it is sometimes charged that, where the headquarters company owns exporting subsidiaries in some countries and importing subsidiaries in others, the prices paid to the exporting subsidiaries may be unduly low so as to yield better profit margins for the importing subsidiaries, again without regard to the welfare of the importing country.

- That the foreign-owned firms are able--by reason of their superior "economic power" or by reason of their affiliations with firms in other countries-- to prevent the production or sale of similar products by locally owned firms.

Unfortunately, such charges can be expressed much more simply than they can be refuted. Yet, refutation is necessary and can always or almost always be achieved, particularly if competent economists are used for the presentation and analysis of all of the facts pertinent to each of the charges. However, the pertinent facts and the appropriate analyses will vary from country to country and from time to time. Furthermore, no single foreign-owned firm can be expected to have all of the facts pertaining to all of the foreign-owned firms. Regular collaboration for this purpose among the foreign-owned firms is therefore necessary.

Five: All U.S. business representatives in Latin America should be encouraged to join, and participate actively in, the many types of local and national business and professional groups, especially the chambers of commerce and industry, in their respective communities.

American-owned firms have certain special problems which can best be handled in the American Chamber of Commerce in their community. But most of their problems are shared by all firms, whatever the nationality of their owners. It is in the best interests of all that the problems which are held in common be considered in common.

It seems to me self-evident, furthermore, that Americans cannot expect to be considered genuinely interested in the welfare of the entire business community and the entire country unless they participate actively in the various local and national organizations where those problems are being discussed. It is worth stressing, again, that the Americans must always try to avoid entanglement in the country's political disputes. This will not always be possible, particularly where the business community as a whole is opposed to some governmental policy. But the hazard of entanglement will not exist with respect to every business problem. And where it does exist, there will rarely, if ever, be any need for an American to play the role of leadership; his role can be limited to concurrence, or abstention, or even opposition. The fact of active participation is likely to be more important than the opinions expressed.

The importance of active participation would be especially great, in my opinion, in those countries--and there are many of them--where the national businessmen are among the leading opponents of foreign investments. Many such businessmen are skeptical about the value of foreign investments because of their credence in some of the charges summarized above. Others believe that the profitability of their own investments is being, or would be, limited by foreign investments in the same area of activity. Sometimes, the opposition to foreign investments derives principally from nationalistic sentiments. Whatever the explanation, however, it is important that the U.S. business representatives take advantage of every opportunity to discuss these problems openly and fully with their counterparts in Latin America.

Finally, I believe that by increasing their participation in local and national business organizations, our businessmen would be able to make a more effective contribution toward demonstrating the many advantages which the system of private enterprise has over socialism. By joining their business knowledge and intelligence to that of the other businessmen and their respective countries, the U.S. businessmen can help provide industry-wide evidence of how private enterprise really functions. They can help demonstrate how it serves, among other things, to promote productive efficiency and low costs, product development and improvement and wide consumer choice.

The businessmen of a country, whether foreigners or nationals, can collectively put together an effective demonstration that private enterprise is desirable not only because it provides maximum opportunity for the spirit of each individual to flower, but also because it is the best means for promoting economic and social development. Businessmen have an important role to play in the war of ideologies which is being waged in Latin America and elsewhere. It would not be proper for the U.S. businessmen who are guests in foreign countries to exercise leadership in this war, but I believe that they can quite properly play a supporting role, if requested. I do not believe that their participation would be resented by any objective citizen of another country as long as that participation is clearly motivated by the principle that knowledge of the truth is a prerequisite for the triumph of democratic institutions.

CHAPTER **10** THE ROLE
OF U. S.
LABOR

One of the most distressing features of the present phase
of the Alliance for Progress is the fact that it has so far received little active support from Latin American labor. In
common with almost everyone else, most unions have welcomed the foreign assistance forthcoming as part of the Alliance. Moreover, most unions are intensely concerned with
various matters covered by the Alliance, such as the formulation and implementation of national development plans and
social reforms. However, their interest in such matters has
been manifested almost entirely by the pressures they have
applied on their respective governments to pursue the policies and practices which the unions consider desirable and
would have considered desirable if the Alliance had never been
created.

They have shown no disposition to consider possible modifications of their recommendations in light of such provisions
of the Charter of Punta del Este as those pertaining to the need
for foreign private investment or to the importance of monetary
stabilization. They have shown little interest in the relation
between the policies and practices of their separate countries
and the requirements for economic integration of the region.
They have shown little interest in the studies being undertaken
by the Alliance for Progress officials of the hemisphere for the
purpose of promoting sound development programs and sound
economic and social reforms. Indeed, they have shown little
interest in any of the inter-American aspects of the Alliance.
And they have even shown far too little interest in the self-help
measures which they could pursue for the betterment of their
own welfare, as well as that of their respective countries. In
general, they have been indifferent to the Alliance, per se, and
some of the unions have actually taken positions against the
Alliance.

Continuation of this state of affairs could well spell the
doom of the Alliance. There can be no Alliance for Progress
mystique if the many millions of Latin American laborers, including agricultural workers and small farmers, remain un-
enthusiastic about the Alliance, despite the fact that the economic

and social objectives of the Charter of Punta del Este were
more specifically designed to meet the needs of that group
than any other group of Latin Americans. Even without the
active support of Latin American labor for a genuine inter-
American alliance, the "winds of revolution" will doubtless
continue to drive the separate governments toward economic
and social reforms. But the synchronization of policy necessary for economic and political integration of the region will
not exist. And in the absence of an effective mechanism for
reaching common and meaningful standards for the formulation and implementation of reforms, the danger of unsuccessful
and harmful "reforms" will be greatly magnified. Indeed,
there is the serious danger that, in the absence of a common
and deeply held ideology calling for the achievement of reforms on the foundation of democratic institutions, some or
many of the separate governments will follow the illusory
paths which the Communists and other Marxists are busily
propounding.

The United States and the rest of the Free World can encourage increased support of the Alliance by Latin American
labor in many different ways. Our universities can do much
to influence the intellectuals who are playing a prominent
role in the leadership of the Latin American unions. U.S.
businessmen can do much to influence both the leaders and
the workers themselves. The U.S. Government can also
have an important impact. In my opinion, however, U.S. labor
can and should make an especially significant contribution
toward this objective by the increased mobilization of its resources and the better coordination of its efforts vis-a-vis
Latin American labor. The U.S. labor movement in general
has a deservedly high reputation among most Latin American
trade unions, and those unions will often be much more willing to
receive advice and assistance from U. S. unions than from any other
organizations. Furthermore, U. S. unions have acquired a much
higher degree of expertise than the U. S. Government has with respect
to many of the special problems confronting the Latin American unions.

The principal measures I have in mind for improving U. S.
labor's contribution toward gaining the active support of the Alliance
by Latin American labor will be discussed below. Before doing
so, however, I consider it necessary to describe the major impediments which exist in the Latin American labor scene:

1. Many of Latin America's laborers share the impression
which is general in Latin America (and in the United States as

well) that the Alliance is an exclusively government-to-government arrangement. They do not know that the success of the Alliance would be facilitated by the active support of their unions, and they do not know the forms which that support should take.

2. Many of them share the general impression that the "Alliance for Progress" is just another title for the U.S. Government's program for providing financial assistance to Latin America, and is related in some bewildering fashion to Point Four, the Agency for International Development, the Export-Import Bank, the International Monetary Fund, Public Law 480, etc. They are for the most part pleased about their understanding that the Alliance is supposed to provide an increase over the amount of aid previously extended to the Latin American governments. But they have not been adequately alerted to the possibility that the unions themselves can be the direct beneficiaries of much of that aid. It is a fact that very few U.S. Government loans have ever been made directly to Latin American unions.

3. They are understandably preoccupied with the problems which they consider to be of the most pressing and most direct relevance to their own welfare. As is a natural function of unions everywhere in the Free World, the Latin American unions are constantly striving to improve the wages, fringe benefits, and the working conditions of their membership through collective bargaining negotiations. In addition, however, almost all of the Latin American unions are constantly engaged, directly as well as indirectly, in the major political struggles taking place in their respective countries. Almost all of the unions control, or are controlled by, one of the major political parties of their country.

4. Even where unions have understood that the U.S. Government would be pleased to consider their loan applications, they have rarely known how to prepare good applications. In particular, they have rarely had the technical competence to formulate economic or social projects which would satisfy the U.S. Government's lending standards.

5. Many labor leaders have been reluctant to become identified as supporters of the Alliance. Sometimes this reluctance stems from a fear of being too closely associated with the Government of the United States. Sometimes it derives from genuine misunderstandings as to what the Alliance is all about. Very few of the labor leaders have risen from the ranks of labor. Almost all of them are lawyers, professors, or other intellectuals.

Many of them are politicians actively campaigning for elective
or appointive public office. Many of them are outright Communists. Many others consider themselves socialists or have
otherwise accepted various Marxist doctrines. On the other
hand, a great many of the labor leaders are truly devoted to
the preservation and strengthening of democratic institutions,
including private enterprise, but have little faith in the practical utility of the Alliance.

6. There are only a few organizations which purport to
represent the interests of the many millions of campesinos
(agricultural workers and small farmers) of Latin America
and which could serve as satisfactory vehicles for acquainting
them with the importance which the Alliance has for their welfare. The workers on the banana and coffee plantations of
some of the Central American countries are unionized, as are
the agricultural workers of Argentina and Colombia. And
there are a few other organizations of campesinos throughout
Latin America, including the organizations which have recently sprung up in northwestern Brazil in opposition to the
Communist-led Peasants Leagues (Ligas Camponesas) in
that large and critical area. In general, however, these organizations have had little financial or structural strength
and have been hard pressed in their struggle for mere survival. They have been ill equipped for the task of inculcating
an Alliance for Progress mystique among their poor and very
largely illiterate members.

It has been a source of considerable disappointment,
under these circumstances, that the United States labor movement has not been making anything like the contribution that
it is able to make, and should make, in support of the Alliance.
Taking into account the financial resources of the American
unions, their large numbers of highly experienced officials, and,
especially, the high regard in which they continue to be held in
Latin America, I am convinced that American labor could do a
great deal more than it has been doing to impress Latin American laborers with the justification for much more active
support of the Alliance.

It is not that American labor is unconcerned about the Alliance. George Meany, Walter Reuther, and other principal officers of the AFL-CIO have all expressed their strong endorsement of the Alliance. Serafino Romualdi, U.S. labor's representative in ORIT (the Latin American regional organization of
the ICFTU--the International Confederation of Free Trade Unions),

has likewise manifested his endorsement of the Alliance. Indeed, the American Institute for Free Labor Development (AIFLD) was established in 1961 by the AFL-CIO, with some support from the U.S. Government and from private business firms, for the principal purpose of helping promote the success of the Alliance.

I have no doubt that American labor is genuinely interested in trying to help promote the Alliance. However, I also have no doubt that it must find much better ways of manifesting that interest than it has yet found. Creation of the AIFLD was desirable, and it has in fact served some useful purposes. But additional measures, requiring the allocation of more money and more people as well as a basic reorientation of approach, are also necessary. The specific measures that I shall here recommend are summarized as follows:

THE NEED TO INCREASE UNION-TO-UNION RELATIONSHIPS

For many years, American labor has relied principally upon various multiunion and, usually, multinational, organizations--especially the ICFTU and ORIT, and, more recently, the AIFLD--to achieve its objectives in Latin America. The usefulness of these organizations should not be deprecated, and I will, in fact, make certain recommendations below for strengthening the role of the AIFLD. However, I believe that principal reliance for representing the views of U.S. labor must be shifted to the major unions themselves. I believe that each major U.S. union should endeavor to arrive at a close working relationship, union to union, with each of its counterparts in the separate Latin American countries which are members of the Alliance.

Joseph A. Beirne, President of the Communications Workers of America and Secretary-Treasurer of the AIFLD, has stated that,

> The Communications Workers of America ...
> through its "Operation South America" is carrying
> on a worker-to-worker program which not only
> provides intellectual and material intercourse but

strengthens the bonds which give succor to free
men everywhere. The more people-to-people, or
person-to-person contacts we can nurture and
develop, the wider becomes the ray of hope in
Latin America.

I consider this a highly encouraging undertaking and one which
should be emulated so far as possible by all of the other major
U.S. unions. To be sure, it may prove to be difficult when,
for example, the workers in a given Latin American industry
are organized on an industry basis whereas their U.S. counterparts are organized on a craft basis, or vice versa. Every
country has its own problems, and the U.S. unions should
not try to foist the organizational solutions which have been
found satisfactory in the United States upon any other country.
The separate U.S. unions trying to strengthen their ties in
Latin America must accept the organizational solutions which
the Latin Americans have found satisfactory, and such juris-
dictional struggles as continue to take place in the United
States must not be carried abroad. However, this kind of
difficulty will not arise often in Latin America, and I believe
it can be surmounted in the few cases where it will arise,
provided that the U.S. unions do not lose sight of their principal objective of helping build active support of the Alliance
for Progress among the workers of Latin America.

Workers in the same industry or same craft are likely to
feel a special kind and degree of closeness to one another,
even when living and working in different countries. The
worker in a copper mine in Chile will undoubtedly share many
of the ideas and attitudes of his countrymen and particularly
those of other Chilean laborers. But he will also feel a
special affinity with those who work in copper mines in the United
States or elsewhere. Indeed, he may feel (and be perfectly
correct in his feeling) that the U.S. miners understand many of
his problems better and can do more to help him overcome those
problems than, say, the steel workers, bank workers, or commercial workers of his own country. Furthermore, everything
else being equal, he will normally feel a much greater affinity
with a U.S. miner than he will with the less-specialized representative of any of the multiunion or multinational labor organizations. I accordingly urge that the major U.S. unions seek to
maximize the benefits which can be derived from the natural
empathy between them and their Latin American counterparts,
just as I urged in Chapter 8 that U.S. professors capitalize upon
the natural empathy between them and their Latin American
counterparts.

My principal concern, of course, is with the war of ideologies. The U.S. labor representatives who succeed in establishing the requisite degree of mutual understanding, confidence,
and respect with their Latin American counterparts can and
should help clarify many of the misunderstandings which have
been impairing the relations between Latin America and the
rest of the Free World. Such understanding, confidence, and
respect will not arise automatically, however, even among
workers in a common industry or craft and even when the U.S.
representatives are able to marshal their facts and argumentation persuasively. They must also be able to demonstrate
that they are genuinely concerned with the pressing problems
of the Latin American workers and workers organizations,
and that they are both willing and able to help relieve those
problems. This means that a U.S. union establishing a working
relationship with its counterpart in a given country must be
prepared to devote both money and manpower to the relationship, since both financial and technical assistance--especially
the latter--are badly needed by many Latin American unions.

The kinds of financial assistance which a U.S. union could
appropriately extend to one of its Latin American counterparts
will not ordinarily be unduly burdensome to the U.S. union,
though the degree of the burden will of course vary from
country to country and from union to union, and though the
collective burden with respect to all of the Latin American
members of the Alliance and all of their unions would doubtless
be substantial. Few Latin American unions have systematic
and effective procedures for the collection of union dues. Accordingly, many of them would benefit greatly from the receipt
of financial assistance which would permit the construction of
meeting halls, health clinics, and even gymnasiums and other
sports facilities, as well as permitting the purchase of type-
writers, filing cabinets, and other office equipment. If free
labor unions are indeed to flourish in Latin America, it is important that the unions be as free as possible from dependence
upon the support of governments or political parties or business
firms. The unions must learn how to become self-supporting, and
I would not encourage foreign assistance to help them meet their
regular operating expenses. But assistance in establishing the bas
physical facilities needed to provide the services required by their
members would often be very helpful, and would not usually be
unduly burdensome to the U.S. union providing that assistance.

On the other h   d   rovision of the kinds of technical assistanc
required by the Latin   erican unions could be very burdensome

indeed, particularly for the U.S. union undertaking to provide
such assistance to its counterparts in each of the pertinent
Latin American countries. Few U.S. unions will have counterpart unions in all of the Latin American countries, but the
technical assistance needs are likely to be large in each of the
countries where there are such unions. And effective assistance will usually depend upon the full-time, and long-time,
assignment of separate experts in different fields of union
activities to work and live in the pertinent Latin American
countries. The kinds of technical assistance needed will of
course vary from union to union, but will often include the following:

> 1. Training in the handling of office work, such as
> the maintenance of good records concerning the ad-
> dress, health, work experience, family size, educa-
> tion, etc., of each of the union members; the organiza-
> tion of an efficient filing system; the establishment of
> routine procedures for collection of union dues; the
> systematic issuance of information concerning em-
> ployment opportunities, government regulations and
> court rulings pertaining to union matters and em-
> ployee welfare; the establishment of acceptable pro-
> cedures for handling workers' complaints against
> their employers; etc.

> 2. The organization of special forms of services
> for the union members. This should often include
> help in the establishment of courses for adult educa-
> tion and in the operation of a health clinic. In certain
> situations, it should also include training in the busi-
> nesslike operation of consumers' cooperatives. The
> initiation of some forms of limited vocational train-
> ing will likewise be desirable in certain cases.

> 3. Assistance in the initiation of various types of
> self-help measures, such as the organization of
> savings and loan associations or union banks to facili-
> tate the acquisition of low-cost housing by the union
> members, or such as the formation of certain types
> of producers' cooperatives.

> 4. Assistance in the preparation of applications for
> loans from foreign governments or international agencies
> for social development projects where foreign assis-
> tance would be necessary, as will frequently be the case,

for example, with workers' cooperative housing
developments.

It will often be possible, and may be very desirable in
certain situations, for the U.S. unions to draw upon experts
who might be made available by the AIFLD (as discussed below) to provide technical assistance in one or more of these
fields. Even so, however, each major union should send at
least one, but usually more than one, of its experts to work
with each of its counterpart unions in Latin America. This
will entail losing the services of those experts in the United
States, and will also entail the costs of sending and maintaining them and their families abroad. I have recommended
that the unions accept these burdens only because of my conviction that their doing so would contribute greatly to the
victory of the Free World in the war of ideologies taking place
in Latin America, including that aspect of the struggle which
pertains directly to the freedom of the Latin American unions--
a subject with which the U.S. labor movement has long
been preoccupied.

I must concur with the frequently made charge that Latin
American unions are in general too tied up in the political
affairs of their countries to be able satisfactorily to exercise their "proper" function as independent and effective
representatives of their membership in collective bargaining negotiations. On the one hand, therefore, the Latin
American workers have generally not had any instrumentality
of their own through which they could effectively negotiate with
their employers; they have had to rely instead upon whatever
political influence they could exert. On the other hand, the intervention of political parties and government officials as
arbiters in labor disputes has increased the power of the governments over both the unions and the owners and managers of the
business firms. Neither the workers nor the employers have
benefited. Only those--principally the Communists and other
Marxists--who want to see the increasing pervasiveness of
government authority have benefited.

I am convinced, however, that the political entanglement
of Latin American labor unions will not be eradicated or even
significantly alleviated by the limited programs upon which the
U.S. labor movement has so far relied. The roots of that entanglement are deeply embedded in certain basic elements of
the current Latin American scene and cannot be loosened by
halfway measures. It is especially important to remember

that the great bulk of the union members have only recently migrated to the urban areas after having spent most of their lives as farm laborers or as the children of farm laborers. They have accordingly grown up under the tradition of paternalism, where the farm owner controls most aspects of "his" workers' lives, while holding himself responsible for supplying their minimum needs. It is hardly surprising, therefore, that these workers--when migrating to the cities--feel a strong craving for the presence of someone, almost anyone, who will continue to make most of their important decisions for them, while guaranteeing their minimum needs. It is hardly surprising that they turn to their unions principally as instruments which can provide assurance that the government will take care of their personal needs. After all, who else can be expected to take the place of the old "patrón"? Given the very inadequate education of most of the laborers, furthermore, it is easy to understand why the leadership of most unions has come from outside of their ranks, and consists very largely of intellectuals whose primary interests are in political rather than labor affairs.

We cannot expect that most Latin American labor unions will modify their basic orientations merely because of the persuasiveness of the labor leaders of the United States or other Free World countries with whom they come into occasional contact, or because of the present programs of the U.S. Government and the AIFLD for training Latin American labor leaders, or even because foreign lending institutions give preferential treatment to free labor unions. Men will not quickly or easily change their basic attitudes because of the impact of argumentation, even when they have confidence in the good intentions of those who are trying to persuade them to change their attitudes, and even when they are promised rewards for doing so. We must not treat our enemies better than our friends, and I would oppose any form of assistance to those Latin American unions which are clearly Communist-controlled. But we must not go to the extreme of offering assistance only to those unions which meet our standards of "free" labor unions and which have publicly committed themselves to oppose Communist or other Marxist influences. Communists and other Marxists are included among the leadership of most Latin American unions and it will be no simple matter to persuade the union membership to eject them or to curb their influence. The offer of rewards will rarely, if ever, bring about a genuine change of attitudes. It will more often be resented than appreciated.

In my opinion, it is essential that the major U.S. unions
make a full-scale effort to help their Latin American counterparts become efficient and effective "business unions," if the
Free World is to win the war of ideologies which is raging at
least as violently among Latin America's laborers as among
other Latin Americans, and particularly if the attitudes of
those laborers toward their unions are to change in the direction
of freedom. It is essential that representatives of the U.S.
unions be present as daily reminders of their genuine desire
to be helpful. It is essential that they be present to provide
whatever information and guidance may be requested of them,
including help in reorganizing the unions' operational procedures so as to enable them to become more self-sustaining
and more effective in collective bargaining negotiations. It
is essential that the U.S. representatives help their counterpart unions provide the kinds of social services which their
members require. And it is essential that the U.S. representatives help them pursue the kinds of self-help measures which
will not only help their members directly, but will enable
them to qualify for appropriate foreign assistance. It is only
through measures such as these that we can reasonably expect the Latin American workers to understand the meaning
of the Alliance for Progress and the advantages which the
Alliance can offer to them as individuals.

THE NEED TO EXPAND THE FUNCTIONS
AND RESOURCES OF THE AMERICAN INSTITUTE
FOR FREE LABOR DEVELOPMENT (AIFLD)

It will be seen that the major U.S. unions can provide an
indispensable series of measures to help assure the success of
the Alliance through strengthening their separate relationships
with their counterpart unions in Latin America. There are
various situations, however, where the U.S. unions can be more
effective through joint, rather than separate, action. The
AIFLD is well constituted for the purpose, though its functions
must be broadened and its resources considerably expanded.

The AIFLD is administered by officials of the AFL-CIO
and is essentially an AFL-CIO organ, though it includes certain
U.S. business executives and certain outstanding Latin Americans
on its Board of Trustees, and though part of its very limited re-

sources (totalling $500,000 in 1962 and estimated annual budgets
of $850,000 during 1963-66) has been contributed by the U.S.
Government and by some U.S. business firms. The AIFLD was
created in October, 1961, for the announced purpose of helping
promote the Alliance for Progress and has so far had two principal functions: to help train Latin American labor leaders and
to help free trade unions in Latin America organize low-cost
housing, credit unions, cooperatives, workers' clinics, voca-
tional training centers, and other community institutions needed
for the development of democratic systems. I shall have more
to say later about these important functions, but I wish first to
recommend the adoption by AIFLD of a vigorous program of assistance to the agricultural workers and small farmers of Latin
America.

In my opinion, the greatest single source of the threat to
democratic institutions in Latin America at this time lies in
the economic and social distress in the cities, rather than in
the countryside. It would be a great mistake, however, to
minimize the seriousness of the threat in the countryside. I
do not believe that the lid is ready to blow off among the campesinos anywhere in Latin America, but I may well prove to be
wrong. Certainly, no one could deny that social and political
turbulence is increasing among those poor people, and no one
could ignore the fact that Communist organizations such as the
Peasants Leagues of northeastern Brazil have been thriving
among them. The campesinos still account for a major percentage of the area's population, but they have been very largely
neglected while their governments have been devoting their
energies and resources to the pursuit of industrialization.

It was for these reasons that the signatories to the Charter
of Punta del Este put a number of provisions into the Charter
calling for land reform. However, effective land reform in
most of Latin America will require much more than the governments
can accomplish alone. The campesinos can do quite a bit to
help improve their own lot, and it is important that they be en-
couraged--and helped--to do so. In particular, I am impressed
by the untapped potential which exists for the organization of
marketing, purchasing, and service cooperatives in many parts
of Latin America.

The peaceful and equitable parcelization of large estates
(latifundia) will generally have important social benefits and
may even have important economic benefits, but it would be
unwise to assume that the economic benefits will necessarily

be large or to ignore the possibility that there might even be
serious economic harm. For the long run, the economic benefits of parcelization are likely to depend upon its synchronization with more productive use of the land. While many of the
necessary steps will have to be governmental (as, for example,
the provision of agricultural extension services) private cooperatives could often be organized to great advantage for the
storage, processing, and marketing of the major produce of a
reconstituted farm area, or for the economical purchase of
farm supplies, or for the collective use of farm machinery,
or for reciprocal assistance in the construction of homes and
barns. Such cooperatives could also contribute greatly toward
relieving the economic and social distress now prevailing in
the many regions where the major land problem is that of the
excessively small landholdings (minifundia) as well as toward
improving the economic and social conditions in many regions
where there does not now appear to be a pressing need for
land reform.

It might appear at first glance that U.S. assistance toward
promotion of a strong and successful cooperative movement
in Latin America could best be effected through collaboration
between separate campesino organizations, on the one hand,
and representatives of the many organizations of large and
successful U.S. cooperatives, on the other. As pointed out
above, however, there are very few campesino organizations
with which we could effectively collaborate in Latin America.
Furthermore, I understand that virtually none of the organizations of U.S. cooperatives has had any experience in Latin
America or with problems of the type generally prevailing on
the farms of that area. On the other hand, some of the U.S.
labor unions are very familiar with the problems on those
farms; indeed, a few of the unions (such as those which are
members of the IFPAAW--the International Federation of
Plantation, Agricultural and Allied Workers) have been
actively--though inadequately--engaged in trying to help overcome those problems. In addition, I believe that the campesinos would feel a greater affinity with members of the U.S.
labor movement that with members of U.S. cooperatives for
the reason, among others, that the economic and social gaps
which separate them from the former are smaller and less
obvious that those which separate them from the latter.

In these circumstances, the AIFLD could, and should,
make a major contribution toward the success of the Alliance
for Progress by establishing technical assistance centers in each

of the principal agricultural centers of each of the Latin American members of the Alliance, assuming, of course, that the
various governments would welcome the establishment of
those centers. The principal function of the experts assigned
to these centers should be to assist in the establishment and
effective operation of private cooperatives of the types mentioned above. If the U.S. unions themselves do not contain
enough experts with the necessary qualifications, they should
recruit them with the help that I am sure could be obtained
from the American Institute of Cooperation.

In addition, the centers should help the establishment and
effective operation of organizations of cooperatives and other
campesino organizations, including, where appropriate, organizations of agricultural workers on large plantations. The
IFPAAW (which is an International Trade Secretariat affiliated
with the ICFTU) has been quite effective with workers' organizations of the latter type, and the AIFLD might be able to
supplement that activity very usefully. The centers could be
particularly helpful in demonstrating the usefulness of the Alliance by assisting the campesino organizations in many of the
ways suggested above for assistance by separate U.S. unions
to their counterpart labor unions in Latin America. Thus, the
AIFLD could help the campesino organizations expand the
range and effectiveness of the services they provide for their
members, and could help them formulate sound applications
for foreign loans to finance specific projects, such as for the
construction of warehouses needed by the agricultural cooperatives.

The technical assistance centers for campesino affairs
would, of course, be different from the regional and national
labor training centers which AIFLD has established in thirteen
Latin American countries. I would like to see the number of
the latter increased so as to cover each of the members of the
Alliance for Progress. Moreover, I would like to see an important increase in the functions of those labor centers, beyond
their present function of training Latin American labor leaders.
Specifically, AIFLD should assign to each of those centers a
full gamut of experts in the many problems with which the separate Latin American unions must deal more effectively if they
are to become free and effective representatives of their membership. These experts should be available, if necessary and
if called upon, to assist and supplement the experts sent by the
major U.S. unions to help their Latin American counterparts.
The experts should be available also to provide necessary techni-

cal assistance to those non-Communist Latin American unions which have not yet consummated satisfactory working relationships with any of the major U.S. unions. I am convinced that union-to-union relationships can be much more effective in creating and sustaining an Alliance for Progress mystique than either confederation-to-confederation or confederation-to-union relationships. However, the AIFLD can supply considerable support to the union-to-union relationships and can even serve effectively as a temporary though inadequate substitute for the U.S. unions.

There is no need to belabor the point that the recommended expansion of the functions of the AIFLD will require a considerable increase of its financial resources. Annual contributions to the AIFLD at the 1963-66 rate of $850,000 would clearly be far from sufficient to cover the costs of sending and maintaining abroad the hundreds of experts who will be needed at both the technical assistance centers for campesino affairs and the labor training centers. Furthermore, I cannot be certain that the U.S. Government and private business firms will be willing greatly to expand their contributions to the AIFLD, though I think it would be desirable that they do so. Of this I feel convinced, however: If the workers and workers' organizations of the United States wish to prove their dedication to the Alliance for Progress and to the principles behind it, they can find no better way to do so than by supporting both the recommended expansion of the AIFLD functions and the recommended union-to-union programs. Some sacrifices by U.S. workers will be necessary, but failure to make them would impart a very hollow ring to the many pronouncements of their union leaders concerning the important role of labor in the war of ideologies and the special importance of the Alliance for Progress in that war. Halfway measures can no longer be considered acceptable. A full-scale program to obtain the active support of Latin American labor for the Alliance must be put into effect, despite the sacrifices it will entail.

CHAPTER **11** THE ROLE OF
THE U.S. PRESS

Indifference and even irresponsibility on the part of much of the U.S. press have substantially impeded creation of an Alliance for Progress mystique. Failure to give due credit to the many Latin Americans who have been trying to promote the Alliance and the unjust denigration of other Latin Americans have compounded the difficulties of many of those whose efforts on behalf of the Alliance might otherwise have been more successful. Unsatisfactory coverage of the Latin American scene has discouraged many Americans from giving the necessary support to the Alliance. And, most important, failure to give Latin Americans a more accurate picture of current developments in the United States has contributed to a deterioration of the bonds of sympathy between us.

A serious and determined effort by the U.S. press along the lines of the measures recommended below could greatly strengthen the Free World forces in the war of ideologies which is raging in Latin America. Conversely, perpetuation of the present situation could undermine or counterbalance the necessary measures of the U.S. universities, business, and labor, as well as those of the U.S. Government. It is no simple matter to overcome the frequently unfavorable impacts which the news stories daily emanating from the United States are having upon the conscious and subconscious attitudes of many Latin Americans. Nor is it a simple matter to maintain enthusiasm for the Alliance among Americans whose understanding of Latin American developments is derived from the sparce and often distorted reports and analyses appearing in some parts of the U.S. press.

This is not meant to be an indictment of the U.S. press as a whole. There have been a few (though too few) competent and conscientious U.S. correspondents in Latin America. Moreover, some U.S. newspapers, such as The New York Times and The Washington Post and Times Herald, have shown a sense of responsibility in their coverage of Latin American affairs.[1] Furthermore, our press is probably just reflecting the interests of the public at large. Our press cannot neglect to report dramatic and disturbing news because that news may mislead some, or many, readers. And our press cannot compel the public to read news reports and analyses in which it is not interested. However, the press is far from being merely a passive agent. It can report even the most dramatic and disturbing news in ways which can enlighten, rather than mislead. It can do much to bring out the drama in news which would otherwise appear to be downright boring. I am most certainly not urging the suppression or sugar-coating of any part of the truth. On the contrary, I am urging only that our press try to present the whole truth, not merely those parts which appear to be the most dramatic. The war of ideologies in Latin America is a deadly serious matter for the United States and the entire Free World, and no part of our press can afford to hide behind the comfortable balm that after all it is our Government's job to handle our country's foreign policy. Many sectors of our society have an important impact upon that policy, and the impact of our press is certainly one of the most important. I accordingly recommend that those responsible for the management of certain sectors of our press pursue the following measures:

THE NEED TO TRANSMIT MORE COMPLETE INFORMATION TO LATIN AMERICA

The ubiquitous evidence of the U.S. press in Latin America must be seen to be believed. Almost all of the major newspapers of the region subscribe to U.S. news services, particularly the Associated Press or the United Press International, and give prominent coverage to the items distributed by those services concerning internal United States matters, as well as international news. The newspapers devote considerable space to any items indicating what we are thinking and saying about Latin America and indicating our intentions with respect to influencing Latin American affairs. Beyond that, moreover, they devote considerable space to current developments within the United States, including interpretive analyses of those developments. The American presence is prominent, as manifested by the fact that many of those newspapers even carry syndicated U.S. comic strips. Not unnaturally, however, the principal emphasis is upon the more dramatic of U.S. developments--just as our own press gives its principal emphasis to such developments. The U.S. news services accordingly have an enormous influence in establishing the image which many Latin Americans have of the United States.

The news services are not responsible for the contents of
most of the news stories which flow into their central offices,
and while they have some discretionary authority in the se-
lection of the stories which they then retransmit to Latin America, I would not want them to use that authority for the purpose
of excluding any story in which the Latin Americans might be
interested. Our objective should be the addition of news, and
particularly of "interpretive news," which will reduce the dis-
tortions deriving from the ridiculous assumption that the Latin
Americans will--unaided--have the same background as Americans in evaluating a spot news item which is written with only
the American readers in mind.

I fully appreciate the danger of mingling straight, "objective" news reports with interpretive, "subjective" analyses.
The news transmitted to Latin America must be as objective as
possible, if the Alliance for Progress is to be founded on truth.
However, inasmuch as a half-truth can be thoroughly misleading,
it is a responsibility of our press to supply the missing ingredients as fully as it can, for the benefit of readers who would not
otherwise have the necessary access to such supplemental information. When truth can be served by transmitting subjective interpretations, they should be labeled as such. Frequently, however, the full truth can be served very effectively by more complete reporting of the facts and without the transmittal of subjective analyses.

To use an old example, our press, including our news
services, had no choice but to report the allegations in the mid-
1950's by the late Senator McCarthy that there were large numbers
of Communists in the State Department, but the news transmitted
abroad could have included equal emphasis upon the fact that he
dodged all challenges to document those allegations. The fact
that the executive branch of the U.S. Government did not at first
meet McCarthy head-on also had to be reported, but the strong
and steadily mounting clamor throughout the United States demanding such a confrontation should also have been reported. Even
"subjective" interpretations by competent and experienced
columnists of the extent to which McCarthyism did or did not
represent a temporary aberration from the fundamental core of
American democracy should have been reported. Transmittal
of the whole truth to Latin America about this shameful episode
in American history would not have eliminated--but would
certainly have significantly alleviated--the damage it did to the
American image in Latin America and the rest of the world.

I accordingly recommend that each of our major news services establish the firm policy of adding "interpretive news" to the reports it transmits to Latin America. If necessary, the staff responsible for selecting the news reports to be passed on to that region should be augmented by persons sufficiently familiar with Latin America to know when the interests of truth will be served by the addition of interpretive news. I do not believe that such additions will be needed frequently. But when they are needed, they are likely to be needed urgently, if not desperately. Any further outbreaks of racial violence in the United States, for example, are bound to have serious repercussions in Latin America--repercussions which might be at least a little less serious if adequately and quickly supplemented by sound interpretive news. The fact of such violence will necessarily be a blot on the American image, but the damage of that blot may be reduced by full reports of the efforts being made-- and the results being achieved--by the American people as a whole, through our Government and through private efforts, in support of racial justice. Full reporting on complex matters such as this will normally require much more analysis than can be expected of our newspapers and news services; books and magazine articles will also be necessary. However, the news services transmitting reports to Latin America must try to make them as complete as possible, because books and magazine articles--though very much needed--can never compensate fully for the hammer-blow effects of the daily news story.

I recommend further that the news services establish the policy of transmitting to Latin America a wide range of different types of information which U.S. newspapers are constantly reporting, but only in a subdued fashion, and which our news services have accordingly been overlooking when selecting items to be transmitted abroad. We in the United States are accustomed to take for granted many facts about our country which are not known, and certainly not taken for granted, in Latin America. What is not important news here may very well be important news there. For example, press stories in the United States should be passed on to Latin America whenever they report on the number and kinds of books and phonograph records sold in the U.S.; and the numbers of concerts and ballets performed, with the numbers of people attending those performances; and the number of churchgoers; and the number of stock owners. Special emphasis should be given, furthermore, to the news items revealing our multiform interests in Latin America, such as the performances of musical works by Latin American composers; the increasing number of college students majoring in Latin American affairs;

the sales of books dealing with that region; and the numbers of
lectures and radio and television programs devoted to Latin
American topics.

One special aspect of our dynamic civilization is worthy of
particular attention when selecting news items for transmittal
to Latin America, though this item is also taken for granted in
our own country. It is the remarkable absence of economic
and social stratification in our country. To be sure, we do not
often see evidence of laborers rising to executive positions.
But highly impressive evidence can be provided of the extent
to which the sons and daughters of those laborers have been
graduating from our universities and moving into positions
of considerable economic, social, and political importance.
It cannot be denied that some barriers to economic and social
advancement continue to exist because of racial and religious
prejudices, but the height of these barriers is unquestionably
declining and there are virtually no barriers because of concern or even interest in the economic or social status of one's
parents. We Americans take this situation for granted, but it
is a fact that would have high dramatic value if known in Latin
America. Few stories have as much interest anywhere, including the United States, as the so-called human interest
story. And few human interest stories about the United States
would have as much value in Latin America--where economic
and social stratification continue to be serious problems--as the
literally millions of "rags to riches" stories which can be
reported about the United States.

I remember very well being told by a Brazilian Finance
Minister and the Governor of one of Brazil's more populous
States that Abraham Lincoln continues to be the most popular
man in Brazil. They told me that pictures of Lincoln continue to
be hung prominently in school buildings all over the country and
that "everyone" is familiar with the story of his life. They
conceded that his role in ending slavery is undoubtedly one
of the most important reasons for his popularity in Brazil, but
they stressed the fact that his having risen from a log cabin to
the presidency is even more important. As they pointed out,
it is the dream of all of the children of humble families in
Brazil (and of Latin America as a whole) that they too will some
day rise to positions of economic and social importance in their
country, in the Lincoln pattern. As I see it, this is the dream
which the Alliance for Progress is trying to make a living reality
for millions of Latin American children who do not now have a
realistic chance to achieve it. It is a dream which has become a

reality for millions of American children under the democratic institutions of our own country and which, indeed, has become much more attainable since the time of Lincoln. It is time that we tell these facts about our country, lest the people of Latin America come to believe that Lincoln's rise was an accident and that capitalism in the United States has stifled the opportunities for advancement by the children of anyone but the rich and powerful.

Clearly, the Spanish- and Portugese-language newspapers and magazines of Latin America are the principal news media in which the full truth about our country must be told. They are the media which have by far the greatest circulation in Latin America among all economic and social classes. It would be a serious mistake, however, to overlook the significance of certain English-language magazines. Many Latin American leaders have studied English and find it helpful to polish their English-proficiency as well as to keep up to date about U.S. and world developments by reading those magazines, especially Time magazine. I do not know the statistics pertaining to the weekly sales of the Latin American edition of Time, but the total must be very large, judging from the prevalence of that magazine on newsstands everywhere in Latin America, as well as the number of times I have seen it in the offices and homes of Latin Americans, and judging also from the number of times I have found myself involved in discussions with Latin Americans about stories appearing in Time.

The popularity of Time is understandable. Its stories are uniformly written in a highly readable style. The scope of its over-all coverage is excellent. Its Latin American edition often deals with Latin American affairs not reported upon elsewhere, even in the U.S. edition of Time. And the events which it covers always seem very current even though it is published only weekly. It is all the more regrettable, therefore, that Time has so often carried stories injurious to the Free World's position in the war o ideologies. I am certain that the editors of Time are whole-heartedly devoted to the democratic institutions of the Free World and that they would never knowingly print any stories designed to harm the image of the Free World in Latin America or to undermi the democratic institutions of that region. The fact that they have often done both must be attributed to the fact that they have not known what they were doing. It is high time, however, that they learned.

The bulk of the Latin American edition of Time is taken
from the U.S. edition. I cannot expect that the publisher of
Time will decide to modify the editorial policies which have
been so commercially successful for the U.S. edition "merely"
out of concern for the Alliance for Progress and the war of
ideologies in Latin America. However, I do not consider it
unreasonable to recommend that more care be taken hereafter in composing the Latin American edition. To the extent
necessary, stories taken from the U.S. edition about complex
matters in the United States and other Free World countries
should be edited by dropping the "good guys--bad guys" syndrome
and concentrating instead upon careful reporting of the basic
issues which are disturbing us but which are almost all being
resolved through the workings of democratic processes, albeit
sometimes awkwardly and even painfully. It may entertain
some readers to convey the impression that the Free World is
being led by a group of buffoons, but the effects of having conveyed that impression to the Latin Americans have been far
from amusing.

Reports about Latin American affairs should likewise be
written with much greater care, omitting, for example, facile
and undocumented references to political figures as "demagogues,"
"leftists," "oligarchs," etc. Labels may make easy reading,
but they are seldom satisfactory descriptions of human beings,
and are often very irritating to the people at whom they are directed. The issues disturbing Latin America are at least as
complex as those disturbing most of the rest of the world and
can rarely be described in a few amusingly written sentences or
by the use of fuzzy and oversimplified labels. Nor can Latin
American attitudes toward the United States be improved by
such irresponsible stories as the inaccurate attribution to a
U.S. Embassy official in La Paz some time ago of the no doubt
"witty," but ridiculous, statement that the only way to solve
Bolivia's problems would be to split up that country and divide
it among its neighbors. If the democratic institutions of Latin
America are to function effectively, it is important that each
country be encouraged to work out its problems by concentration on issues rather than on personalities or on nationalistic
emotions. Time can significantly help those institutions, if it
feels so inclined.

THE NEED TO TRANSMIT MORE COMPLETE
INFORMATION ABOUT
LATIN AMERICA TO THE UNITED STATES

Current events in Latin America are reported to the United States primarily by a mere handful of correspondents stationed in that large area by our major news services and a few newspapers and magazines and, to a less significant extent, by "stringers" (usually citizens of the country in which they live) who receive separate payment for each report which they send to the United States and which is printed. I have known a few highly competent and conscientious men among those correspondents, and have generally found their reports to be trustworthy. However, the bulk of the reporting about Latin America has focussed too heavily on the more obviously dramatic of the political events, with far too little attention to the changes which have been taking place in the underlying economic and social factors influencing those events. In particular, far too little attention has been given to the many forward steps which have been made under the Alliance for Progress, as summarized in the appendix to Chapter 2. There has been inadequate coverage even of the more important inter-American conferences concerning Alliance matters. And while the most dramatic political events have been reported, the motivations of the dramatis personae have often been distorted, whether because of oversimplification or because of the reporter's unawareness of the substantive issues involved.

Furthermore, far too much stress has been placed on the influence of Cuba and Castro in Latin America as a whole. The Cuban problem is indeed a serious one, and there is no doubt about the fact that it has significantly disturbed the political situation all over the hemisphere. However, the fundamental economic and social changes which have been in process in many Latin American countries carry very important long-term implications which should not have been slighted by our correspondents, as they have been, just because of our concern over Cuba. Some of the most important aspects of the Cuban problem should be considered primarily (though not exclusively) within the context of U.S. relations with the Communist bloc, rather than as problems which are primarily Latin American in character. The problems of the Alliance for Progress countries are very different from those of Cuba, and warrant close and separate attention. In the long run, the developments which are now unfolding in those countries will undoubtedly have far greater importance to the United States and the rest of the Free World

than what is happening inside of Cuba--barring, of course, the
outbreak of a major war because of Cuba.

The fact that the U. S. press has been doing a poor job of
covering Latin American affairs is certainly responsible in part
for the excessive disappointment and frustration which many
Americans feel over the slow progress of the Alliance. The rate
of progress has indeed been slower than any of us would have wanted
and I for one believe that we must all redouble our efforts to achieve
progress more rapidly, as reflected throughout these pages. However, there has been progress, and I am confident that the widespread disappointment with the Alliance would not have been so great
if the U. S. press had been doing a better job of telling the American
public about it. Support of the Alliance by the Congress and by the
public at large might accordingly have been greater if the press had
been doing a better job.

It is important to remember also that virtually any kind of story
in the U. S. press concerning a specific Latin American country is
given feature status in the newspapers of that country. Stories written about a Latin American country by U. S. correspondents and
journalists primarily for publication in U. S. newspapers and magazines are regularly played back to Latin America, where they often
have a considerable impact, not only because most Latin Americans
assume that the American public believes those stories, but also because many Latin Americans have greater confidence in the reliability of the U. S. correspondents than in that of their own newspapermen.

The morale of the numerous Latin Americans (in the legislative,
as well as the executive, branches of their governments) who have been
trying to promote the success of the Alliance despite formidable political and economic problems would therefore have been better if they
had known that their efforts were being publicly recognized in the United
States. Indeed, such recognition could in certain cases have made their
tasks less difficult, if only because it will usually be easier to get support for perpetuation of a measure publicly recognized as strengthening
the Alliance for Progress than for a measure which is being ignored by
the press while it is being attacked by others. It is still a sound rule
that nothing succeeds like success. The prospects for success of the
Alliance will accordingly brighten considerably when the press begins
to show some awareness, and even due optimism, over the progress
which is being made, instead of bemoaning the progress which is not
being made.

Just as stories in the U.S. press giving due credit to a
Latin American government for its efforts in behalf of the Alliance can help reinforce that government's determination and
ability to further its efforts, undue criticism of a government

in the U.S. press can weaken its determination or ability to
collaborate with the United States in the Alliance for Progress
or in any other way, for such criticism may often be a useful
tool in the hands of the political opponents of that government.
I hasten to add that I would not recommend on that account
that U.S. newspapers or magazines play down any stories
critical of a Latin American government when they are reasonably confident about the veracity of the stories. Indeed, the
interests of the Alliance may be served best by bringing the
public's attention to any evidence that some government (including our own, if the shoe fits) is misconducting itself or
otherwise doing less than it should be doing to try to promote
the Alliance. However, determination of the veracity of a
story in Latin America may be very difficult, especially for a
small corps of correspondents each of whom is charged with
the task of covering every type of story which may appear in
any of the several countries which make up his "beat." It is
accordingly incumbent upon the U.S. press to take special care
to avoid improper criticism of a Latin American government.

    I have very much in mind an interview that I had not long
ago with the President of one of the Latin American countries.
For one hour and twenty-seven minutes, and almost without
interruption, he expressed his strong indignation over what he
considered the unfair treatment he was receiving in the U.S.
press. He stated that he was being identified as an "oligarch"
and a "reactionary" because his Government had not yet enacted the land reform and tax reform measures which some
people, including some foreigners, believed appropriate. He
then pointed out that, first, only his Congress could enact the
necessary legislation and that various proposals were under
active consideration at that very time by the appropriate committees of the Congress in consultation with the responsible officials of his Government; that, second, there was considerable
room for honest difference of opinion over the measures which
would be most appropriate to the special circumstances of his
country; that, third, he had enforced a number of important
administrative measures for which the U.S. press did not seem
inclined to give him any credit; and that, fourth, some of his
political opponents in the Congress were deliberately withholding
their collaboration on the proposed reforms because of their
belief--based on the U.S. press reports--that continued delay in
the enactment of those reforms would not only destroy his standing with his own public but would also provoke the U.S. Government to cut back the economic assistance required by his country,
thereby leading to the downfall of his Government. In my opinion,

there was a great deal of justification for the indignation which that President was expressing. His situation illustrates the need for special care by the U.S. press in reporting about complex situations in Latin America.

I accordingly recommend that each major U.S. news service greatly expand the number of its correspondents assigned to Latin America so as to permit much more complete coverage of the complex situations in each of the separate, and very distinct, countries of the region. I recommend also that a large percentage of those correspondents be instructed to focus upon signs of changes in the economic and social conditions of those countries, with special emphasis upon the Alliance for Progress, leaving coverage of the more obvious political events to the other correspondents. Changes in the economic and social scene will often have greater long-term impact, even on fundamental political developments, than the more dramatic political events of the moment. Moreover, adequate reporting even on political events will often be impossible in the absence of reasonably full knowledge concerning the underlying economic and social scene, which is invariably much more complicated than can be described by mere reference to poverty and social injustice.

Furthermore, I am convinced that high drama can almost always be found by competent reporters covering the economic and social changes in Latin America. I am convinced also that the U.S. public will recognize that drama when well-written stories describing it begin to appear in U.S. newspapers and magazines. Significant changes in the "right" direction will seldom take place until after difficult battles have been won over the opposition of important, and frequently dangerous, forces resisting those changes. Any changes in the "wrong" direction likewise carry important, though contrary, political significance. The Alliance for Progress is not merely an economic and social venture superimposed on a fundamentally political scene. The Alliance itself has enormous political implications.

CHAPTER **12** THE ROLE OF
THE U.S.
GOVERNMENT

It has been a serious error since the inception of the
Alliance for Progress to have ascribed predominant responsibility to the U.S. Government for assuring the success of
the Alliance. The success of the Alliance depends upon the
total involvement of the people of Latin America, the United
States, and the rest of the Free World. Accordingly, I have
already described the principal measures which should be
pursued by the private sector of the United States in support
of the Alliance, and I shall describe the proper role of the
rest of the Free World in Chapter 13. However, no emphasis upon the importance of those sectors can logically de-
tract from the need for full participation, and indeed leadership, on the part of the U.S. Government. As the representative of the entire American public, only our Government can
deal adequately with the governmental representatives of our
partners in the Alliance. Only our Government can act for
the people of the United States in determining when we should
extend financial, economic, and technical assistance to supplement the efforts of other countries to help themselves.
Only our Government can speak for the American people as a
whole in the war of ideologies.

For the most part, I believe that the Government has been
performing its proper role reasonably well. However, I also
believe that the Government can improve upon its performance
in five principal ways, described below:

THE NEED FOR BROADER RELATIONSHIPS
WITH THE MILITARY LEADERS
OF LATIN AMERICA

The economic and social development of Latin America has
unquestionably been retarded by the excessive allocations of
economic resources for the maintenance of unnecessarily large
military establishments in most of the countries. Moreover,

many governments have been overthrown or substantially controlled by the use, or threatened use, of military force by the leaders of those establishments. The most rapid possible success of the Alliance for Progress accordingly requires reduction of the separate military establishments to dimensions commensurate with the realistic requirements for defense from external agression and internal insurrection, and reduction of the role of the military leaders as the dominant powers behind the throne. However, neither of these interrelated objectives can be accomplished without considerable opposition, not only from the military forces themselves, but also from many other groups--including many people who consider themselves genuinely dedicated to the basic principles of the Free World. For the war of ideologies is intimately involved in the military problems, as in virtually all other problems, of Latin America.

Many Latin Americans, alarmed by the growing strength of Communist forces in their countries, look to their military leaders to restrain the civilian leaders from the adoption of policies or practices which would "unduly" change the status quo. Sometimes, they even look to their military leaders to prevent the constitutional accession to power of men who they believe to be either pro-Communist or susceptible to control by the Communists or other Marxists, as when some of Brazil's military leaders tried (unsuccessfully) to prevent then Vice President Joao Goulart from assuming the Presidency following the resignation of President Janio Quadros in August, 1961, and as when the military forces succeeded in preventing Haya de la Torre from taking office in Peru after he had apparently won the Presidential election in June, 1962.

On the other hand, many Latin Americans look to their military leaders to assure the preservation of their national sovereignty, sometimes endorsing the "nationalistic" policies which they consider appropriate for this purpose, even when those same "nationalistic" policies happen to coincide very closely with policies being recommended by the Communists. Moreover, the Communists themselves, as well as other Marxists, have recently made substantial inroads directly within the ranks, including some of the leaders, of the military forces of some Latin American countries.

Beyond the objectives of using their military forces as "activist" instruments in some of the broader aspects of the war of ideologies, furthermore, many Latin Americans (including many of the military leaders themselves) have simply not had sufficient faith in the competence and integrity of the democratically elected

officials to allow them to administer their governments without
"supervision." I have participated in several conversations
with Latin Americans who have argued vehemently that while
they strongly endorsed the formal practice of full democratic
processes in their country, they did not consider their country ready for "complete" democracy. I recall particularly
one conversation in which a Latin American friend pointed to
the large percentage of the voters in his country who were at
best semiliterate and who had had virtually no previous experience in self-government. "Is it any wonder," he asked,

> that they elected that unprincipled demagogue,_____,
> as our President? Would you want me, as a patri-
> otic citizen, to sit idly by and let that man ruin my
> country? Do you really blame me and some of my
> friends for working with General ____ _____ and
> General _____ _____ to make sure that the
> President behaves himself?

I firmly believe that one of the prerequisites for effective
democracy is that the people be allowed to govern themselves
and to learn from experience, including their mistakes, how
to govern themselves better. I firmly believe also that, while
the elite of a country--whether in private life or in some
branch of the government--may have a better idea than the
rest of their compatriots of what is best for the country, there
is a substantial possibility that they will at least subconsciously
tend to think of the country's interests in terms of their own. I
accept no rationale, or rationalization, as justification for the
use of military force to limit the right of a people to govern
themselves through their freely elected representatives. Having
said this, however, I must go on to say that I cannot simply
dismiss any of the "justifications" for military involvement
outlined above by designating them as undemocratic, or venal,
or oligarchic, or stupid. Many intelligent, patriotic, unself-
ish, and generally pro-democratic people believe in one or more
of those "justifications." If their opinions are to change, it will
only be because they have been persuaded of the logic of other
opinions.

Our universities, businessmen, labor unions, and press can
all make significant contributions toward such persuasion by
improving their participation in the war of ideologies through the
various measures recommended in previous chapters. By helping create an Alliance for Progress mystique, these different
segments of our society can help dissuade many Latin American

civilians and even some military personnel (primarily through the impact of the press) from reliance upon military force to "guide" governmental conduct. In order to solidify the Free World concepts of the Latin American military leaders, however, I consider it important that our Government do a better job of cultivating its direct relationships with those leaders.

Specifically, I recommend that the functions of the Army, Navy, and Air Force attachés of our Embassies in Latin America be expanded so as to include the responsibility of supporting an Alliance for Progress mystique among the military leaders of that region. To be able to carry out this responsibility effectively, the quality of our military attachés and their staffs will have to be modified by the assignment of personnel who are not only competent to handle their present military responsibilities, but who are also competent to participate in technical discussions of the economic, social, and political matters embraced within the Alliance for Progress. Furthermore, the military attachés of each Embassy will have to work closely with the civilian officers of that Embassy who are more intimately involved in administration of the Alliance so as to obtain all available information about current developments under the Alliance and so as to attain full coordination of U.S. positions under the direction of the ambassador.

I do not expect, or desire, that the military attachés will actively try to "propagandize" the military leaders of Latin America in any way. To do so would be inconsistent with their other functions as diplomatic representatives of the U.S. Government, and might very well be resented by the Latin Americans. Moreover, while many military leaders of that region have been disposed to use their power to enforce the governmental policies which they consider desirable in areas other than the strictly military, many others are content to concern themselves exclusively with military matters. The objectives of our military attachés should be to encourage reduction, not expansion, of military participation in civilian affairs. However, the attachés can be very helpful to the Alliance without recourse to propagandizing.

Where any Latin American government is seeking to enforce economic or social reforms or other economic or social measures which are intended to further the Alliance, but which some military leaders consider dangerously upsetting to the status quo or otherwise undesirable, and where those military leaders

initiate discussion of these matters with our attachés, the attaches should be competent to discuss the technical aspects of
those measures and their relation to the Alliance. The attachés should likewise be capable of making useful technical
contributions to discussions concerning the merits of any
measures which some military leaders may be trying to
coerce the civilian authorities to adopt and which run counter
to the objectives of the Alliance. In general, our attachés
should be as conversant as possible with the many different
aspects of the Alliance and should do all that they can appropriately do to encourage active support for the Alliance among
the military leaders of Latin America.

Almost every Latin American military officer whom I
have known has been genuinely patriotic and intellectually
honest, though usually very ill-informed about economic and
social matters, and often very distrustful of the judgments of
the civilian officials of his government about such matters. I
believe that those officers will frequently have more respect
for the opinions of other officers, even though in the uniform
of another country, than they have for the opinions of their own
civilian colleagues. In any case, those civilian officials will
have no basis for complaint as long as the opinions expressed
by our attaches are unmistakably motivated by the desire to
help further the common interests of the Free World in promoting the success of the Alliance, and as long as those opinions
coincide with the opinions of the civilian authorities, as they
normally will in these situations. The readiness of some
military leaders to refrain from interference in civilian affairs
will often depend upon their confidence in the competence of
the civilian officials, and anything our attachés can do properly
to strengthen that confidence will be helpful.

THE NEED TO PUBLICIZE AND DRAMATIZE
THE ACHIEVEMENTS OF
THE ALLIANCE FOR PROGRESS

The United States Information Agency (USIA) should do a
much better job than it has been doing of publicizing, and dramatizing, the achievements of the Alliance for Progress in Latin
America. Care must be taken to avoid exaggerating those achieve-

ments and to avoid encouraging the concept that the success of the Alliance should be measured by the monuments to which one can point as "proof" of its success. However, a well conceived publicity program would demonstrate that much more has been accomplished than is generally recognized by the people of Latin America, thereby tending to restore faith in the long-term success of the Alliance, while giving a more accurate perspective of the measures which must be employed to assure that success. The three principal areas in which I recommend that USIA improve its program are as follows:

First, USIA should give much more extensive and intensive publicity to the many types of economic, financial, and technical assistance which the Government of the United States is extending to Latin America in fulfillment of its commitments under the Charter of Punta del Este. I do not expect that better knowledge of that assistance will provoke gratitude on the part of its beneficiaries, nor do I believe that the publicity should be designed to obtain such gratitude. However, it is important that the people of Latin America realize much better than they now do all that the U.S. Government is doing to fulfill its commitments under the Charter. It is necessary that the people recognize that fulfillment of their commitments will be in their own interests, but it is necessary also that they realize that the U.S. Government is proving its good faith, and that they are honor-bound to prove their own good faith. The commitments which are assumed by each of the signatories of the Charter lie at the heart of the Alliance for Progress, and it is important that there be constant reminders of those commitments and of the seriousness which the U.S. Government attaches to them.

I am particularly, though by no means exclusively, concerned with the need for much better publicity concerning the various types of financial assistance we have been extending to Latin America. At present, the publicity with respect to an Export-Import Bank or AID loan to a Latin American country is ordinarily limited almost entirely to an undramatic announcement coming out of Washington that a loan for certain more-or-less specified purposes has been approved, under the Alliance for Progress, in the amount X for Company Y in Country Z or for the government of Country Z. Considerable publicity is generally given to the loan in the country concerned on the day of the announcement, but the publicity normally ends right there. Other news captures the headlines thereafter, and the loan is quickly forgotten by the general public.

If the publicity given to U.S. financial assistance is to be
satisfactory and have lasting effect, it must include many or
all of the following features: When announcing a loan for a
specific project, the pertinent press release should name the
site on which the project will be located; the estimated number
and annual incomes of the people to be employed in construction and, later, in operation of the project; the estimated annual expenditures for procurement of domestic raw materials
and other supplies required by the project, and, if feasible,
the major locales from which those supplies are to be obtained; the extent to which the end products will reduce the
country's dependence upon imports from abroad or contribute
to the production of other commodities, thereby advancing
the rate of the country's industrialization; and the direct and
indirect social benefits, as when the project provides for the
construction of low-cost housing. In general, each announcement should contain details of the kind that have more vital
pertinence to the people of the country than the antiseptic an-
nouncements the Government is now issuing.

Furthermore, the publicity should not stop with the announcement of a loan. Photographs should be released covering the ceremonies at which loan contracts are signed. An-
nouncements should be made of contracts concluded for procurement of the equipment and supplies to be utilized in construction of the project, and photographs should be released as
the supplies are loaded aboard ship, then unloaded, and finally
delivered to the site of the project. Later, full publicity should
be given to inauguration of the project and its entry into actual
production. Periodically, news stories and even documentary
films should be prepared showing the impact of the U.S.-financed
projects in terms of their effects upon the human beings involved as well as on the economy as a whole. To be sure, the
newspapers and other news media of the country concerned may
find that some of these releases do not have enough news value
to warrant printing. If so, little harm will have been done by
having issued the releases. I am confident, however, that they
will want to print the releases more often than not.

The extension of U.S. Government loans for balance of payments or budget support or "development program" purposes,
rather than for specific projects, affords some special technical
and public relations problems, inasmuch as such loans are not
directly related to any specific, tangible projects that can be
identified as being financed by the U.S. Government. Indeed,
the difficulty of identifying the specific results deriving from
such loans is one of the more persuasive arguments that are

sometimes offered against making them at all. However, inasmuch as there are various circumstances in which such loans
will be the most effective way by which the U.S. Government
can help another government help itself, we must not rule them
out simply because of the difficulty of obtaining satisfactory
publicity.

We must, instead, make sure that any agreements providing
for such loans contain provisions that will facilitate appropriate publicity. Ordinarily, this can be accomplished by the
device (which has already been tried in a few cases) of requiring that the beneficiary government set aside a special banking
account in its local currency equivalent to the dollar assistance we are providing, on the understanding that loans will then
be made out of that bank account for specific Alliance for Progress
projects, the financing of which will be attributed to the United
States. While this is not a new device, it has not been employed
as often as it should have been, and--in practice--there has
never been the necessary follow-through, whether by USIA or
by any other U.S. Government agency, to assure that the appropriate publicity has in fact been emitted at the time of each
local currency loan and thereafter, in the manner recommended
above for direct project loans by the U.S. Government.

It is important that USIA be given over-all responsibility
for publicizing in Latin America all U.S. Government financial assistance (and all U.S. Government economic and technical assistance as well). Only in this way can we be certain
that there will be a continuously integrated and coherent picture
of the totality and interrelationship of all U.S. assistance in
support of the Alliance. It is accordingly necessary that intra-
Governmental procedures be established pursuant to which USIA
will become much more than the transmission belt it now is for
press releases written by the press officers of the Export-Import Bank, AID, the State Department, the Treasury Department, and the Agriculture Department.

USIA officers, in Washington or in Latin America, should
participate as a routine matter in the drafting of each press
release announcing the extension of assistance to Latin America,
and should be given primary responsibility for all subsequent
publicity. They should be given ready access to all pertinent
information, such as the names of the firms supplying the equipment and other supplies to be used in the construction of a
U.S.-financed project, plus shipping schedules for the delivery
of those supplies. In general they should be charged with the
responsibility of obtaining the maximum publicity that is de-

sirable in any country (subject to the determination of each
pertinent Ambassador) with respect to each form of assistance
under the Alliance for Progress and with respect to any sum-
mations and analyses of that assistance.

In addition to publicizing U.S. assistance under the Alliance, USIA should, second, give maximum appropriate assistance to each Latin American Government in publicizing
and dramatizing the achievements of that country under the
Alliance. The Alliance is a joint venture of twenty Western
Hemisphere countries, and every significant achievement of
any of them in promoting the success of the Alliance serves
the interests of all the Alliance partners and should receive
the appropriate publicity. Unfortunately, few of the Latin
American governments are well equipped to prepare this
type of publicity, and USIA should accordingly be prepared
to give them all appropriate assistance, not only with respect
to the specific projects formulated, financed, or implemented by those countries, but even with respect to economic and
social measures undertaken by them in fulfillment of their
commitments under the Charter of Punta del Este.

To be sure, the USIA officers in each country must
follow the instructions of the Ambassador as to the appropriate assistance which they can render to the host government. USIA must never undermine its own reputation for
integrity by participation in any form of exaggeration or
misrepresentation. Moreover, it must carefully avoid any
appearance of trying to propagandize the public of any country into support of any controversial and sensitive policy
determinations of the host government. The U.S. Government must be highly scrupulous in handling its public relations in the United States. It must be no less scrupulous
in assisting the public relations efforts of other governments.
However, sensitive and controversial issues will rarely be
involved in publicity concerning the Alliance for Progress
achievements of another country, and it is important that
those achievements be made known in order that confidence
may be created in the long-term succes of the Alliance.

Third, the USIA officers in each country should help
publicize, and dramatize, the Alliance for Progress achievements of each of the other members of the Alliance, including any successes in promoting more effective economic,
social, and political collaboration among them, as called for
in the Charter of Punta del Este. The creation of an Alliance

for Progress mystique depends upon many different types of
vigorous efforts and by many different sectors of the Free
World, as described in this book. The USIA officers in each
country can be very helpful by giving appropriate publicity
to the efforts of many of those sectors, including the efforts
in each of the other Latin American countries. They should
draw their information from the many sources available to
them, including their USIA colleagues in the other countries,
as well as the information transmitted by USIA headquarters
in Washington, by the Inter-American Development Bank and
by the OAS, the latter of which has been given special responsibility for keeping the public currently informed about the
state of the Alliance. USIA can in this way contribute greatly
toward creating the necessary understanding of the Alliance
as a true alliance of all of its members in a common undertaking for the common good.

THE NEED FOR LONG-TERM SCHOLARSHIPS
FOR GRADUATE STUDIES IN THE UNITED STATES

The critical importance of strengthening the intellectual
bonds between the Latin Americans and the rest of the Free
World has been emphasized throughout this book. Free World
concepts will be victorious in the war of ideologies in Latin
America only when the people of that area are genuinely
convinced that adherence to those concepts is in their own best
interests, as well as in the best interests of humanity as a
whole. The predominance of such convictions will not grow
easily or quickly. Above all, it will depend upon fortifying
the mental and spiritual affinity which the intellectual leaders
of Latin America feel with the rest of the Free World. Accordingly, no U.S. Government program can do more to
further the long-term success of the Alliance than a program
designed to support the many other measures which must be
pursued by Free World forces to improve their relationships
with the intellectuals of Latin America. The U.S. Government
program can and should contain many facets, but I shall here
focus on the special importance of modifying and greatly ex-
panding the Government's program for granting scholarships
to Latin American students wishing to do graduate work in the
United States.

The sorry state of university instruction in Latin America and the extent to which Communist and other Marxist influence has prevailed in those universities and has spread from them into the other sectors of public and private activity were described in Chapter 7, along with my recommendations for measures which U.S. universities should pursue in order to help alleviate this situation by facilitating the enrollment of Latin Americans, primarily (though not exclusively) for graduate studies in economics. One of those recommendations was that the U.S. universities grant to Latin American students a much larger percentage of the total number of scholarships granted to all foreign students than they have been granting up to now. I am convinced that fulfillment of that recommendation would have important benefits in Latin America. At the same time, however, I recognize that the maximum number of scholarships that one could reasonably ask the universities to allocate to Latin Americans would still not be large enough for the objectives I have in mind. Furthermore, the universities would have special difficulty in granting the kinds of scholarships that are needed.

I accordingly recommend that the U.S. Government supplement the measures recommended for the universities by instituting a new and large-scale scholarship program with the following principal features:

The administrators of each of the 120 Latin American universities would be advised that they may act as agents of the U.S. Government, if they so desire, in distributing a given number of four-year scholarships each year for a specified minimum number of years thereafter for studies in United States graduate schools to be designated by the United States Government in collaboration with the graduate schools. They would be advised that they would be expected to select the students to receive those scholarships from among the highest ranking students graduating from their university and majoring in certain specified subjects, primarily economics. If, for example, ten four-year scholarships are allocated to a given university, it would be expected to distribute, say, five among the top ten graduating students who have majored in economics; two from among the top four or five who have majored in political science; two from among the top four or five who have majored in sociology. When necessary, expansion of the panels from which the scholarship students are selected should be permitted, but only after approval by the U.S. Ambassador. Provision might be made also for some scholarships to professors as well as students.

I am especially anxious that the scholarships be granted for four-year periods (subject to the maintenance of passing grades) and that they cover not only travel and tuition costs, but also reasonable living allowances. One of the most serious deficiencies of the many different scholarship programs now being carried out by the U.S. Government is the fact that none of them (with very minor exceptions) provides for scholarships which can be given for more than one year. Provision is sometimes made for the extension of a scholarship for an additional year and (very rarely) for still an additional year, but the Latin American students receiving such scholarships rarely know in advance that the scholarships will be for more than one year. The attractiveness of the scholarships is accordingly impaired for the reason, among others, that no student can ever be confident that he will be able to complete his work even for an M.A., much less for a Ph.D.

Graduate work for anything less than four years will ordinarily fail to meet the most important objective which should be sought for the Latin American students: truly intensive education in their respective subjects, such that upon return to their separate countries they can serve as effective leaders in their chosen professions, as university professors or government employees or businessmen or in some other capacity important to the success of the Alliance for Progress. The undergraduate student in a Latin American university who would like to be awarded one of the four-year scholarships and who believes that he has a good chance to get one may be expected to make an especially strong effort to increase his proficiency in English while striving for that scholarship. Even so, however, it is unlikely that most of such students will acquire sufficient mastery of English while living in Latin America to be able, during their first several months or more in the United States, to deal with the more subtle nuances of the language which must be mastered for effective graduate work, particularly in abstruse subjects such as economics. Most Americans require four years of graduate work to earn a Ph.D., even after having had the benefit of undergraduate work in a good U.S. university. Can we expect most Latin Americans to require less time, handicapped as they will be by a language problem and by inadequate undergraduate training?

Knowledge that this program will continue for an indefinite period should serve as a stimulus to the best possible preparation for graduate work in the United States. And knowledge

that the administrators of their own universities will make the
scholarship awards--with rank in the graduating class serving
as much the most important, if not the only, criterion--should
allay any suspicions of political favoritism on the part of the
U.S. Government or their own government. I foresee only one
serious administrative problem: the McCarren Act, denying
visas to most foreigners who are believed to be Communists.
However, I doubt that many Communists would rank high enough
in their graduating class to qualify for a scholarship. The
possibility of embarrassment on this score seems to me to be
too small to justify rejection of a program as important as
this one.

     To have maximum effectiveness in promoting the Alliance
for Progress, several hundred scholarships should be awarded
each year. This will, of course, be expensive, particularly
since the cost will be accumulative until it reaches its peak
(for a constant annual number of new scholarships) in the
fourth year. However, I am convinced that no expenditure by
the U.S. Government can have more long-term effectiveness in
promoting the Alliance, keeping in mind the considerations
discussed in Chapter 7.

                  THE NEED TO HELP THE FORMULATION
                  OF SPECIFIC DEVELOPMENT PROJECTS

     As indicated in Chapter 5, implementation of the Alliance
has been seriously impeded by the dearth of specific developmental projects. Even when agreement has been reached concerning the scale and general types of investments which would
best promote a country's economic and social development
and even when the effectuation of such investments has been
made possible by the measures taken to promote the availability of the necessary internal savings and external assistance,
no development plan can be implemented in the absence of blueprints for specific investments of the general types contemplated
in the development plan. The Alliance has accordingly suffered
greatly from the fact that almost none of the Latin American
countries--including their private business firms as well as
their governments--has shown the necessary capacity to formulate large numbers of specific development projects.

Where developmental investments have been made, they have often been for highly desirable purposes. However, they have in many cases been made instead because the pertinent projects could be formulated relatively simply or because an especially influential agency director, who is naturally interested in the formulation of projects of interest to his own agency, has been able to capture the services of the few people competent to formulate development projects. The effective implementation of a well-conceived development plan depends upon the existence every year of substantially more blueprints for sound development projects than can be carried forward with the available resources that year. It is only under that circumstance that the process of determining relative priorities among different investment expenditures can be meaningful. Funds may be spent on low-priority, or even unsound, projects when the funds are available and higher-priority projects are not at hand. Conversely, the availability of high-priority projects may prevent the misuse of funds for less desirable purposes and may even serve as an important inducement for fiscal and financial reforms in order to increase public and private savings.

Those officials of the U.S. Government who have been responsible for promoting the success of the Alliance for Progress have long been concerned about the dearth of specific development projects and have been urging the Latin American governments to focus their energies heavily on this problem. In addition, AID has made loans to various Latin American governments to finance feasibility studies to provide the necessary guidance in determining, first, the types of projects which are likely to prove most helpful in promoting economic and social development and, second, the specific form in which such projects should be formulated, i.e., the most appropriate size of each project, the best site for it, the quality of product or service to be produced, etc. Pursuant to AID policy, contracts for the performance of feasibility studies in any Latin American country are awarded only to firms controlled by U.S. citizens or to firms controlled by citizens of the specific Latin American country in which the feasibility study is to be performed. Thus, a feasibility study to be performed in any given Latin American country cannot be financed under an AID loan by a consulting firm, however well qualified, of any other Latin American country.

The fact that the present system of financing feasibility studies has not fostered anything approximating a satisfactory number of sound development projects may be attributed to many defects of that system.

   Despite the recent increase in the number of qualified consulting firms in Latin America, it frequently has been impossible to rely upon the consulting firms of various Latin American
countries to perform all of the feasibility studies needed in their
respective countries.   Some of the consulting firms have not
had the necessary technical competence to deal adequately with
all of the essential aspects of certain specific feasibility
studies.   Others have had the necessary technical competence,
but have not had the experience required by AID as a guarantee
that the desired studies would be fully reliable.   Still other consulting firms have had both the technical competence and the
experience, but have been disqualified for specific feasibility
studies because the firms have had proprietary or managerial
relationships with the only construction firms considered qualified to implement the projects in question; doubts have accordingly existed concerning the impartiality with which the
consulting firms could be expected to conduct the pertinent
feasibility studies.

   It has likewise not proven practical to rely upon U.S. consulting firms to conduct all of the feasibility studies needed in
Latin America, or even a large percentage of them.   Inevitably,
it is extremely costly to send teams of qualified Americans
to any Latin American country to perform feasibility studies,
even assuming that personnel with the necessary language
and other qualifications can be found for such assignments--an
assumption which too often has proven to be unwarranted.
Furthermore, it is very cumbersome and time-consuming for
any government to negotiate separate contracts with U.S. consulting firms for each of the many studies that must be made.
Some governments have found it politically difficult to conclude contracts of certain studies because of the opposition of
domestic firms which have argued that it is improper to
award the contracts to U.S. firms as long as the domestic
firms are willing to do the jobs, and at much lower costs.

   There has even been resistance in some Latin American
countries to the obtaining of AID loans for the financing of
feasibility studies because of the government's obligation to
repay those loans even though the feasibility studies might
lead to the conclusion that the projects to be studied are not
sound and do not warrant foreign loans, or because the government must ultimately repay the costs of the feasibility studies
even when the projects in question pertain to the private sector
rather than the public sector.   One result of the latter problem
is the fact that the Latin American governments have not gen-

erally found it proper to contract for studies designed to determine the feasibility of projects which <u>private</u> firms might later
undertake; the studies are normally concerned only with the
feasibility of <u>government</u> studies.

Furthermore, certain special problems will ordinarily
derive from the fact that separate teams of U.S. experts and
even separate teams of U.S. firms are usually engaged in the
different studies. To do a good job of determining the feasibility of projects of the type it has undertaken to study, each team
must have an accurate understanding of the economic and social
conditions of the country as a whole, as well as the country's
development plan and the probable relationships of the potential
projects in question to other potential projects. The understanding of these matters is likely to be very uneven among the
different teams. It is not unlikely therefore that some or many
of the teams, being as enthusiastic about the merits of their
own specialities as experts normally are, will tend to consider
as feasible the types and dimensions of projects which would
indeed be feasible if considered exclusively on their own merits
but which would not be considered feasible if evaluated within
the context of an accurate appraisal of the total country situation.

Many, if not all, of the foregoing difficulties could probably
be overcome or greatly alleviated if satisfactory arrangements
for distribution of specific job assignments within individual
feasibility studies could be concluded among qualified American
and Latin American consulting firms. However, in the absence of such arrangements, and in order to be of maximum
assistance to the Latin American countries in formulating
specific projects for economic and social development, the U.S.
Government should, in my opinion, institute a new program
along the following lines:

The Government should contract for the service of a separate and large team of engineers and economists to be assigned
directly to each United States AID Mission (USAID). Each
team would be subject to over-all direction of its activities by
the USAID Director, always acting under the general supervision of the Ambassador, and would be expected to accept
guidance from the Director and his staff concerning the general
economic and social circumstances of the country. However,
inasmuch as the team members would be working on contract
rather than as Government employees, they would be expected
to make their analyses and recommendations as pure tech-

nicians and without binding the U.S. Government in any way to
some future course of action.   Each contract would be for a
period of at least two years, the full cost to be borne by the
U.S. Government, except for the partial reimbursement that
might occur, as indicated below.

The initial function of each team would be to determine,
after appropriate consultation with USAID and with the host
government, where feasibility studies pertaining to both governmental and private development projects might most usefully be undertaken. It would submit its recommendations for
such studies, including recommendations for the specific terms
of reference which would apply to each study, to both USAID
and the host government.   After consulting with the host government, USAID would then publish the team's recommendations
for the conducting of any feasibility studies concerning projects that should be of interest to private business firms--
but without accepting any U.S. Government responsibility.
Where the host government desires to do so, it should be
encouraged and assisted to negotiate contracts for recommended
feasibility studies in the public and/or private sector with
qualified consulting firms of that country or the United States,
on the understanding that AID would pay, without reimbursement, for any public sector studies which USAID has approved
because it considers them to be of high priority and pertinent
to projects considered appropriate for governmental investment.   Alternatively, and after USAID consultation with the
host government, the USAID consulting team itself could be
instructed by USAID to conduct any of such public sector feasibility studies, with the understanding that the team would employ
any additional, specialized, technicians needed for a specific
feasibility study, also at U.S. Government expense. If the
host government or any private firm (U.S.- or domestically
owned) wishes to negotiate a contract with a qualified national
or U.S. consulting firm to effect any of the private sector
feasibility studies recommended by the USAID consulting
team, it should be encouraged to do so, on the understanding
that the host government or the private firm would pay for
50 per cent of the costs and would reimburse the U.S. Government by way of a long-term loan for the remaining 50 per
cent if the study culminates in a private investment. If requested to do so, the USAID consulting team could itself effect
any of the private sector feasibility studies, on the same understanding with regard to payment of their costs.

If the host government decides to move forward with the formulation of any public sector project the feasibility study of which has proven to be favorable, the government should be encouraged to seek an AID loan to finance the performance of that work by a qualified domestic or U.S. firm. Alternatively, it could ask USAID to instruct its consulting team to formulate the project, again on the understanding that the team would employ such additional personnel as it considers necessary for the purpose and on the additional understanding that the host government would reimburse the U.S. Government for 100 per cent of the costs of the team's services by way of a long-term loan from the U.S. Government. Any U.S. - or domestically owned private firm could likewise ask USAID to instruct the team to formulate a specific project, but on the understanding that the firm would pay for 50 per cent of the team's costs and would reimburse the U.S. Government for the remaining 50 per cent through a long-term loan if the firm later undertakes the project. If the private firm preferred to make its own arrangements for formulation of a project, USAID could agree to extend a loan covering 50 per cent of the costs.

Whatever the method by which the blueprints for a governmental or private project might be formulated, USAID should instruct its consulting team to render all reasonable assistance in the preparation of an appropriate application for a loan from external lending institutions, always on the understanding that the team cannot speak for the U.S. Government in any way.

CHAPTER **13** THE ROLE OF
OTHER FREE
WORLD COUNTRIES

Whereas the unpleasantnesses during Vice President
Nixon's trips to Peru and Venezuela in 1958 and the Castro
takeover of Cuba in January, 1959, awoke the United States
to the existence in Latin America of a serious threat to the
security of the Free World, those events had little impact
in the rest of the Free World. Most of Europe* did not
awaken to the dangerous situation in Latin America until
the world arrived at the brink of war in October, 1962, because of the form that Cuba's ties to the Communist world
had taken. But where the United States--having awakened--
was galvanized into action, the Europeans have not found it
possible to do much more than observe and lament.

The Europeans have extended very little long-term
financial assistance and even very little technical assistance
to Latin America since the inception of the Alliance for
Progress, despite various efforts by the Latin Americans
and by the U.S. Government encouraging them to do so.
They have shown little readiness to reduce their tariffs
or excise taxes on Latin American products. Most important of all from some points of view, they have carefully
avoided direct involvement in the Alliance. I have heard
many Europeans express their enthusiastic endorsement of
the Alliance, but almost exclusively in private conversations.
A few government officials, such as German Minister of
Development Scheel, have expressed approval of the Alliance
publicly, but no European government has seen fit to join in
the psychological as well as the material aspects of the Alliance.

---

*For purposes of convenience, I shall generally hereafter
speak of Europe as if it comprised all countries of the Free
World other than the United States and Latin America. Frequently, the references made to Europe will be pertinent
also to such countries as Canada, Israel, and Japan.

The failure of the Europeans to play the role that they are capable of playing in the war of ideologies in Latin America may be attributed to three principal factors. I would list as first among them the fact that most Europeans continue to think of Latin America as being primarily within the United States' sphere of influence. They believe that the United States is both willing and able to carry the responsibility for protecting the general interests of the Free World in that region. Moreover, they believe that the United States would resent, and might in some way retaliate against, any effort by a European nation to take some part of that responsibility away from us. They know very well that we would like them to extend much more assistance to Latin America, but they believe that we would refuse to share with them in any significant degree the right to decide the amount, kind, and distribution of assistance among the Latin American countries, as well as the prerequisites for assistance. They believe that we and the Latin Americans want to retain the decision-making powers, while expecting of the Europeans only that they will help implement those decisions.

Secondly, most Europeans, being as preoccupied as they are with problems much closer to home, have been quite satisfied to defer Latin American problems to the United States. The problems of Berlin and a divided Germany; the forces working for, and against, the ultimate economic and political integration of Europe; the persistence of inflationary pressures in almost all of the European countries and of balance-of-payments difficulties in several of them; the United Kingdom's problems with some of the commonwealth countries and the problems of several European countries with their previous and their remaining dependencies in Africa and the Far East; the domestic political, economic, and social problems within each of them; their relations with the Iron Curtain countries and with the United States-- these and many other problems are dominating the minds and energies of most Europeans. They consider Latin American problems peripheral and see no need to get involved in those problems, particularly as long as the United States appears willing to do so.

Thirdly, the European organizations which were designed to facilitate assistance to other areas have not been well implemented, particularly so far as Latin America is concerned. Assistance for some purposes is necessary on a scale or with a composition which is beyond the capacity of any one country

to provide alone, and which no country will accordingly be prepared to extend unless the procedures for extending collective
assistance are improved upon. Where assistance can usefully
be extended by separate countries, furthermore, each country
will wish to avoid both the wasteful duplication of assistance
being provided by some other country and the provision of
assistance which will be considered of lesser importance than
that being provided by some other country. There is accordingly a need for improvement of the procedures for coordinating the separate assistance efforts of the European countries
with one another and with the United States.

It is important to realize that while most Europeans would
prefer not to get involved in Latin American problems, there
are many influential Europeans who are prepared to get involved. Some Europeans are interested primarily in taking advantage of the trade and investment opportunities which now
exist in Latin America and which may be expected to become
much greater with the success of the Alliance for Progress.
Others are genuinely interested in helping win the war of
ideologies in Latin America because of a compassionate desire to help improve the economic and social levels of the
people of that region while helping them resist subjugation
to Communist tyranny, and because of an awareness that the
winds of revolution in Latin America can provoke a terrible
world-wide war unless guided along democratic lines. I have
been impressed by the deep concern over the war of ideologies
in Latin America which has been expressed to me by almost
all of the large number of Foreign Office officials of Europe
with whom I have spoken about Latin American problems.
This same concern has been manifested privately and publicly by the important and enlightened businessmen who are
members of UNIAPAC (International Union of Catholic Employers Association), a private organization dedicated to the
furtherance of Christian ideals. It has been expressed also
by the leaders of various labor unions adhering to the ICFTU
(the International Confederation of Free Trade Unions) and
the IFCTU (the International Federation of Christian Trade Unions).

It is, accordingly, necessary that the U.S. Government
make it clear to the governments and peoples of Europe that
we would greatly welcome their participation in the Alliance
for Progress. It is necessary, furthermore, that we clarify
the fact that we do not contemplate by inviting their participation that they will serve as mere appendages to the total
Alliance effort. It is important that the Europeans understand

that the success of the Alliance requires their involvement not only by the extension of material and technical assistance, but also, and perhaps more significantly, by the extension of spiritual and intellectual assistance, as discussed in Chapter 4. It is important that effective arrangements be made for European participation in the critical decision-making processes, as well as the implemental processes, of the Alliance.

However, effective and helpful participation by Europeans in both the decision-making and the implemental processes of the Alliance does not depend exclusively upon their being invited to do so by the governments of Latin America and the United States. It is necessary also that the Europeans pursue various measures to provide reasonable assurance that such participation will in fact be both effective and helpful. The organizational improvements which are necessary in order to facilitate maximum collective assistance by the Europeans and better coordination of their separate assistance efforts with one another and with the United States will depend primarily upon measures which the Europeans, rather than the Americans, must take. And no spokesmen other than the Europeans themselves can effectively communicate to the Latin Americans an understanding of the spiritual and intellectual concepts of the Free World as interpreted by the different European countries.

I believe that European performance of their proper role in the Alliance for Progress would be facilitated by their pursuit of the principal measures described below:

THE NEED TO IMPROVE EUROPEAN PROCEDURES FOR COLLABORATION ON LATIN AMERICAN PROBLEMS

Collaboration among the European countries with respect to Latin American problems will inevitably be complicated by the many complex and, to a large degree, divisive forces now at work among and within the European countries themselves. Such collaboration will inevitably be complicated also by the preferential arrangements which several of those countries are continuing to maintain with certain independent countries and dependent overseas territories, particularly in Africa and the Far East. It

cannot reasonably be expected that under present circumstances the European countries will be able to block out a full-
scale long-term program for collaboration with one another,
with the United States and with Latin America toward facilitating the success of the Alliance for Progress. The scale
and composition of the European effort will inevitably have to
evolve along with many other changes in the world scene.

On the other hand, the manner in which European collaboration evolves is likely to depend, in no small degree, upon
the quality of the procedures established for effectuating that
collaboration. It is accordingly of considerable importance
that neither of the two principal instrumentalities which have
been explicitly constituted with the responsibility of improving
the form and content of European economic relations with
other areas has been effective in fulfilling that responsibility
with respect to Latin America. One of these instrumentalities--
the Organization for Economic Coordination and Development
(OECD)--has in practice been concerned primarily with allevi-
ation of intra-European problems, despite the fact that its
membership includes not only most of the governments of western Europe, but also those of the United States, Canada, and
Japan, and despite the fact that its responsibilities include that
of recommending collective and coordinated policies of its
members regarding economic relations with Latin America
and other underdeveloped regions and countries. The other
instrumentality--the Development Assistance Committee (DAC),
which is technically a subcommittee of OECD and which is constituted of most of the members of OECD, but which acts inde-
pendently of OECD though it is administered by OECD staff
personnel--has formulated some broad policy guidelines pertaining to the desirability and terms of financial assistance to
underdeveloped countries, but has in practice had little effect
in promoting either the expansion or the better coordination of
the assistance efforts of its members toward Latin America.

During the numerous occasions on which I represented the
State Department and AID at meetings in Europe concerning
Latin American matters, I frequently found a desire among
some of the Europeans to be helpful. The fact that little
European assistance was provided to Latin America following
any of those meetings was due, in my opinion, to two major
factors: First, the European (including the Canadian and Japanese) representatives at those meetings were rarely well informed about the matters under consideration. Second, they
never came to those meetings with authorization from their

respective home governments to agree on any form of collective or coordinated assistance efforts. The governmental representatives at OECD and DAC meetings on Latin American affairs have normally consisted of the Ambassadors or Ministers who are stationed in Paris as the permanent representatives of their governments to those organizations and who therefore have little specialized knowledge of the current Latin American scene. Their function has been to participate in general discussions about the subjects at issue and to report the substance of those discussions to their home governments, perhaps with general recommendations. However, neither OECD nor DAC has been designed to serve as an operative, decision-making organization so far as Latin America is concerned.

Yet, it is only if OECD and DAC become operative that European collaboration can become both effective and helpful. Two measures are necessary for this purpose:

First, the OECD staff structure should be revised so as to permit the staff to gather and disseminate the information needed by the member governments for effective collaboration with one another on Latin American problems. Reportedly, only 3 of the 1,600 people comprising the OECD staff are now engaged full-time on Latin American affairs. I believe that that number should be increased to the extent necessary to permit fulfillment of the following functions:

- The maintenance of up-to-date analyses of the current economic and social situation in each Latin American country plus the progress of economic integration among them.

- The transmission of such analyses to each OECD member, with special attention to the specific matters in which a member has expressed interest or in which the OECD staff believes it is likely to be interested. This could include, for example, information concerning the status of a Latin American government's development planning or the enactment of legislation necessary for the implementation of a development plan or the rate of progress on specific projects the lack of which has served as a significant bottleneck to the kind of additional project in which the OECD member might be particularly well qualified to participate.

● The collation of up-to-date information from each
OECD member concerning the status of its separate
assistance efforts vis-a-vis each Latin American
country, and the transmission of that information
to each OECD member.

● Communication with the Latin American governments
and the inter-American or international agencies
concerning possible OECD or DAC collaboration.
The staff might, for example, be instructed to make
such separate analyses of each Latin American
government's development program as would be of
special interest to the OECD or DAC members,
and the fulfillment of that assignment might require
the maintenance of close contact between the staff
and the Latin American government concerned or
between the staff and, perhaps, the Inter-American
Committee for the Alliance for Progress or the OAS
or the Inter-American Development Bank or the International Bank for Reconstruction and Development.

Effective staff work along the lines suggested above would
provide reasonable assurance that the governments which are
prepared to take meaningful positions concerning a Latin
American problem at any OECD or DAC meeting will have
been fully informed about all of the facts pertinent to the
subject to be discussed prior to that meeting. Neither OECD nor
DAC can be a decision-making, operative organization in the
absence of such staff work.

Second, the European governments must arrive at the broad
policy determination that they want OECD and DAC to be operative organizations concerning Latin American problems. The
recommended staff work would help each OECD and DAC member
improve the quality of its own financial, economic, and technical
assistance efforts in Latin America, even if neither OECD and
DAC becomes an operative organization. But improvement of
their collective assistance efforts and better coordination of their separate assistance efforts will only transpire if
and when the member governments give their representatives
at OECD and DAC meetings the authority and responsibility to
participate in decisions about these matters. Under certain
circumstances, the permanent representatives to OECD and
DAC could be principal spokesmen of their governments. Under

other circumstances, high-ranking officials of the home governments would have to attend the meetings as the principal
spokesmen. Whatever the implemental procedure, however,
the organizations must become operative, rather than merely
consultative, bodies.

This would not require that operative decisions concerning
assistance to Latin America be made at every OECD or DAC
meeting on a Latin American problem. Many meetings may be
required with respect to a given problem before the members
have reached the point where they are ready to commit themselves to a specific course of action, and no member can be
compelled to make any such commitment before it wishes to
do so. It is important also that each meeting be held under
conditions which will protect each member from possible
embarrassment through unnecessary disclosure of any disagreement it may have had with the other members. However, fear of possible embarrassment can no longer be accepted
as justification for lack of collaboration. If collective and
coordinated assistance for Latin America is to be sought, the
member governments must plan to hold as many meetings as
may be necessary before arriving at operative decisions on any
problem. But the meetings must be held with the ultimate
objective of arriving at such decisions.

Furthermore, while every effort must be made to avoid
embarrassment of any member government by unnecessary
and improper disclosure of positions taken at any OECD or
DAC meetings, a certain amount of publicity concerning the fact
that meetings about Latin America are being held would be very
desirable. It is important that the people of Latin America be
made aware of the European desire that the Alliance for Progress
succeed. It is important that the European endorsement of the
Alliance objectives of economic and social reform and self-
help be made known. It is important that the Latin Americans
be made aware of the fact that it is the Free World as a whole--
not just the United States--which subscribes to the ideology
embodied in the Charter of Punta del Este, and which wants
to help assure that that ideology prevails, while recognizing
that the Latin Americans themselves bear the major share
of the responsibility for their own fate.

THE NEED FOR BROADER EXPRESSION OF
EUROPEAN INVOLVEMENT IN THE
ALLIANCE FOR PROGRESS

I have no doubt about the fact that every government of
western Europe, plus the governments of Japan and Canada
and those of almost every other country which may be said to
comprise the Free World, subscribe to the objectives and
ideology of the Alliance for Progress. I have heard vehement
endorsement of the Alliance expressed by representatives of
the Foreign Offices of many Free World countries. Moreover, I have even heard the economic and financial representatives of these countries stress the importance of social reforms, as well as economic reforms and self-help, as prerequisites to greater and more effective external assistance.
Indeed, it has often been the European--rather than the United
States--representatives at the International Monetary Fund
and the International Bank for Reconstruction and Development
who have been most inflexible in tieing assistance by those institutions to certain Latin American countries to better performance on such self-help measures as the maintenance of
monetary stability and the encouragement of private enterprise.

Many European countries have learned, from their own
experiences, of the serious economic, social, and political
harm done by inflation; they can testify further to the fact that
while the measures necessary to curb inflation quickly are
likely to be painful, the pain is likely to be much less severe
and to end much sooner than many Latin Americans have been
led to believe. All of the European countries can testify to
the enormous contribution which private enterprise has made
to their phenomenal growth since the end of World War II; even
most European socialists have been discouraging government
ownership and operation of any but a few business enterprises.
Most Europeans are very much aware of the important economic and political benefits they have derived from the various
measures that have been employed to promote intra-European
trade and economic integration. Most Europeans are very
familiar with--and deeply concerned about--the nature of the
threat which Communism and the Communists represent to
their individual liberties and their national preservation. And
those Europeans who are familiar with the economic and social
problems of Latin America and the winds of revolution that
are blowing in that region are, in general, as enthusiastic about
the Alliance for Progress and as anxious that it succeed as we are.

It is not enough, however, that the Europeans be enthusiastic about the Alliance or even that they extend material and technical assistance to promote its success. It is necessary also that the Europeans extend their intellectual and spiritual assistance. It is necessary that they join with the Government and the private sector of the United States in meeting the challenge of the war of ideologies in Latin America with words as well as with actions.

Many Latin American officials are familiar with the European views concerning the importance of self-help and economic reform. They have heard expressions of those views by European officials during the course of their private bilateral discussions, and they know of the inflexible and controlling positions usually taken with respect to such matters by the European Directors of the International Monetary Fund and the International Bank. But the people of Latin America do not know that the Europeans have those views, or that the European votes predominate in those institutions. The belief is current throughout Latin America that the International Monetary Fund and the International Bank are controlled by the U.S. Government. "Proof" of this alleged fact is seen in the fact that the U.S. Government, and only the U.S. Government, continues--publicly as well as privately--to stress the importance of many of the same types of economic reform and self-help measures as are stressed by those institutions. The fact that there is genuine and deep conviction within the rest of the Free World on the critical importance of those measures to the economic and social development of Latin America is not known, just as the rationale in support of those measures is not understood.

I accordingly consider it important, for several reasons, that the Europeans enter fully and publicly into the war of ideologies in Latin America. They should want to do so, if only because many of the strains in the relations between the United States and Latin America will be alleviated when the people of Latin America come to realize that the United States is only one of the many countries of the Free World which have established various difficult reform and self-help measures as prerequisites to financial assistance. The rest of the Free World has a great deal at stake in the maintenance of good relations between the United States and Latin America. Their self-interest, as well as their sense of fair play, should impel them to be of all possible help in this regard, particularly inasmuch as I am only asking of them that they say publicly what they have long been saying privately.

It is perhaps even more important for the long run to recognize, furthermore, that the readiness of many Latin Americans to pursue the types of reform and self-help measures
which are necessary for the economic and social development
of their countries might be greatly increased if they were made
aware of the strong endorsement of those measures by many
Free World countries other than just the United States, as well
as the reasons for that endorsement. As explained in Chapter 4,
a line of argumentation by a European may be much more persuasive to many Latin Americans than the same line of argumentation by an American; and the more widespread the endorsement
of a concept among the countries of the Free World, the less
will the Latin American who endorses that concept be susceptible
to the charge that he is an American Puppet.

There are three principal ways in which the rest of the
Free World (Europe) can express its involvement in the
Alliance for Progress, in addition to the extension of im-
proved economic, financial, and technical assistance.

What is needed, first and foremost, are loud and clear
statements by high-ranking spokesmen of each European
country, endorsing the objectives and ideology of the Alliance
for Progress and conveying that country's desire to help further the prospects for its success. Such statements could be
made most effectively by the Presidents or Prime Ministers
of the European nations during their visits--hopefully on a
much increased scale--to Latin America. Leaders of that
rank could be very effective in dramatizing the spiritual affinity between their countries and those of Latin America, while
clarifying the nature and significance of the bonds among all
the countries of the Free World and placing the Alliance for
Progress in its proper perspective as the Free World's alternative to Communist tyranny in Latin America.

Second, the European ambassadors in Latin America should
begin to participate in the war of ideologies in that region. No
ambassador will wish to become "improperly" embroiled in
the domestic political controversies of his host country, and I
know that I am in effect recommending that the European ambassadors assume the risk of being charged with such embroil-
ment. However, I do not believe that a sharp line can always
be drawn in practice between "proper" diplomatic representa-
tion and "improper" interference in the domestic affairs of a
host country. Ideological conflicts have pervaded virtually
every field of public affairs in Latin America. The European
ambassador who wishes to avoid the risk of being charged with

improper interference must refrain from public statements or must resort to the expression of nothing but banalities. Meanwhile, our antagonists in the war of ideologies will continue at work, and the basic spiritual and intellectual bonds between his country and the country to which he is accredited will have been undermined. Every ambassador must be prepared to assume some risks if he is to succeed in his objective of fostering the best possible relations between his country and his host country.

The risks should not be exaggerated, furthermore. There is no need for any ambassador to offer public (or private) opinions concerning controversial matters at issue in the host country. He can quite properly speak of the ideological concepts of the Free World as interpreted and applied in his own country. Indeed, he should consider it to be one of his major responsibilities to provide public clarifications of past and current events in his country and between his country and others. The role played in his country by the Communists; the ramifications of inflation and the means his government has employed to combat it; his country's experiences with government-owned or government-controlled business enterprises; the role of free labor unions, the universities, and the military forces in his country; the relations between his country and the other countries and international institutions of the Free World as well as the relations between his country and the Communist world--an ambassador may properly discuss all these and many other subjects for the purpose of improving the understanding and appreciation of his country among the people of the host country.

The fact that some or much of what an ambassador has to say is pertinent to the war of ideologies in the host country should not deter him. He should, if anything, interpret that fact as manifestation of the need for what he has to say. Ideological differences account for the most serious strains in international relations. The interests of no European country can be well served by reliance upon the United States or any other country to speak for the entire Free World.

To be sure, the various countries of the Free World do not have the same points of view with respect to every subject. There is some danger, therefore, that an inconsistency of viewpoints would appear among the different Free World ambassadors. Expressions of sharp differences with regard to important matters could convey the impression of serious

disunity among the Free World countries or could otherwise
confuse the Latin Americans. However, I do not believe that
there are many basic differences in viewpoint among the Free
World countries on the issues which are important in the
Latin American war of ideologies, and I do not believe that
any European ambassador would knowingly magnify the degree
of the differences that do exist. Furthermore, some diversity
of viewpoint within the Free World is not only acceptable; it is
desirable. The free expression of individual and national differences in one of the most attractive and critical characteristics of the Free World.

Third, each European government should encourage the
fuller involvement of the private sector of its country in the
war of ideologies in Latin America, along the general lines
recommended in Chapters 7-11 for the private sector of the
United States. The form which such involvement might appropriately take will vary from country to country. It is a
safe generalization, however, that all of the European-owned
business firms in Latin America would benefit, and that the
Alliance for Progress would likewise benefit, if the managers
of those firms would pursue the type of measures recommended
in Chapter 9, separately and in conjunction with other foreign-
and nationally-owned business firms. The European labor
unions which are members of the ICFTU or the ICFTU could
well strengthen their relationships with their counterpart
unions in Latin America. And the European universities could
help the Alliance for Progress in several ways, including encouragement to the authorship of books and articles which are
likely to be particularly helpful in solution of the technical
problems of economic and social development in Latin America. For example, French treatises on the relationships between government development plans and private investment
would be helpful in Latin America, as would Swedish treatises
on the scope for cooperatives and Japanese treatises on land
reform.

To repeat the point made throughout these pages, the Alliance for Progress is the Free World's alternative to Communist
tyranny in Latin America. Anything which the governmental or
private sector of any European country can do to help promote
the success of the Alliance would be in the interests of the Free
World as a whole.

THE NEED FOR EUROPEAN PARTICIPATION
IN THE ALLIANCE FOR PROGRESS MACHINERY

Despite the fact that Europe will benefit along with the rest of the Free World by the success of the Alliance, it is understandable that many Europeans have been considerably less than enthusiastic about the idea that Europe should extend important assistance to the Alliance, but only in such forms and for such purposes and under such conditions as are determined by the governments of Latin America and the United States, or by a strictly inter-American organization. No country with a well-developed sense of its own dignity and importance will happily pursue policies which it has had no part in formulating, however sound those policies may be. There can be no doubt about the fact, furthermore, that European knowledge and experience could contribute a great deal toward assuring the soundness of the decisions made by the Alliance authorities, if ways could be found to draw upon that knowledge and experience. Some suggestions will be made in the next Chapter, therefore, for obtaining European participation in the decision-making processes of the Alliance machinery.

There will be little point in providing for such European participation, however, unless the Europeans are prepared to accept the responsibility that would necessarily go along with their participation in the decision-making processes. It is necessary that the Europeans themselves decide that they want to assume that responsibility.

PART

III

THE ALLIANCE MACHINERY

CHAPTER **14** THE FUNCTION
OF THE INTER-
AMERICAN SYSTEM

The old maxim that "money is the root of all evil" is
certainly not appropriate to the Latin American situation.
Money is an indispensable tool for achieving the highest
possible levels of personal income and well-being everywhere.
And the flow of large quantities of money from the rest of the
world to Latin America is essential if the goals of the Alliance for Progress are to be achieved. The Latin Americans
are perfectly justified in seeking to encourage the largest possible inflow of money. They are perfectly justified, furthermore, in believing that the readiness of any foreign country
to extend monetary assistance to Latin America is an important
index of that country's true desire to help promote the success
of the Alliance for Progress. Accordingly, I have no quarrel
with the fact that the Alliance machinery--in particular, the
newly created Inter-American Committee on the Alliance for
Progress (CIAP)--has been designed to help stimulate an increase of that assistance from as many countries and international agencies as possible.

Unfortunately, however, CIAP has in my opinion allowed
its proper concern with maximizing foreign assistance to divert
its energies from an even more necessary concentration upon
the other prerequisites for the success of the Alliance. It is
not that the Alliance leaders are any less impressed by the
importance of the other prerequisites than they once were. I
am convinced that there is a growing awareness in several of
the Latin American countries of the need for basic economic
and social reforms and increased self-help, and the leaders of
the Alliance have been trying very hard to stimulate both that
awareness and the kinds of actions that should follow. The
emphasis of the Alliance leaders in this regard, however, has
been upon stimulating the separate Latin American countries
toward the necessary awareness and toward taking such
actions as the separate countries themselves consider best,
while the actions of the Alliance machinery, per se, have
been directed predominantly toward strengthening the influence of the Latin Americans upon the foreign aid decisions
reached by foreign government and international institutions.

The necessary emphasis has not been given to what I consider the most critical requirement of the Alliance machinery: multinational, inter-American formulation of the standards by which to measure the degree to which the reform and self-help measures of the separate Latin American countries are fulfilling the separate national requirements.

To be sure, no Latin American country is likely to adopt any self-help or reform measure merely because that measure has received the blessing of any other country or international body. The political leaders normally consider themselves much more knowledgeable about the general problems of their own country than any foreigner or group of foreigners can hope to be, and consider it incumbent upon themselves to govern their country in the light of their own general knowledge. Likewise, no lending country or international financial institution is likely to accept uncritically the judgment of any other country or international institution concerning the soundness of the measures which any Latin American country is taking. Each lending government (and international agency) considers itself responsible to its citizens (and member governments) for the best possible use of its lending resources, and accordingly feels that it must make an independent judgment as to whether any particular loan applicant has, or has not, taken the measures which would qualify it for loan assistance.

The fact that no governmental or international agency is prepared to yield authority to any other governmental or international agency over matters for which it considers itself accountable to its own constituents should not, however, be accepted as a logical justification for perpetuation of the present state of confusion and frustration concerning the self-help and reform objectives of the Alliance for Progress, as described in the Introduction. It is necessary, even for strengthening the collaboration of the external agencies, that agreement be reached on the standards for measuring progress toward self-help and reform. It is important that the Alliance machinery be the instrument through which such agreement is reached.

I accordingly recommend that CIAP be reorganized for the purposes of, first, establishing consistent (though not necessarily identical) standards by which to determine the kinds of "reform" and "self-help" measures which are most appropriate to the specific circumstances of each of the different Latin American countries, and, then, actually evaluating the performance records of the different countries in pursuing the reform and self-help measures appropriate to their specific circumstances.

There is fairly universal agreement that external assistance under the Alliance for Progress should be correlated with the extent to which each separate Latin American country implements the economic and social reforms called for by the Charter of Punta del Este and pursues such self-help measures as will enable it to make the best possible use of its own resources. As pointed out in Chapter 5, however, there is considerable confusion and difference of opinion among the Latin Americans and even among the foreign governments and international lending agencies over how to determine whether a country is adopting and implementing the self-help and reform measures appropriate to its special circumstances. Self-help is not necessarily being achieved, and may even be impeded, when a government passes a law designed to raise more tax revenue, inasmuch as the law may never be implemented and, indeed, may even be counter-productive, as by having loopholes leading to an actual decline of revenue or by discriminating seriously against foreign investors or even domestic investors. Similarly, a law labeled "land reform" would not necessarily constitute reform just because of its label; conceivably, it could even worsen the situation of the small farmers by, for example, establishment of farm units so small (minifundia) as to be uneconomic. Moreover, a self-help or reform measure appropriate to the circumstances of one country may be completely inappropriate to the circumstances of another country.

THE FORMULATION OF REFORM AND
SELF-HELP STANDARDS

CIAP might well consider several alternative procedures for the formulation of self-help and reform standards. It might, for example, ask the OAS staff to prepare draft proposals for for the consideration of CIAP. Or CIAP might hire the most highly qualified consultants it can find from universities in Latin America, the United States, Europe, and Japan to prepare the draft proposals. Or each of the member governments of CIAP might be asked to prepare the draft proposals on one or more of the possible reform or self-help measures. Something can be said in favor of each of these alternatives, and others. My own preference is summarized below:

CIAP should first charge "special committees" of the type created at the First Annual Meeting of the IA-ECOSOC in Mexico City in October, 1962, with responsibility for formulating draft proposals for various general standards for fiscal reform, land reform, education reform, the elements of a favorable climate for private enterprise, the bearing of price movements on economic and social development, etc. The OAS staff would be charged, as it is at present, with preparing working papers for consideration by each of the special committees, and would be authorized to contract the services of outside consultants to assist in the preparation of those working papers.

Then, after each of the special committees has given CIAP the report or reports for which that committee was responsible, CIAP would review the reports separately and collectively, with the objective of revising them so as (a) to adapt the general proposals, which were prepared by the high-level technicians of the different countries which comprise the special committees, to the broad political considerations which must ultimately be taken into account if the proposals are adequately to reflect the will of the people of Latin America, and (b) to give the necessary assurance that the various reform and self-help proposals are not only sound in themselves, but also mutually consistent and even, so far as possible, mutually reinforcing. CIAP should, for example, accept the responsibility for determining the best possible reconciliation among the various measures designed, on the one hand, to promote economic development and those desig on the other hand, to promote social development. Some suggestions for the kinds of general proposals which the special committees and CIAP might come up with appear as Appendix B (on fiscal reform) and Appendix C (on the bearing of price movements on economic development).

Having approved general proposals on reform and self-help, CIAP should then charge the OAS staff with the responsibility of adapting those reports to the special circumstances of each of the Latin American countries, in consultation with the designated representatives of each of the countries concerned. The reports pertaining to each country would then be submitted to CIAP for its consideration and approval.

While the foregoing procedure may be a bit cumbersome, I believe that it would lend maximum assurance that the standards established for "reform" and "self-help" are not only sound, technically and politically, but are also Latin American standards--standards formulated by the Latin Americans themselves in their own interests and for the purpose of promoting the objectives of the Alliance for Progress. Much would thereby have been achieved toward Latinization of the Alliance, as urged in Chapter 6. Indeed, the fact that the standards have emerged not only from the studies and analyses of the OAS staff and from the exchange of viewpoints among the country representatives in CIAP, but also from the interchanges of experience and viewpoint among the high-level technicians representing different countries in the special committees should do much to help promote the ultimate economic and political integration of Latin America.

THE EVALUATION OF PERFORMANCE

The formulation of standards by which to evaluate the self-help and reform measures of the Latin American countries would be only the first step--though a critical first step--toward Latinization of the Alliance. The necessary second step, in my opinion, would be the establishment of procedures whereby the Latin Americans themselves would accept the burden of evaluating the performance by each of their countries in implementing the measures necessary to meet those standards. Many Latin Americans have been understandably displeased with the fact that the U.S. Government and other governments and international agencies, including the International Monetary Fund and the World Bank, have been making independent (and frequently conflicting) judgments concerning the extent to which each of the Latin American countries has, or has not, been implementing appropriate self-help and reform measures. The need for independent judgments by the lending governments and international agencies can doubtless never be eliminated. However, I am convinced that the latter will give increasingly greater weight to the judgments reached by the Latin Americans themselves once the Latin Americans have demonstrated that their judgments can be relied upon for objectivity and soundness.

Accordingly, I recommend that after CIAP has approved
the reports establishing the standards for self-help and reform
which are appropriate to the special circumstances of each
Latin American country, the OAS staff be charged with the
maintenance of records summarizing the extent to which each
country has, or has not, been meeting the standards established for it. The records would be made available to CIAP, at
its request, to enable it to determine the qualifications--and
particularly the relative qualifications--of the different countries for external assistance. It is in this way--and, I believe,
only in this way--that CIAP can hope and expect to have a
major influence upon the total amount, and the distribution, of
the external assistance extended to Latin America. It is in
this way, moveover, that CIAP can have the greatest impact
in guiding and helping the various Latin American countries
toward implementation of those internal measures that will
be most effective in reaching the goals of the Alliance for
Progress.

The burden which I am recommending be assumed by the
Alliance machinery will not be a light one. It will project
that machinery into the middle of substantial controversy of
a political, as well as a technical, order. However, if the
Latin Americans are to obtain the degree of self-mastery over
their own fate that they so understandably desire, while achieving a high rate of economic and social development in accordance with the basic principles that they share with the rest of
the Free World, it is necessary that they assume the recommended burden. There can be no substitute for self-discipline.

THE NEED FOR EUROPEAN INVOLVEMENT

I am not optimistic about the extent of assistance which
Latin America can expect to obtain from the various governments
of the Free World other than the United States. I have no doubt
that each of these governments would like to see the Latin American countries reach the goals of the Alliance for Progress. And
I consider it possible that some of those governments will be
prepared to extend more assistance, including more financial
assistance, to Latin America if they can be satisfied with regard

to some of the doubts that have so far discouraged them from
extending more assistance.   But I cannot ignore the fact that,
to date, the various other members of DAC (including several
European countries, plus Canada and Japan) have been willing
to consider almost no financial assistance except insofar as
that assistance would entail the promotion of their own exports
to Latin America.   They have not yet taken seriously either the
importance of the Alliance for Progress to the welfare of the
Free World or the great assistance which they could render
toward the success of the Alliance, as indicated in Chapter 4.

Nevertheless, I consider it highly important that the
Latin Americans do everything possible to encourage the
Europeans (including the Canadians and Japanese) to participate in the Alliance machinery.   Accordingly, I recommend that
the OECD and/or DAC be invited to designate representatives
to serve in CIAP as nonvoting members.   Their advice on
reform and self-help measures would be useful.   And the fact
that they have participated in the discussions leading to the
formulation of standards, and even in the discussions concerning the performance of the Latin American countries in implementation of those standards, should do much to clarify
European doubts about whether their active participation
would be welcome.   Furthermore, if CIAP works as I hope it
will, the deliberations in CIAP may have a considerable impact upon the total assistance, and the distribution of the assistance, extended to Latin America from Europe as well as from
the United States and the official international agencies.

APPENDIXES

APPENDIX A SUMMARY OF THE
UNDERSTANDINGS AND
RESULTS OF THE
PUNTA DEL ESTE
CONFERENCE

(Appendix to Chapter 2)

A mere summary of the remarkable understandings reached
at Punta del Este must do violence to many significant ingredients
of the Alliance for Progress. Nevertheless, the following high-
lights will reveal the fundamental elements of the very new and
critical venture on which the members of the Alliance embarked
at that time:

Recognizing the paramount need for self-help, the Alliance
calls upon each Latin American member to formulate and implement a national development plan based on democratic principles. Each plan is to provide for the fullest possible mobilization of the country's economic resources and for the allocation of those resources according to the country's highest priorities for economic and social development. Each plan is to
provide for more rational utilization of the government's resources and for the measures necessary to encourage private
enterprise in support of the plan. Moreover, each plan is to
call for whatever legal and administrative measures are necessary to achieve the reforms which will not only encourage the
most rapid possible increase of national income but will promote the equitable distribution of that income among all the
people and will help overcome other social injustices. Thus,
the plans are to provide for: raising the general levels of education and health; improving the standards of governmental
administration; strengthening the physical, financial, and
technical bases of agricultural production while correcting unjust systems of land tenure; reform of tax structures and fiscal procedures, including the severe punishment of tax evasion,
so as to distribute the burden of supporting governmental expenditures more equitably while promoting private savings and
investment; maintenance of price stability; measures to encourage the inflow of foreign private investment; and measures
to increase competition and reduce monopolistic practices.

Furthermore, the Alliance calls upon the Latin American nations to do even more than "just" to reconstitute their separate economic and social structures in the manners summarized above. It also calls upon each of them to collaborate with, and to reinforce the efforts of, each of the others. "The participating Latin American countries recognize that each has in varying degree a capacity to assist fellow republics by providing technical and financial assistance. They recognize that this capacity will increase as their economies grow. They therefore affirm their intention to assist fellow republics increasingly as their individual circumstances permit." They agreed, moreover, that "presently existing differences in income levels among the Latin American countries will be reduced by accelerating the development of the relatively less developed countries and granting them maximum priority in the distribution of (external) resources and in international cooperation in general."

Collaboration among the Latin American countries is also to take the form of measures to attain the economic integration of Latin America. The basic Alliance documents accordingly provide for: increasing the membership of, and strengthening the relations between, the Latin American Free Trade Association and the Central American Treaty of Economic Integration; priority allocation of external assistance to those countries and for those purposes where the assistance can best be employed for attaining the objective of economic integration; promotion and coordination of transportation and communications systems; coordination among the Latin American nations of "their actions to meet the unfavorable treatment accorded to their foreign trade in world markets"; and, perhaps most important, "appropriate" coordination of the separate national development plans.

Neither of the basic documents of the Alliance provide for any date on which it is to terminate. However, there is frequent reference to the objectives to be sought and the means to be employed during the ten-year period following its inception. It was estimated that achievement of the specific objectives spelled out for that period would require a rate of economic growth in each Latin American country of at least 2.5 per cent per capita per year (or an increase of something over 5 per cent per year in each country's total economic growth, allowing for an average annual population increase of 2.5-3.0 per cent). It was further estimated that this growth rate will require investments totalling at least $100 billion over the ten years and that the Latin American countries should be able to finance as much as 80 per cent of those investments out of their own resources if they pursue the pertinent self-help measures as strenuously as can reasonably be expected of them.

The Alliance accordingly calls upon the Latin American countries to carry approximately 80 per cent of the total estimated financial burden. Recognizing the low average incomes of the area, it will be appreciated that that responsibility will not be easy to meet. The importance of the remaining burden, estimated to be at least $20 billion and available only from foreign sources, will also be appreciated. The $20 billion will be important simply because of the 25 per cent it will add to the Latin American investment effort. It will be important also because it is expected to be used for the importation of machinery, equipment, materials and services (including know-how) not available in Latin America. It will be important, finally, for the manifestation it will provide that the United States and the rest of the Free World are genuinely determined to help the Latin Americans help themselves because they are our neighbors and our friends and because we have much in common.

In light of these considerations, the United States Delegation at Punta del Este was happy to be able to approve those portions of the Declaration to the Peoples of America which read:

> The United States, for its part, pledges its efforts to supply financial and technical cooperation in order to achieve the aims of the Alliance for Progress. To this end, the United States will provide a major part of the minimum of twenty billion dollars, principally in public funds, which Latin America will require over the next ten years, from all external sources in order to supplement its own efforts,

and

> The United States intends to furnish development loans on a long-term basis, where appropriate, running up to fifty years and in general at very low or zero rates of interest.

No effort was made publicly at Punta del Este to break down the $20 billion figure, or the United States contribution toward that figure, more precisely. Various public statements made subsequently, however, permit the following amplification:

Subject to satisfactory self-help by the Latin Americans, the U.S. Government is committed to the extension of direct financial assistance of "over" $10 billion to Latin America during the ten-year period. No statement has been made concerning the precise amount the Government is committed to provide in excess of $10 billion, but the Government evidently considers the commitment to be for something less than $1 billion. There has been no commitment that the $10 to $11 billion will be divided evenly over the ten-year period, but both the executive and legislative branches of the U.S. Government have been lending support to the conclusion that the assistance will in fact be divided evenly, and the Latin Americans appear satisfied with such a distribution.

No commitments have been made with regard to the remainder of the $9 to $10 billion. However, U.S. Government officials have considered it reasonable to assume, primarily on the basis of past experience, that about one-third will consist of private investment by United States nationals; about one-third will consist of loans from various international organizations, including the International Bank for Reconstruction and Development (IBRD), the International Development Association (IDA), and the Inter-American Development Bank (IDB); and about one-third from the governments and private investors of other capital-supplying countries (primarily in Europe). No commitments have been made to cover the contingency that these assumptions would prove to have been overly optimistic; that is, the U.S. Government is not committed to help cover any shortfall. On the other hand, the U.S. Government commitment of $10-$11 billion is explicitly to be the minimum assistance. The hope has been held out that the total of U.S. Government assistance might in practice substantially exceed the the amount committed.

Moreover, the basic Alliance documents call for the collaboration of the U.S. Government with more than the provision of U.S. public funds alone. The Government committed itself at Punta del Este to extend the following additional principal types of support: (1) collaboration in requests for financial support of the Alliance by other capital-supplying countries and international institutions; (2) provision of technical assistance to help formulate specific development projects as well as national development plans and tax and agrarian reform programs; (3) the reduction or elimination of all restrictions and discriminatory practices in the United States tending to reduce the consumption and importation of Latin American primary

products;   (4) the improvement and strengthening of
international commodity agreements, including encouragement to the participation of other producing and consuming
countries in such agreements, in an effort to stabilize the
prices of the major Latin American export commodities; and
(5) cooperation in efforts to induce other importing countries
to reduce their import duties and internal taxes applicable to
Latin American basic products and to terminate the preferential agreements and other measures curtailing Latin
American access to their markets, "especially the markets
of Western European countries in process of economic integration, and of countries with centrally planned economies."

The organizational and procedural arrangements established at Punta del Este for coordinating and integrating the
Alliance efforts of all of its members plus the numerous
inter-American institutions are of special interest. Most
important among those arrangements were those pertaining
to the disposition of the national development plans. The
Charter of Punta del Este provided for the creation of a completely autonomous Panel of nine high-level experts to be
appointed without reference to nationality (although the
Panel as finally constituted contained seven Latin Americans, one British citizen, and one U.S. citizen) and encouraged each Latin American government to submit its
development plan to that Panel for its expert appraisal. The
Panel would then discuss possible modifications of the plan with
the government concerned and would later report its conclusions to the Inter-American Development Bank and to other
governments and institutions that might be prepared to extend
financial and technical assistance in support of the plan.
Neither the Bank nor any other potential source of financing
would be bound by the Panel's conclusions. However, Secretary
Dillon made it clear that the United States Government, at
least, would give great weight to those conclusions.

* * * *

Neither the accomplishments nor the failings of the Alliance since Punta del Este are susceptible to full and accurate
measurement. Subjective judgments are necessary for evaluation of some "accomplishments," such as certain self-help
or reform measures. Furthermore, it was never expected
that some objectives, such as that of raising greatly the level
and quality of Latin American education, would be achieved in
just five years, or that progress toward that objective could be

measured statistically. Nevertheless, some indication of the
results of the Alliance may be shown by the following summary,
which is derived primarily, though not entirely, from the annual surveys by the Secretariat of the OAS and the annual evaluations of the Alliance by the IA-ECOSOC:

It has been estimated that the increase per capita in the
gross domestic product at constant prices for the nineteen
Latin American countries collectively amounted to 2. 9 per cent in
1964 and 2. 5 per cent in 1965. Accordingly, the minimum goal
of an annual increase of 2. 5 per cent per capita which was
established in the Charter of Punta del Este was met by the
area as a whole in those two years, following increases aver-
aging 1. 8 per cent during 1955-60 and increases of 2. 3 per
cent in 1961 and 0. 9 per cent in 1962 and a decline of 0. 8 per
cent in 1963. However, use of the collective data is somewhat
misleading inasmuch as the relatively high rates of increase of
just seven of those countries--Argentina, Peru, El Salvador,
Guatemala, Nicaragua, Bolivia, and Mexico--served to increase substantially the over-all average increases in 1964
and 1965. The other twelve countries, which include the
majority of the population of the area, did not reach the minimum Alliance goal of 2.5 per cent in those years. Moreover,
as concluded by the IA-ECOSOC at its Buenos Aires meeting
in March-April, 1966, "It is clear that despite the substantial progress in some countries and sectors, the region as a
whole has not yet attained a rapid and sustained rate of economic development. "

Almost all of the nineteen countries have prepared some
sort of development plan, as called for in the Charter of Punta
del Este. In general, the plans have been useful, even important guides for national policy, and almost all of them have
been worthwile first steps. However, the plans differ widely
in scope and depth. Many of them are limited to the public
sector alone. Some apply only to the short-run of perhaps
two or three years. A serious defect of almost all of them is
that they are essentially of the econometric, model-building
type where emphasis is placed on national income accounts
and sectoral goals, with little attention to the relative priorities of specific development projects, either in terms of
time sequence or in terms of specific allocations of specified
amounts of real or financial resources. In fact, there is
little consideration in any of the development plans to the
specific actions to be taken for achievement of the development
goals. As pointed out by the Economic Department of the

OAS, "Usually lacking is an evaluation of the operative capacity of the administrative machine to accomplish that part of the
over-all development plan that is the responsibility of the public
sector." The plans have uniformly been produced by the planning offices of the respective governments, and the government
agencies which must necessarily play the major role in implementation of those plans have rarely considered themselves
legally or morally responsible to do so. There have been especially serious divergencies between the development plans,
on the one hand, and the federal budgets and bank credit allocations, on the other.

All of the nineteen countries have made noteworthy efforts
to meet the monetary stabilization goals called for in the Charter
of Punta del Este. This has been especially true of Brazil,
Argentina, and some of the other countries which had most con-
spicuously been suffering from inflationary pressures. Nevertheless, many factors, including the desire of these countries
to speed up their rates of economic and social development
through increased public spending, have impeded achievement
of monetary stability. The Secretariat of the OAS reported
in March, 1966, that "During the Alliance period, inflationary
tendencies have been greatly intensified in the larger countries
of the region."

Many of the countries of the region have enacted laws designed to effect basic tax reform. The revised tax laws and
improved tax administration have together been largely responsible for the fact that tax revenues at constant prices have been
increasing in all of the nineteen countries except Argentina and
Uruguay, and for the fact that there are evidences of improved
tax equity. Nevertheless, the OAS Secretariat has pointed
out that "While the objective of the Alliance for Progress of
'demanding more from those who have more' through 'fair and
adequate taxation of incomes' is well on its way in most Latin
American countries ... it is still rather far from being achieved."
Also, "The existing systems of taxation tend ... to perpetuate a
demand structure unfavorable to the development of mass production, on which many aspects of development depend." It continues to be true, in addition, that many of the national budgets are
far too dependent upon the revenues derived from import duties--
a fact which renders those countries excessively vulnerable to
balance-of-payments fluctuations and impedes achievement of
the economic integration objectives of the region. Furthermore,
the tax laws of many of the countries are poorly designed from
the point of view of their impact on private investment. As

pointed out in the IA-ECOSOC report in March, 1966, "industrialization in the urban centers has been insufficient to absorb
the annual increases in the active urban population. In consequence, unemployment has shown a tendency to increase in
many countries, or at best to stay stable at high levels."

The export earnings of the nineteen countries as a whole
increased at an average annual rate of 5.8 per cent during
1961-65, representing the highest and most sustained rate of
growth since 1950. The increased export earnings have been
due to many factors, including the effectiveness of the International Coffee Association, of which the United States and
various European and African countries are members, along
with most of the Latin American countries. The markets that
accounted for most of the expansion of Latin America's exports were the members of the European Economic Community
and other Latin American countries plus Japan. Trade among
the Latin American countries alone increased from a total of
$569 million in 1961 to $643 million in 1962, $733 million in
1963, and $945 million in 1964, or an average annual increase
of about 18 per cent. However, exports to the United States
during that period only increased from $3,175 million in
1961 to $3,227 million in 1962, $3,342 million in 1963, and
$3,404 million in 1964, or an average annual increase of about
2 per cent, while exports to the United Kingdom declined
from $688 million in 1961 to $279 million in 1962, and only
partially recovered thereafter to $355 million in 1963 and $431
million in 1964. Furthermore, the over-all statistics conceal
the relatively poor export rates and the sharp export fluctuations of several of the countries. It is important to note also
that while the over-all growth rate of Latin America's exports
during 1961-65 was impressive, the region's share of total
world exports has declined from an average of 8.8 per cent
during 1950-59 to 7.1 per cent in 1960, 6.9 per cent in 1961,
7.0 per cent in 1962, 6.8 per cent in 1963, 6.5 per cent in
1964, and 6.3 per cent in 1965.

The determination of the Latin American countries to
raise the levels and quality of education is reflected in the
fact that the ratio between educational expenditures and gross
domestic product increased considerably in many countries
during 1960-64 and did not decline in any country. The number
of students in elementary schools increased from 24 million in
1960 to 27 million in 1962 and 30 million in 1964. Data are not
available concerning the over-all increase of students at the
secondary levels since 1960, but the OAS has estimated that

the increase ranges between 22 per cent in the case of Chile to
76 per cent in the case of Peru. "Of the fifteen countries on
which recent information is available, eleven showed an increase of more than 50 per cent." The number of students
enrolled in Latin American universities increased from 470,000
in 1960 to 522,000 in 1962 and an estimated 675,000 in 1964.
None of the foregoing information, however, alludes to the
quality of the education being provided, and impressive as the
increase in the number of students may be, it must be conceded that the number of students relative to the total school-
age population continues to be very low almost everywhere.
It is important to remember also that few of the elementary
school students complete more than four or five years of
schooling. The OAS report in March, 1966, concludes that
"Little has been done" to accelerate education since the
Alliance for Progress was launched, and buttresses this conclusion by the following statements, among others:

> The results of the human resource research done
> by the Institute Torcuato Di Tella in Argentina
> point up the shortage of technical and scientific
> personnel.

> The results obtained in Chile are similar
> to those in Argentina. In addition, the high pro-
> portion of persons in Chile's actively employed
> population who have had only five years of elemen-
> tary school (59.7 per cent) is a definitely ad-
> verse factor.

> The Colombian educational system is unable to
> train the number of professional persons required
> by the development plan. The shortage of professors
> appears to be the major bottleneck.

> The figures obtained in the study made by CSUCA
> (Consejo Superior Universitario Centro-Americano, or
> the Superior Council of Central American Universities)
> in Central America on the educational level of that
> region's active population are alarming.

In summary, those figures indicated that of the economically
active population of Central America, 0.7 per cent had a university education, 2.1 per cent had a secondary school education,
9.4 per cent had an elementary school education, and 87.8 per
cent had not completed their elementary school education or had
had no education at all.

School-construction and teacher-training programs
have been initiated in Latin America since the Alliance was launched, but these investments still represent a very small proportion of the public expenditure for education.

Educational planning is a prerequisite to the
most effective use of resources devoted to education.
Unfortunately, progress to date is very limited.
All available national and external resources have
not been exhausted in designing and implementing
educational plans, nor have many essential aspects
been taken into account in the urgent overhaul of the
educational systems, particularly secondary education.... Although all existing plans emphasize the
need to adjust the study plans and programs in order
to improve the quality of instruction being given, none
has reached the stage at which the reforming, salu-
tary effects of planning are felt in the daily activities
of the various educational institutions.

The Latin American university is far from
having established a functional link with the
society it serves. The perpetuation of obsolete
patterns in professional training have caused the
student to be frustrated, to feel left out of the main
stream of national life.

Almost every one of the nineteen Latin American countries
has promulgated agrarian reform laws, has created the necessary
administrative bodies for implementation of those laws, and has
taken some initial steps toward that implementation. However,
the over-all progress has been a drop in the bucket even with respect to the noncontroversial aspects of agrarian reform.
From the point of view of land redistribution--the most widely
accepted, though not necessarily the soundest, meaning of agrarian reform--only a few countries have done anything at all, and the
few that have done anything have done very little. In general,
agrarian reform has been retarded, according to the IA-ECOSOC,
principally by "deficiencies in legislation, inadequate internal
and external financing, and lack of understanding about the
nature and benefits of agrarian reform.... In the majority of
the Latin American countries, there is an almost total lack of
attention to the rural sectors." Agricultural-livestock production is estimated to have increased about 20 per cent since 1960,
representing a cumulative annual increase of about 4 per cent and
a per capita annual increase of less than 1 per cent.

The OAS Secretariat has estimated that total housing construction under the Alliance program in both urban and rural
areas amounted to 116,000 units in 1962-63, 71,024 units in
1964, and 118,315 units in 1965. This is a substantial figure,
but its significance should be evaluated in light of the OAS
estimate that the need for new housing units in the urban areas
alone amounts to about 1,000,000 units annually. It is estimated that about 400,000 new units are needed annually because of the influx of families from rural areas to the urban
zones, and that an additional 600,000 new units are needed annually because of population increases.

It has been estimated that during 1961-64, 10 million
people were supplied with potable water under the Alliance
programs, reflecting substantial progress toward the original
Alliance target of providing potable water to 45 million people.
In addition, another 40 million people, including those living
in rural areas, have benefited from improvements in the quality
and quantity of the water services (including sewage) available
to them.

Total loans authorized by the United States Government
under the Alliance for Progress amounted to $1,348 million in
1961, $563 million in 1962, $622 million in 1963, $1,062 mil-
lion in 1964, and $847 million in 1965, as compared with av-
erage annual loans to Latin America of $218 million during
1950-55 and $375 million during 1956-60. Loan authorizations
for Latin America by the official international institutions (the
International Bank for Reconstruction and Development and its
affiliates, the Inter-American Development Bank, and the International Monetary Fund) averaged $834 million annually dur-
ing 1961-65, as compared with annual averages of $117 million
during 1950-55 and $272 million during 1956-60. Data are not
available concerning the flow of private capital to Latin America or concerning official loans from Europe and other areas,
but it is generally believed that neither of these categories has
reached the level anticipated at Punta del Este. Furthermore,
the rate of disbursements of the loans authorized by the U.S.
Government and the official international institutions has been
substantially smaller than the rate of authorizations. Disbursements of official international agency loans averaged $466
million during that period as compared with average authorizations of $834 million.

APPENDIX B FISCAL REFORM

Broadly speaking, the objectives of economic and social development measures are twofold: (a) to increase the percentage and improve the composition of the gross national product which is devoted to <u>investment</u> in economic and social development, and (b) to increase the extent to which the rich contribute to that investment and to which the poor benefit from it. The following brief outline, to be discussed in detail below, summarizes some of the ways in which fiscal reform may under certain circumstances contribute toward the achievement of those objectives:

A. By increasing federal tax revenue,

    1. In order to permit the federal government to finance the local costs of its economic and social development program, thereby avoiding undue reliance upon foreign financial assistance.

    2. In order to avoid monetary instability.

B. By making better use of federal tax revenue,

    1. In order to give higher priority to the development program.

    2. In order to avoid absorbing so much of the national income for federal expenditures as to constitute an excessive drain upon domestic purchasing power (needed to provide markets for industry and agriculture) or upon domestic savings (needed to finance private investment).

C. By distributing the burden of tax payments more equitably,

    1. In order to increase the share borne by the Latin American rich relative to that borne by the Latin American poor.

2. In order to increase the share borne by the Latin American rich relative to that sought from the American taxpayers, most of whom are very much less wealthy than some of the richer Latin Americans.

D. By increasing the tax incentives, or reducing the tax impediments, to increase investment and higher productivity, thereby facilitating attainment of many targets, including agrarian reform.

E. By increasing the tax revenues of local communities,

1. In order to foster and finance local initiative in development planning.

2. In order to promote a higher degree of tax equity.

3. In order to reduce the public's dependence upon central government decisions, thereby strengthening democratic forces.

4. In order to increase the incentives for collection of taxes, with the consequence, among others, of promoting agrarian reform.

The major difficulty which I find with the aspects of fiscal reform suggested above is the fact that they are not necessarily mutually consistent and are indeed likely to be mutually conflicting in many countries. I believe that those accepting the responsibility of urging any Latin American country to undertake fiscal reform must also accept the obligation of arriving at a rigorous determination of precisely which aspects of fiscal reform are most needed and most appropriate in that country. The fiscal system of every country inevitably impinges to a greater or lesser degree upon every facet of the country's mode of life. A modification of the fiscal system may have important indirect as well as direct effects. We would not, and do not, recommend such modifications casually in our own country. We must not be less careful when recommending them for other countries, particularly when those countries are so much less resilient than our own.

Let us, then, probe more deeply into the problems of fiscal reform in Latin America, following the general outline, above, so far as practical:

There is probably no limit to the number of ways in which
the various federal governments of Latin America could usefully spend an increase of tax revenues. Economic and social
development might be promoted in every country of that area
by an increase of federal expenditures on roads, railroads,
hydroelectric power facilities, warehouses, school buildings
and teachers' salaries, municipal sewage and water supply
systems, etc. It may therefore appear at first glance to be
obvious that the more revenue the federal government has to
spend on such projects, the better.

In my opinion, however, it would be a great mistake to
accept that conclusion uncritically. The basic problem of
economic and social development, indeed the basic problem of
strengthening the economic and social position, of any country is how best to allocate the economic resources of that
country among alternative forms of employment. Certainly,
there is no lack of sound purposes to which the limited, the
necessarily limited, internal resources of any country can be
put. Obviously, federal expenditures for education, roads,
warehouses, etc., may all be highly desirable. Indeed, I know
that even after all pertinent factors had been given their due
consideration, I would still recommend that the federal governments of certain Latin American countries be encouraged
to expand their tax revenues so as to permit increased expenditures for such purposes. However, the need of each country
to make the best use of its limited resources points to the
need to delay formulation of any recommendations on this subject until after all pertinent factors have in fact been given their
due consideration. I believe that the result of careful thought
may well lead, in the cases of some Latin American countries,
to recommendations against increased tax collections and might
even lead to recommendations in favor of decreased tax collections. The principal factors in question may be summarized
as follows:

(a) Some Latin American governments could considerably
increase their expenditures on economic and social development
if they were to make better use of the tax revenue already being
collected. A careful and objective analysis of the military expenditures in many Latin American countries would undoubtedly
reveal opportunities for great savings without significant im-
pairment of the military security of those countries. Considerable savings could also be effected in some countries by reduction
of government payrolls, which have become heavily padded through
political patronage. Some countries could greatly reduce expendi-

tures now being devoted to subsidizing government-owned corporations: The number of employees on the payrolls of these
corporations frequently can be reduced without damage to, and
even to the benefit of, the output of the enterprises; it would
frequently be economically reasonable to increase the fees or
other prices charged for the product of the corporations so as
to compensate for increased costs, thereby reducing or elim-
inating the need for subsidization from federal taxes; it might
even be desirable to turn some corporations over to private
enterprise in order to relieve the government of the need to
subsidize them and possibly in order to permit improvements
in their productivity or the quality of their products. Finally,
some countries might be encouraged to do a better job of establishing priorities in the allocation of expenditures explicitly
designed to promote economic and social development. The
construction of a long paved highway through a forest may be
much less productive than, say, the construction of a large
number of local roads.

(b) It seems evident that the rationale supporting a recommendation for increasing federal tax revenues in some
countries cannot be applied with equal validity to other countries with different economic, political, and social conditions.
Thus, federal tax revenues now absorb a very much larger
percentage of the gross national product in some Latin American
countries than in others with roughly equivalent per capita incomes. In some countries, the sum total of federal plus state
and municipal taxes aggregates a larger percentage of GNP
than in others, although federal revenues alone may not weigh
as heavily in the first group as in the second. The distribution of national income in some countries is less uneven than
in others, so that an increase of tax revenues in the first
group of countries might have to be more heavily at the expense of the poor than in the second group, and the political
feasibility of tax increases may be less in one group of countries
than in another. Furthermore, the need for federal tax revenue in the different countries may vary greatly among them
in accordance with the different stages of economic and social
development already achieved, their different geographies,
and even their different attitudes. A country which welcomes
and is receiving private investment in, say, the meat-packing
industry may need less tax revenue than one where the public
wants governmental ownership of, and investment in, that
industry.

(c) The resources available to any country, even including
any external resources which may be made available to it, are
necessarily limited. While there is probably no limit to the
number of developmental projects to which the various Latin
American governments could devote an increase of tax revenues, each government must set a limit somewhere to the
number (or value) of projects it will finance if it wishes to
leave any resources for investment, or even for production,
by private enterprise. Except in completely socialist countries (none of which exist in Latin America, except Cuba),
private investment is necessary not only for the satisfaction
of consumer needs, but even for economic and social development. Just as there may be no limit to sound governmental
projects, there may be no limit to sound projects for private
enterprise. Investments by private enterprise may be necessary for such diverse economic and social development projects as steel mills and the fabrication of steel products, the
manufacture of radio and television transmitters and recep-
tors, paper manufacture and book publishing, the production
of electric wires and light bulbs, cattle husbandry and the
distribution of pasteurized milk, etc.

After allowing for the consumption needs of a country,
its savings (income less consumption) are available for investment by government and private enterprise. Each country must decide for itself what sort of distribution it wants as
between investment by the government and by private enterprise. I shall engage in a further discussion of this question
below, limiting my present comments to two points:

Firstly, any recommendation for an increase of tax revenues implies a prior judgment to the effect that governmental
investment should be increased at the expense of private investment and/or consumption; that judgment might be valid in
some Latin American countries, but such judgments are too
important to be made casually--they should be reached only
after careful examination into the specific circumstances of
each country.

Secondly, the effort to increase tax revenues may have
important consequences beyond that of transferring savings
from the private community to the government. In particular,
it is important to remember that taxation of the savings of
private investors may, at some tax level, serve to reduce
private investment by more than the amount of savings which
the government hopes to capture. The tax level at which in-

vestors will be discouraged from investment obviously varies
among countries, in accordance with their differing economic,
social, and political situations. However, it is clear that the
greater the hazards of any potential private investment, the
larger must be the contemplated return to the investor after
taxes if he is to undertake that investment. Given the profit
prospects for any investment, there will be some tax level
beyond which potential investors will be unwilling to take the
risks involved.

It should not be forgotten that one of the characteristics
of most underdeveloped countries--indeed, one of the factors
frequently accounting for the fact that they are underdeveloped--
is the hesitancy of the public to invest in those countries.
Where the supplies (and/or prices) of raw materials, equipment,
parts, power and labor are unreliable and when the effective
market is limited, the risks of investment may be great. Where
there are social or political disturbances, the risks will be
even greater. Since all of such conditions unfortunately are
prevalent in Latin America, it is obvious that the tax levels of
those countries should not be set so high as to discourage the
desired rate of private investment, whether that investment is
desired for itself or as a source of the savings needed to finance
governmental investment.

(d) An increase of the federal tax revenue in any country
not only provides the means for increased expenditures for governmental development projects, but also--and as a consequence
of that very fact--increases the role of the federal government
in the country's total economic and political life. In my opinion,
we might reasonably be prepared to accept the risks associated
with an increase of governmental power in Latin America when
we believe that, in the case of a given country or given countries, those risks are small and the advantages to be obtained
in the form of economic and social development are large. However, I consider it important that the risks be fully appreciated,
lest they be dismissed too lightly:

In the first place, the greater the extent of governmental
power, the greater, in my opinion, will be the threat to individual
liberties. I believe that most sociologists and political scientists who have studied Latin America agree that the social and
political ills of that region derive in large part from the tradition,
inherited from Spain and Portugal, of excessive dependence upon
central authority, be it the head of the central government or
the local cacique. I think it is remarkable that the striving for

individual liberties has been as successful as it has been in
Latin America in the past few years, but I do not think we
should be complacent about it. The tradition of reliance upon government officials to make all important decisions is
deep-seated in Latin America, and anything done to strengthen
the economic and political power of the central government
would also serve, in my opinion, to jeopardize maintenance of
the individual liberties so recently gained in Latin America,
and to jeopardize even more the prospects for the much-to-be-
sought increase of those individual liberties. Strong governmental leadership is clearly necessary in the present stage of
world affairs. But I consider it no less necessary that special
efforts be made, under these circumstances, to preserve and
if possible to strengthen the extent to which individuals are
free to rely upon their own abilities and desires.

Secondly, there is the risk that an increase of federal tax
revenues will lead to a <u>retardation</u> of economic and social development, even assuming the exercise of great care to avoid
excessively high tax levels. Conceding that there is probably
an infinite number of ways in which the various Latin American
governments could <u>theoretically</u> spend an increase of tax revenue so as to promote economic and social development, it
does not necessarily follow that any specific government will
"therefore" be <u>able</u> to do so. The relative priorities among
alternative projects cannot be easily determined. It is a difficult and complicated task to formulate all the plans necessary
for the implementation of specific projects and for integration
of the specific projects into the rest of the economy. And
effective implementation of the detailed plans of a project generally depends upon dedicated and highly trained governmental
personnel, as well as upon the willingness and ability of the
government officials to resist the pressures for logrolling,
patronage, etc. Experience in Latin America and other underdeveloped parts of the world suggests that while the necessary
skills and other qualities necessary for planning and implementing development projects <u>do</u> frequently exist, it would be unwise
to assume that they exist <u>in</u> every Latin American country and in
adequate quantity to make the best possible use of expanded tax
revenues. The transfer of savings from the public to the government will not be desirable unless the government can reasonably
be relied upon to invest those savings to better national advantage than potential private investors.

I should perhaps emphasize at this point my belief that an
increase of federal tax revenue would be desirable in some Latin

American countries, even after giving due allowance to the considerations discussed above.   An increase of federal tax revenue
may be the only practical means in some countries, or may be
necessary in addition to other measures such as the feasible reduction of military expenditures, for raising the amount of money
necessary to finance high priority economic or social development projects.   It may be a necessary means of acquiring the
local currency necessary to cover the local costs of economic
or social development projects for which foreign financial institutions are prepared to finance the foreign exchange costs.   The
spirit of private enterprise may be particularly moribund in some
countries.   Governmental economic or social development projects may be critically important in some countries for the purpose of creating or improving the climate and opportunities
for private investment.

If any conclusion is appropriate, it is that no general recommendation should be made for an increase of federal tax revenue
in each country of Latin America.   The economic, political, and
social circumstances differ greatly among them, and an increase
of federal tax revenue may have net unfavorable consequences in
some of them, just as the net consequences may be favorable in
others.   The specific circumstances of each country should be
carefully examined before any conclusion is reached as to the
desirability of increasing federal tax revenue in that country.   We
are very cautious about such conclusions in our own country.
We should be no less cautious in others.

* * * *

Let us turn now to another aspect of fiscal reform, that of
distributing the burden of tax payments more equitably.   Those
concerned with increasing tax equity in Latin America usually
have one or both of two principal objectives in mind: (a) to increase the share of the tax burden borne by the Latin American
rich relative to that borne by the Latin American poor, and
(b) to compel the Latin American rich to bear a greater responsibility for the economic and social development of their countries, thereby relieving to some extent the degree of the responsibility being shouldered by foreign (predominantly, American)
taxpayers, most of whom are far less wealthy than the richer
Latin Americans.   These objectives are sought not only because
the present tax structures seem to be obviously unfair, but also
because it is believed that the achievement of greater tax equity
will reduce social discontent in Latin America.

Concepts of "justice," "fairness," "equity" are obviously of great importance. A poor man who believes that the rich
and powerful control the government for their own advantage
and to his disadvantage will normally want to change that government, and will sometimes be willing to do so by force if
that seems to be the only practical means at hand. Conspic-
uous consumption by the rich may well serve as a red flag to
the poor, particularly if the poor believe (rightly or wrongly)
that their poverty is being aggravated by excessive taxation,
while the rich are relatively tax-free. It undoubtedly is of
great importance that such feelings of injustice be reduced to
a minimum, and the United States should quite properly, in
my opinion, associate itself with a strong recommendation
for greater tax equity in Latin America.

Before recommending any specific measures for the
achievement of tax equity, however, I think that the following
considerations should be taken into account:

(a) Reliance upon private enterprise to help promote economic and social development may well be inconsistent with
United States concepts of tax equity. To tax corporate profits
at rates of 50 per cent and then to tax personal incomes at rates
rising to 80 per cent might well destroy whatever willingness
Latin Americans might otherwise have to engage in private investment. As pointed out above, the risks faced by private
enterprise are particularly large in underdeveloped countries.
There must be some hope of large returns after taxes if those
risks are to be taken. It is not irrelevant to point to the historical economic growth of the United States, and even to the
current growth of Puerto Rico which until very recently was
considered one of the least developed areas of the world, under
structures of taxation which most of us would consider quite
inequitable if applied to the United States in its present state of
economic development. In fact, it may be argued that income
tax rates in some Latin American countries--countries which
have been quick to copy the social legislation adopted in the
more advanced countries of the world--are already too high in
terms of their present economic, social, and political situations.

(b) The concept of "equity" is a subjective one. Remembering that the social, historical, religious, cultural and other
facets of every country's background differ from those of every
other country, it is to be expected that the definition of equity
will vary from one country to another. It would be just as pre-

sumptuous of us to aver that our concept of equity is "the" right
one as it would be of any Latin American country to aver that its
concept is "the" right one. The present U.S. attitudes concerning "progressive" taxation and taxation according to "ability
to pay" are not necessarily shared by the people of each Latin
American country. The fact that there is little evidence reflecting a desire of the Latin American people to modify their tax
laws so as to achieve greater tax equity does not necessarily
manifest their true desires; they may simply be too mute or too
unsophisticated to be able to express their desires. It might
even be argued that we should urge them to adopt our concept of
tax equity for their own good and as a manifestation of our interest in the well-being of the poor. However, it might also
be argued that we should conduct some research into the basic
attitudes of the people of each country before seeking to obtain
their adoption of our attitudes; it may be easier to foment
social unrest than to quell it.

John Kenneth Galbraith has stated, "In our prescription
for the improvement of other countries, we have a little-
recognized but highly persistent tendency to advocate what
exists in the United States, with no very critical view of its
appropriateness to the situation or stage of development of the
other country."[1] He directed that statement toward our technical assistance advisers overseas and toward those who stress
the need for external financial assistance to supplement the internal resources of the underdeveloped countries. In my
opinion, his statement can be directed at least as appropriately
toward those who stress the need for social reforms in
those countries. Social reforms are necessary (just as foreign
technical and financial assistance are necessary) in each of the
Latin American countries. Fiscal reforms, in particular, are
necessary. But the specific composition of the necessary reforms and the means of accomplishing them vary from country
to country. Before recommending any specific measure, we
should take a "very critical view of its appropriateness to the
situation or stage of development of the other country."

(c) While there is little evidence reflecting a strong desire of the Latin American people to modify their tax laws so
as to achieve greater tax equity, there is some (though not
very much) evidence of dissatisfaction over the widespread
evasion of the tax obligations under the laws which have already been enacted. It is generally a reasonable presumption
that the laws existing in any country reflect the will of the
people. Therefore, the United States can properly support

recommendations designed to foster enforcement of those laws, particularly where we believe that the laws would, if properly enforced, contribute to economic or social development.

It may be stated as a general proposition that tax evasion is wide spread in Latin America (as in many other countries, even in Europe) because (1) the likelihood of being caught is low, and (2) the penalties which are likely to be applied to the tax evader, if caught, are too low. In my opinion, an attack upon the second factor is much the more necessary. I believe that much of the advice given by the U.S. tax advisers assigned to certain countries, and much of the equipment provided to implement that advice, has had little value because the focus has been on detecting tax evasion, whereas the critical problem has been the reluctance of the governmental officials--including the courts--to apply punishment which is sufficiently severe so as to frighten those who are contemplating evasion. To my knowledge, no one has ever received a jail sentence for tax evasion in any country of Latin America. Frequently, the "penalty" consists of nothing more than the requirement that the tax be paid, perhaps with interest. Such penalties can hardly be considered frightening, particularly when the evader expects inflation, so that the longer the interval between the payment date established by the tax law and the court order requiring payment, the less will be the real burden of the payment, even allowing for interest charges.

Obviously, even a willingness of the tax authorities and the courts effectively to punish tax evaders may be insufficient where the means of detecting tax evasion (including the technical competence and integrity of the tax collectors and assessors) are inadequate. Where the willingness exists, the U.S. Government might appropriately assign tax advisers to assist any Latin American government in improvement of its assessment and collection procedures. However, the major problem is that of stimulating the necessary willingness. And here, as elsewhere, we run up against the differences between our cultural, historical, religious and other backgrounds and those of the various Latin American countries.

We consider tax evasion a crime against society; a form of theft warranting not only social disgrace but also severe punishment, including imprisonment. We consider it to be the obligation of our citizens to know the tax laws or, if they do not, to employ lawyers or accountants to explain them; "ignorance of the law is no excuse." We expect our citizens to maintain

careful records of their gross income and gross expenditures.
Our jurisprudence is closely knit, the rules of law being defined with reasonable precision for the purpose of protecting
the constitutional rights of the individual, while protecting
society from what we consider improper abuses by the individual.

The situation in Latin America is different in every respect, though varying somewhat from country to country. In
no country of Latin America is tax evasion considered as
serious an offense as it is in the United States; in some countries it is almost considered a game to see who can evade the
law most cleverly; "The government is entitled to whatever
it can collect, but a man would have to be a fool to pay any
taxes he can escape paying." Moreover, if a man does not pay
all of the taxes called for by the law because he did not know
all the complicated provisions of the law, who can properly
accuse him of deliberately evading the law? Why, then, should
he be punished for it? And how can anyone be expected to
keep accurate records when business transactions are so complicated, when so many transactions are handled by cash rather
than check, when there are so many fees, discounts, sur-
charges, rebates, commissions, bribes, gratuities, etc. , that
have to be paid in addition to the quoted prices? And how can
a man know what to expect of the courts where the rules are
so ill-defined?[2]

I do not mean to imply a belief that the United States should
sit by idly while tax evasion continues rampant in Latin America.
I believe that one of the most fundamental types of social reform
necessary in Latin America is acceptance of the rule of law. I
believe that "rule by law rather than by man" is one of the key
pillars of democracy and that we should do all that we can to support that concept. I believe also that when the people of any
Latin American country have adopted laws establishing concepts
of equity which in themselves provide for an important type of
social reform, the United States should be particularly anxious
to do what it can to encourage enforcement of those laws.

Fortunately, there is some evidence of a desire in Latin
America to overcome tax evasion, and we may be able to reinforce it. However, we should not deceive ourselves as to the
complexity of the task. In particular, we should remember
that the democratic goal, "rule by law rather than by man," is
more complex than it may seem. For, men must interpret law,
and the interpretation itself is often tantamount to law, just as
is the nature of its enforcement. It is very likely, for

example, that the people of Latin America would be much more
angered by tax evasion by foreigners who have invested in their
country than by tax evasion by one of their own countrymen.
The violation of <u>any</u> national law by a foreigner is considered an
insult to their country, a sign of ingratitude for the nation's
hospitality. Foreign investors are acutely conscious of this
fact and it is the foreign investor who is accordingly the most
discouraged by highly progressive tax rates, especially since
he believes that his domestic competitors can be expected to
evade payment at those rates. If, therefore, we believe (as
I do) that foreign private investment can make an important contribution to the economic and social development of Latin America, we cannot shut our eyes to the fact that highly progressive
tax rates may be harmful by (1) worsening the competitive position of foreign vis-a-vis national producers as well as by (2)
reducing the attractiveness of all private investment for the
reasons explained under (a), above. Since this second consideration would apply even if there were any reasonable likelihood
of changing the attitudes of government officials so as to induce
them to enforce their tax laws impartially against foreigners
and nationals alike, we are brought to something of a dilemma:
If highly progressive tax rates are fully enforced only against
foreigners, foreign investment will certainly be discouraged by
the discrimination. If enforced against foreigners and <u>nationals</u>
alike, national investors will be discouraged, and even the fact of
equality of treatment may not be sufficient to overcome the discouragement to <u>foreign</u> investors.

* * * *

The structure of any country's tax system is important also
for the encouragement or discouragement which it may provide
for investment and/or production in specific fields of private
enterprise. A government may devise its tax structure deliberately
with that thought in mind. It may exempt a given industry from all
or some taxes and may impose extremely high taxes on some
other industry. It may levy high import duties on some commodities and low ones on others. It may impose high sales or excise
taxes on some goods (e.g., cigarettes) or services (e.g., night
clubs) and exempt others (e.g., food).

On the other hand, the tax structure may have unintended consequences in encouraging or discouraging different types of economic activity. Thus, the effects of a turnover tax may be of little
importance to the manufacture of simple products such as hand-

made wooden ash trays, but may be extremely burdensome to
the manufacture of complex items such as bicycles, each of the
components of which may have been taxed and which may in
fact consist of subsidiary components each of which was taxed.
The ultimate sales price of some products may often, in fact,
represent the effects of taxes upon taxes, to the point where
the sales prices might be out of the range of many consumers
who might otherwise have been part of the market for those
products, even though it is not the government's intention that
this be the case. The tax-imposed market limitation can in
fact be so severe as entirely to discourage production of some
commodities or to permit production only on a scale so small
as necessarily to be very high cost.

Where taxes have the effect of discouraging or encouraging certain types of investment and/or production because of
the deliberate choice of the government, the results may be
considered salutory as reflecting the peoples' wishes, even
though the effect upon the national income may be negative.
In most cases, however, the tax structure just grows, as one
tax law is superimposed upon another. Sometimes, indeed, taxes
are imposed for a publicly accepted purpose without public recognition
of important, and unwanted, ancillary consequences. Thus important
duties are sometimes established at extremely high levels for the purpose of discouraging the importation and consumption of commodities considered luxuries. In such cases, the national
objective might have been better met by high excise taxes applicable to the commodities in question, whether imported or produced domestically. For the import duties may have the effect
of providing a protected market for the domestic manufacture
of those commodities even at very high costs, thereby serving
to foster uneconomic utilization of the country's resources,
i. e. , serving to reduce the nation's real income.

On the other hand, taxation may be a useful instrument for
stimulating production, particularly agricultural production. I
shall not attempt to analyze the problems of agrarian reform
here. However, it is pertinent to point to my conclusion that
agrarian reform may fail in its major objectives unless it helps
promote an increase of agricultural income, and the use of
taxation--graduated in accordance with the size of the farm--
may be a particularly useful means of encouraging the efficient
use of land, and therefore an increase of agricultural income.

There is no doubt in my mind that the tax structure of every
Latin American country (as is perhaps true of every country of

the world) could be so revised as to promote an increase of
national income. In some countries this type of fiscal reform
may even be among the foremost measures needed for economic and social development. I accordingly hope that CIAP
will encourage and assist the Latin American countries to
adopt these measures. Again, however, I feel it necessary to
caution against oversimplification and undue optimism. It
may be necessary also to point out that great care should
normally be taken in giving advice on such matters, lest that
advice stir up a nest of hornets against the advisers and without benefit to anyone:

It is important to recognize, first, that the fiscal system
of every country is only a part, albeit a very important part,
of that country's governmental mechanism. The good effects
of a sound fiscal system may be offset by the harmful effects
of a bad banding or foreign exchange system or by price
or trade controls, just as the good effects of an otherwise sound governmental mechanism can be offset by the
harmful effects of a bad fiscal system. A given industry may
suffer from excessive taxation while benefitting from especially favorable exchange rates for its imports or exports. Private enterprise--industry, agriculture, commerce--always ad-
justs somehow to the milieu established for it by the com-
posite of governmental regulations, whether the regulations
reinforce, supplement or conflict with one another. A change
in any regulation, however desirable that change may appear
when considered by itself, may nevertheless have net undesirable effects in view of its impact upon the total milieu confronting those affected by it.

Consider, for example, the case of Brazil where, a few
years ago, income derived from agriculture was virtually exempt from income tax, but where almost all other governmental
regulations (bank credit policy; road construction; price controls on foods; the foreign exchange system, including the multiple rate structure as well as the policies established for foreign
exchange rationing; etc.) were designed to favor industry. Let
us suppose that a group of foreign experts was assigned to the
Brazilian Government at that time for the purpose of advising
on broad governmental policies. Any tax expert would quickly
have recognized the desirability of reforming the tax structure
so as to eliminate the preferential tax treatment accorded to
agriculture, presumably by applying much higher taxes upon
agricultural income. However, the other foreign experts would
probably have pointed to the desirability of providing greater

advantages to agriculture (better credit facilities and foreign
exchange treatment; increased governmental expenditures for
rural roads, irrigation, warehouses, etc.; elimination of
price controls on foods and, perhaps, even establishment of
agricultural price supports; extension services; etc.) so as to
correct a chronic balance-of-payments problem, so as to improve the national diet, so as to achieve agrarian reform, so
as to restrain excessive urbanization, etc. A recommendation
for reform of the tax structure alone would probably have run
counter to Brazil's national interest, even though tax reform
in conjunction with other reforms would probably have been
very desirable. In considering the measures appropriate for
promoting the economic and social development of any country, it is clearly necessary as a first step to compartmen-
talize the country's problems. In my opinion, however, no
recommendations should be made vis-a-vis any particular
compartment, such as the tax structure, until after careful
consideration has been given to the interrelationships between that compartment and the major other compartments.

It is important to recognize also the importance which
should be attributed to definition of the word, "taxation."
If we wish to be very precise, we can use textbook definitions of taxation. In the area of actual public administration, however, we must acknowledge that taxes may be obtained, in effect if not in name, by many different types of
measures which are not normally accepted as being taxes
per se.

Note, for example, the impact of multiple foreign exchange rate systems. A multiplicity of exchange rates applicable to different kinds of imports may have all of the
essential characteristics of a differential scale of taxation on
those imports or of a range of subsidies on imports effected
at rates of exchange more favorable than "the equilibrium
rate" and a range of taxes on imports effected at rates less
favorable than "the equilibrium rate." Similarly, different
rates of exchange applicable to exports may have all of the
essential characteristics of subsidies on some exports and
taxes on others. Even a differential between the average import rate and the average export rate may be defined as a
form of taxation (on imports, or exports, or both) if only
because of the fact that that differential may constitute a
source of "profits" or "revenue" to the government or central bank. It seems logical to conclude that anyone considering the desirability of reforming the tax structure of a coun-

try should devote careful attention to this form of taxation even
though its impact upon the country's balance of payments may be
even more important.

Special reference should also be made to the "prices" or
"fees" or "tariffs" charged by government-owned firms. It
often happens, particularly in underdeveloped countries, that
such charges are insufficient to cover the costs of the goods or
services being provided by those firms, thereby causing business losses which must be covered by tax revenues or deficit
financing. Since an obvious alternative to increasing tax revenues from other sources for the purpose of meeting such losses
would be to increase the charges by these firms, it seems equally obvious that this problem warrants the careful examination
of those considering tax reform, even though these charges are
not usually defined in the textbooks as "taxes."

* * * *

To me, one of the most important aspects of fiscal reform
would be that of strengthening the fiscal positions of the state
and municipal governments of the various Latin American
countries. The primary responsibility for promoting economic
and social development undoubtedly rests upon the shoulders
of the federal government of each of those countries. In my
opinion, however, the burden of that responsibility would often
be greatly lightened if the local communities were able to fulfill the role which they are best fitted to play. The manner in
which the federal government seeks to carry out its responsibility often depends upon the kind of support it can expect to get
from the local communities. The degree of the federal government's success may itself depend not only upon the support which
its program receives from the local governments but also upon
the extent to which the local governments have helped guide the
direction of the federal program. Furthermore, there are
certain types of measures which are important to economic and
social development and which can be designed and implemented
far better by local than by federal governments. However, the
fiscal strength of the local governments is an absolute pre-
requisite--though not the only prerequisite--if they are to make
effective contributions in these various directions, and such
fiscal strength is with few exceptions lacking throughout Latin
America.

The construction of a federal highway may be very desirable, but may in practice accomplish very little except to the extent that local roads are constructed so as to link with that highway.

The contribution made by a hydroelectric power project will often depend upon the availability and efficiency of the local distribution mechanism. The use made of the power may depend also upon the quantity and quality of the services needed to attract industry into any community (reliable water supply, healthy and efficient labor, paved streets, good ports, etc.).

The success of a federal education program may depend upon the construction of local schools and payment of adequate salaries to school employees (supervisors, teachers, janitors, etc.).

The success of a federal health program (such as the construction of hospitals and clinics and a concerted effort to eradicate certain diseases including malaria and typhoid) may depend upon the ability of the local communities to attract doctors and nurses and upon the local government's ability to provide healthy water and efficient sewage and garbage disposal. The health program may even depend in part upon adequate housing, including the availability of sanitary facilities for the disposal of human waste.

A federal program for increasing the availability of credit, or reducing its cost, to small farmers may be greatly affected by the differing local conditions in which that program must operate. As is true of everyone else, farmers differ among themselves in their honesty and in their knowledge and ability to make efficient use of credit. They differ in their knowledge of farming and marketing. There are local differences in the availability of warehousing and the need for warehousing. The sound administration of agricultural credit programs accordingly requires heavy reliance upon support from the local communities: support in providing information about credit applicants; support in providing information to the applicants; support in analyzing the local production conditions--probable rainfall, irrigation problems, transportation problems, marketing problems, etc. The construction of local roads, warehouses, and irrigation facilities may also be essential for the success of the credit program in many communities.

Agrarian reform is, in my opinion, especially dependent upon the support of local governments. I believe that the undesirable

patterns of land ownership and the equally undesirable economic and social relationships between landlord and tenant in Latin
America are very largely or predominantly attributable to the
weaknesses of the state and local governments.

The picture of the typical rich Latin American landowner
as a malevolant exploiter of the poor is, in my judgment, a
melodramatic distortion of reality.   There are heartless landowners.   No doubt, there are even landowners who cruelly and
deliberately take advantage of the poor, ignorant and defense-
less peasants working on their lands.   From all that I have seen,
read, and heard, however, I have been led to the conclusion
that the typical landowner feels and manifests a greater or lesser degree of paternalism toward his peasants.   The typical
peasant feels a certain affinity, frequently even gratitude, toward his "patron," for the various types of assistance given
to him by the patron in times of special need.   This subject is
too complex for full discussion at this point.   Nevertheless,
I wish to express the opinion that one of the evils deriving from
that paternalism is the fact that the landowner and the peasant have each been trapped by it.   The state and local governments (which are obviously in a far better position than the
federal government to be familiar with the needs of individual
members of their communities) must be able, financially and
otherwise, to meet the needs now being met by the landowner
if the bonds of dependence and subservience which at present
tie the peasant to his patron are to be broken by means other
than force.

It seems appropriate now to say a few words pertaining
to the "planning" of economic and social development.   I
believe that in some cases the sharpest impetus to economic
and social development through governmental expenditures may
be those expenditures which are made by state and municipal
governments, even apart from the question of whether those
expenditures are related to any national plan.   It is possible,
for example, that industry or agriculture may best be encouraged in some countries by development of local roads or
by improvement of local water supply systems or by school
construction.   There is a need for federal governments to concentrate upon over-all development plans, but there is also a
need for local governments to concentrate upon the specific and
detailed problems of their separate communities.

After all, it is inevitable that the people of the local communities will be more familiar with their own special problems than
federal officials can be.   Moreover, the people of those commun-

ities will often, if not usually, have a clearer conception of
what is needed to overcome their problems than federal officials can have.   Unfortunately, however, it is the federal
governments which collect the bulk of the total tax revenues
of the Latin American countries.   The local communities generally find that they can finance economic and social development projects only (or primarily) by seeking federal contributions.   The local governments can rarely count on federal
financial support on more than a yearly basis, at best.   This
fact is thoroughly debilitating to the kind of intellectual drive
necessary if the local officials are to focus effectively on
development planning.   It results in uneven, spasmodic and
unfruitful efforts.

For all these reasons, therefore, I believe that one of
the most important aspects of fiscal reform in Latin America
should consist of strengthening the financial positions of the
state and local governments.   I do not mean to imply that
financial strength would be sufficient to meet the problems
of the local communities.   The financial strength of any
state or municipal government will itself be limited by, among
other things, the level of the income produced in that state
or municipality.   Furthermore, the availability of money does
not necessarily mean that the money will be well spent.   But
the money is obviously needed if development projects are to
be undertaken.   It obviously is needed if competent officials
are to be employed for the formulation of those projects.

Assuming agreement that fiscal reform for the purpose
of strengthening the fiscal positions of the state and local
governments of Latin America is highly desirable, it should
not be assumed that such reform can easily be attained.   In an
important sense, the federal governments are competitors of
the state and local governments for whatever tax revenues
can be extracted.   Indeed, the constitutions of some countries
explicitly delimit the types of taxation which may be levied by
the different levels of government.   Moreover, some of the tax
powers relegated to the state and local governments are extremely difficult to enforce, especially where the enforcement
officials are poorly educated and/or subservient to those having
the economic or political power in their communities.   Nevertheless, I believe that CIAP should make a special effort to
persuade the various Latin American governments to work
vigorously for this aspect of fiscal reform.   In my opinion,
there will otherwise be little prospect for its achievement.
It is natural, if not inevitable, that each federal government

will wish to <u>increase</u> its fiscal strength relative to that of the state and local governments. It will require a convincing exposition by CIAP, and perhaps more than just a convincing exposition, to persuade most federal governments to <u>reduce</u> their relative fiscal strength.

My conclusions:

      1. When recommending economic and social reforms in Latin America, we should focus on the desirability of <u>fiscal</u> reform rather than <u>tax</u> reform alone.

      2. I believe that CIAP's general recommendations should include the following points:

    (a)   That each Latin American government should devote special attention to the desirability and possibility of increasing the tax revenues of their state and municipal governments.

    (b)   That each government should recognize that individuals and firms failing to comply with their government's tax laws are committing a serious offense against the economic and social welfare of their country. Accordingly, each government should agree to take all feasible measures to apply sufficiently severe punishment to tax evaders so as to discourage further evasion.

    (c)   That each government should reexamine its federal tax structure with the objective of reforming that structure so as to minimize the features discouraging and to strengthen the features encouraging desirable private investment and production.

    (d)   That each government should reexamine its entire fiscal system with the objective of (1) reducing or eliminating expenditures of a relatively low priority from the point of view of economic and social development, and (2) arriving at a judgment of the dimension of tax revenues which should be sought so as to maximize the joint contribution

which the government, on the one hand,
and private enterprise, on the other hand,
can best make to the promotion of economic and social development.

APPENDIX C   THE BEARING OF
PRICE MOVEMENTS
ON ECONOMIC
DEVELOPMENT

There is a general consensus of opinion among professional economists as to the critical importance of monetary stabilization in providing the necessary preconditions for economic development. Furthermore, the need for monetary stabilization has frequently been stressed by such official lending institutions as the Export-Import Bank of Washington and the International Bank for Reconstruction and Development. Indeed, it would be difficult to find anyone who openly recommends that governments should deliberately pursue the policy of seeking inflation (although many would argue for the policy of promoting a "very small" rate of price increases).

Yet, monetary instability has long prevailed in many Latin American countries, and in some of those countries "monetary stabilization" is a dirty word. Even in the United States, there are many who believe that it would be wrong to place much emphasis upon monetary stabilization as an index of self-help because they consider it of less importance than various other indexes or because they believe that political considerations render concentration on monetary stabilization inadvisable.

This appendix is concerned primarily with the economic aspects of monetary stabilization. These may be divided into two broad categories and summarized briefly as follows: (a) The question of whether monetary stabilization is "too conservative"; whether it is a "Wall Street" concept which may be of prime importance in developed countries, but is of secondary importance in those countries the primary goal of which is to become developed; whether it is true that while inflation and balance of payments deficits are evils, they are evils which the Latin American countries must endure as necessary by-products of the developmental process; and (b) the question of whether monetary stabilization is a sufficient, as well as a necessary, condition for economic development.

ARE INFLATION AND BALANCE-OF-PAYMENTS
DEFICITS NECESSARY BY-PRODUCTS
OF THE DEVELOPMENTAL PROCESS?

In my opinion, the anwer is clearly a resounding negative. I believe, in fact, that there is every reason for the conclusion that the economic development of Latin America as a whole has been greatly retarded, especially since the end of World War II, by both the inflation and the balance-of-payments difficulties which have afflicted most of those countries. As I shall explain later, there has been some economic growth during that period. In my opinion, however, the economic growth would have been much greater (and much sounder) if monetary stabilization had also prevailed.

The relationship between monetary stabilization and economic development may best be evaluated by reflection upon the many respects in which the economic development of Latin America has in fact been retarded as a result of inflation and balance-of-payments deficits (i.e., by the lack of monetary stabilization). They may be summarized as follows:

1. The incentive for the ordinary person to save his money for a rainy day or for his old age has been destroyed or greatly weakened in many Latin American countries. Why save money when prices are going up so fast that the purchasing power of that money is declining (as it has been in much of Latin America) at the rate of 20 per cent or 30 per cent or even 50 per cent every year? A person might be willing to save his money even under such inflationary conditions if he could earn equivalent rates of interest on his money, but such rates of interest are not ordinarily available. For, while everyone may be confident that the inflation, per se, will continue, no one will be confident about the precise degree of inflation. Interest rates are usually fixed obligations, and borrowers (including banks which accept savings deposits) must obviously undertake such obligations very conservatively. Few borrowers will promise to pay 30 per cent interest per year if there is any significant chance that the prices of the goods or service they propose to acquire with the borrowed money might rise "only" 15 per cent. It is the experience of most Latin Americans, therefore, that the interest rates available for their savings are far too low to protect them against the probable loss in real value of the money saved. So why save money?

As will be discussed more fully below, many people find gainful ways of employing their "excess" money even during inflation. However, the ordinary person, seeing no point in saving his money and knowing of no gainful way of employing it, either (a) will spend on consumption of "unnecessary goods and services, the money which he would have preferred to save, or (b) will work less hard in order not to earn money in amounts beyond what he feels that he needs to pay for "necessary" goods and services.

In either case, the goods and services which could have been available to the economy for investment will have been lost.

2. The gainful ways of investing money during inflation are frequently of a character which tends to retard, rather than to promote, economic development.

Try for a moment to put yourself into the frame of mind of a man who has lived through years of inflation and expects that inflation to continue at a heavy, though uneven and unpredictable, rate for years into the future. To the extent that you earn more money than you choose to spend on consumer goods and services, you may decide to exchange your "excess" money for something that you expect to increase in price at least as fast as, or preferably faster than, the expected increase in the general price level.

Hoarding

One method of exchanging "excess" money which is very often chosen is the purchase and hoarding of items considered likely to become scarce. When, for example, inflation is associated with balance-of-payments difficulties (as it almost always is, especially in underdeveloped countries) many people will seek to convert their own currencies into foreign exchange. They might then hold that foreign exchange (usually, dollars) abroad in expectation that depreciation of the internal value of their own currency (I shall call them all "pesos") will be matched by an equal or even greater depreciation of the peso-dollar exchange rate. Or they might use the dollars to finance the importation and hoarding of certain commodities in expectation that the internal supply of those commodities will become scarce (with especially sharp price increases as a result) as

the balance-of-payments difficulties impede their importation;
such curtailment of importation will be especially likely if
the commodities in question are of a "luxury" character, such
as expensive automobiles, and are therefore low on the government's list of import priorities. In either case, whether it is
the country's supply of dollars or of import goods that is being
hoarded, the very fact of the hoarding means that the country
is not making use of its dollar resources for purposes which
will promote its economic development. (And, incidentally,
the purchase of dollars as a hedge against inflation is itself
one of the forces aggravating the balance-of-payments difficulties of some Latin American countries, and increasing
their need for balance-of-payments loans from foreign financial institutions.)

Of course most Latin Americans seek to protect themselves against inflation by using their "excess" money for the
purpose of hoarding domestically produced, rather than imported, items. Every merchant stockpiles as large a supply
of merchandise as possible, in full expectation that he would
otherwise have to pay higher prices for that supply later. Every
housewife does the same thing. The result for the economy as
a whole is, of course, that more goods are being kept off the
market at any given moment than would be the case under monetary stabilization. That is, real resources--the product of land,
labor, and capital--which could and should be available to promote economic development are instead being kept idle in warehouses, cellars, and closets because they are acceptable hedges
against inflation.

Misdirected Investment

One consequence of Latin American inflation which has perhaps been even more harmful than the discouragement of savings
or the encouragement of hoarding has been the misdirection of
such investment as has taken place. As I will attempt to explain
more carefully below, Latin American investment has to a very
great extent been motivated by the opportunity to obtain large
profits quickly in certain types of enterprise (but not in others)
on the basis of low-volume production; without much concern for
the efficiency of production; and directed toward meeting the limited current demands of the domestic market, rather than the
demands of foreign markets. Inflation has discouraged investment directed toward most types of agricultural production and

toward production for export markets. It has even discouraged industrial investment directed toward potential, as opposed to assured, domestic markets. In summary, inflation has guided investment toward the production of high-cost goods and services, thereby contributing too little to the welfare of consumers or to the development of other industries.

I am convinced that if monetary stabilization had prevailed since World War II, there would not only have been more investment in Latin America by Latin Americans as well as by "foreigners," but that that investment would have been much sounder than what in fact took place. Let me broaden the picture so as to describe the principal factors which have been in the minds of Latin American investors:

(a) Expecting inflation at the rate of, say, 30 per cent annually, the annual rate of profit expected from any investment obviously must be very much higher than 30 per cent if the investment is to be made at all. Why go to the trouble and assume the risks associated with investment in a factory for the production of wood furniture at an expected profit of 30 per cent per annum on the pesos invested if you could instead put the same amount of money into the purchase and stockpiling of a commodity (raw lumber, for example) with reasonable expectation of a 30 per cent per annum "profit" just from the rise in the price of that commodity? You have to run fast just to stand still during inflation.

(b) The longer it takes for the investment to result in production, the greater must be the expected profit return, if only to compensate for the imputed "profit" which could alternatively have been gained by hoarding during the investment-production time gap.

(c) Investment geared to low-volume output has a number of special inducements under conditions of monetary instability: First, it is desirable to avoid dependence upon large supplies of raw materials where scarcities may result from hoarding by others or (when those raw materials must be imported) from balance-of-payments crises. Second, there is generally a pattern of

sporadic wage increases, frequently associated
with governmentally-determined increases of
minimum wages, following a more or less prolonged period of cost-of-living rises. The markets for most consumer goods therefore show
corresponding sporadic increases and prolonged
periods of decreases, even culminating sometimes in the virtual disappearance of the demand
for some commodities as income squeezes force
shifts in demand. In view of the wide fluctuations
in markets and the high cost, real and imputed, of
maintaining idle capacity during inflation, investors
tend to gear their capacity to something near the
lower levels of demand. After all, advantage can
ordinarily be taken of sudden increases of demand
by increasing prices instead of increasing volume.
Third, the prices of different goods and services
rise at uneven and unpredictably uneven rates
during inflation. An investment which appears
likely to be profitable on the basis of today's cost
and price structures might prove to be unprofit-
able as cost and price structures change over
time. It is therefore dangerous to put too many
eggs into any one investment basket. Fourth, the
greater the planned scale of investment, the longer is the investment-production gap likely to be and
the greater will be the hazard of miscalculating the
cost of the investment itself. This factor is especially serious for foreign investors, including
foreign lending agencies, who normally desire
fairly reliable estimates of the ultimate investment as well as ultimate production costs before
committing themselves to an investment project.

(d) Governmental intervention in the control of prices
and costs as well as the allocation of supplies may at
any time be exercised in such fashion as to reduce
or eliminate the profit possibilities of any investment. This threat is especially great under the following circumstances: First and most perversely,
when the investment is directed toward production
of "essentials," such as electric power, meat-
packing and the provision of other basic foods (rice,
beans, wheat, etc.), and urban and interurban
transportation, for the general discontent associated with inflation inevitably leads to price controls

over those goods and services which are considered
essentials by the general public. Second, when the
investment is by foreigners, inasmuch as foreign
investors are usually considered rich and powerful,
and it is normal to consider the remittance of profits abroad as unnecessary drains on the internal
economy especially when those profits are associated with price increases. Third, when the balance-
of-payments difficulties are severe. For such difficulties usually lead to the rationing of the amounts
of foreign exchange available for "nonessential"
imports, thus provoking especially sharp increases
in the costs of such imports, and/or direct import
rationing and price controls over "essential" imports. Only a relatively few investors can be confident that the governmental controls will be so administered as to benefit their particular enterprises.
It is true that governments can normally be depended
upon to try to avoid the social and political strains
that would result from shutting off the importation
of the supplies and the parts and equipment needed
to maintain production and employment in any established industry. But foreign exchange shortages
may become so severe that the government may be
compelled to cut the imports needed by some or many
investors. The strong likelihood that the government
will try to prevent "excessive" depreciation of the
peso-dollar exchange rate (an "excessive" increase
in the number of pesos required to pay for each
dollar) in an effort to avoid an increase in the
peso prices of imported commodities is an especially
serious threat to those agricultural and industrial
enterprises devoted to production of export goods
and therefore dependent upon foreign markets, for
the prospective peso receipts of such enterprises
would then be relatively fixed while inflation was
driving up their costs of production.

(e) While monetary instability thus serves to discourage
investment in many types of enterprise, it often
leads to investments in other types of enterprise,
such as those believed to be attractive means of
hedging against inflation. One of the more widely
recognized types of such investment is investment
in real estate--especially, apartment buildings,
office buildings, and hotels--in view of the generally

held belief in Latin America that, with the trend
towards increased urbanization along with rapidly
increasing population, real estate values may be
expected to increase even more rapidly than the
general price level. Furthermore, real estate
ventures are frequently excellent income-earners
and, once completed, usually require relatively
little maintenance expenditure. On the other hand,
rent controls may serve to reduce the income-
earning potential of some types of real estate.
This has, indeed, been one of the major factors
impeding construction of low-cost housing in Latin
America.

(f)   The balance-of-payments difficulties which have
generally been associated with inflation have stimulated a considerable portion of the industrial investment which has taken place in Latin America
during recent years. This stimulation has derived
essentially from the fact that when faced with demands for foreign exchange which cannot be satisfied out of reserves and current earnings, the various governments have uniformly considered it
politic as well as economically wise to debar the
importation of certain goods of a type considered
competitive with nationally produced goods. If any
commodities can be produced nationally (and even
though the national products might be inferior in
quality and/or higher in price than comparable
foreign products) they have a guaranteed market,
founded on virtual certainty of protection from
foreign competition. [1] However, it is important
to realize that domestic consumers and industrialists
frequently press for the importation of items considered to be "essential" and only available abroad
at satisfactory prices (e. g. , wheat, petroleum and
other raw materials, fertilizers, and parts and
equipment for established industries). Accordingly,
the protectionist effect of exchange controls is usually applied with special force against the importation of "nonessentials" (e. g. , radios, toys, refrigerators, high-quality textiles, automobiles, etc.).
In summary, monetary instability is normally manifested in balance-of-payments difficulties, which
usually lead to exchange controls, which are usually
directed toward excluding the importation of "non-

essentials," thereby stimulating domestic investment in the production of "nonessentials," by protecting the producers of those commodities from
foreign competition. Potential investors in the
production of "essentials" cannot look forward
to the same benefits from exchange controls.

(3) I have summarized above various ways in which monetary instability has either discouraged investment in Latin
America or has stimulated investors to focus on enterprises
other than those which are most fundamental for economic
development. I shall now summarize various other respects
in which monetary instability has interfered with economic
development in Latin America:

(a) It has minimized the operation of competition as
a force for productivity. Exchange controls, in
particular, have encouraged trends toward autar-
ky. If something can be produced domestically,
it can be assured of freedom from foreign competition unless the community considers that commodity so essential that it insists upon acquisition
at the lowest possible price. There are strong
drives in most Latin American countries to en-
courage--and, if necessary, to subsidize--the
production of any commodity which would otherwise have to be imported. High prices or poor
quality are generally accepted as undesirable,
but necessary, first steps in the developmental
process. And since there is virtually an infinite
number of commodities for which there is some
effective demand, there is likewise a virtually
infinite number of opportunities for investment
in the production of each one of those commodities. There is accordingly almost no incentive
for investors to concentrate in any given industry or industries in competition with one another.

Moreover, where foreign equipment is needed
in a given industry, as is usually if not always the
case, the exchange control adminstrators usually
seek to limit the scale of investment in that industry. Why, they say, should we waste our limited foreign exchange resources by financing the
importation of more equipment than is needed
to satisfy our present market? Why buy equipment which will be operated at less than full

capacity? If foreign loans are needed to finance
foreign equipment, why burden our future balance
of payments in order to acquire equipment which
is not needed for satisfaction of our current requirements? Even in the case of foreign equity
investments which involve no commitments
for balance-of-payments servicing, why permit
the foreigners (who no doubt possess greater
experience, more know-how and probably more
advanced equipment) to invest on a scale greater
than required by our present market, since the
effect of their investing on such a scale would
probably be to take over some of the market
previously open to other investors, thereby
forcing them to put up with some unutilized productive capacity?

Accordingly, monetary instability serves to
limit the number of investors, and the scale of
investment, in any given industry, thus elimina-
ting the main spur to competition--the hope of an
individual producer of capturing part of someone
else's market or the threat of losing part of the
market for his own product unless he can meet
the price and quality of a competing product.
Where everyone produces at or near his capacity,
what advantage would he derive by trying to capture part of someone else's market?[2] Furthermore, how would one go about increasing the
productivity he can obtain from his existing capacity? It is very difficult to predict the ultimate
effect of a change in productive processes when all
prices and costs are increasing, but at uneven,
and unpredictably uneven, rates.

(b) Managerial skills are slow to develop. Most investment projects in Latin America are personal or
family affairs, for a number of historical and
social reasons as well as because of the fact that
monetary instability encourages small-scale investment. There is no clear line of demarcation between ownership and management, as there is in
more developed countries. Accordingly there is
almost no group of professional managers, "business administrators," who continue available for
employment by other firms when the firms with
which they are associated fail.

And let there be no mistake about it: There are a great many business failures annually in Latin America despite the fact that business enterprises are not normally undertaken except on the basis of assured markets. For the markets are assured only in the sense that the absence of competition is assured. An investor undertaking a new enterprise may find that his production costs are far greater than he had anticipated or that his effective market at the prices he must charge in order to cover his costs is much smaller than the market which had earlier existed for the similar commodity which had formerly been imported at a much lower price. Remembering, further, that the prices and costs of different goods and services increase during inflation at uneven rates, it is hardly surprising that individual investors frequently find themselves in embarrassing financial situations.

It is especially important to remember that each of the Latin American countries is poor by U.S. standards, and that the increased production of goods that earlier were imported does not necessarily make any nation richer, and may even have the effect of making that nation poorer. The fact that production costs are high and result is sales prices higher than those of comparable imported commodities means (assuming that this is not the infant industry exception and that the rate of exchange is the "correct" one), that the land, labor, and capital resources which are being applied to the production of those commodities would better have been applied in some other way, preferably in the production of export commodities which could yield the foreign exchange to pay for expanded imports. Uneconomic production will tend to lower any nation's income, and it is to be expected that the investors engaged in such production will to some extent share the loss of income which the country as a whole experiences.

(c) Monetary instability has seriously impaired the opportunities for broadening markets across national lines within Latin America. Inflation has been proceeding at differing rates among the different Latin American countries, and each

country has been following that separate foreign
exchange policy which it considers appropriate
to its own balance-of-payments position. It would
accordingly have been extremely difficult, if not
impossible, to find a reasonably reliable and
reasonably stable set of foreign exchange rates
and exchange control policies to be used for promotion of inter-Latin American trade, even if any
of those countries had really been anxious to promote such trade. In fact, there has been little
interest in promoting a Latin American market
and there has even been little genuine interest
in promoting regional markets, except among
a few of the more economically stable countries
of Latin America. It is possible that this lack of
interest has itself been the result of the fact that
there is no acceptable yardstick (no acceptable
way to measure the relative values of their currencies) by which even to determine how their
respective national interests would be affected
by the creation of regional or continental markets.

(d) The operations of the price mechanism have been
so badly distorted as to have upset even the governmental efforts to promote economic welfare
in Latin America. Prices represent measures
of value, and are the guiding lights by which en-
trepreneurs are enabled, in a private enterprise
system, to allocate a country's resources in the
best possible directions for the maximizing of
national income. Almost all of what has been
said so far in this chapter can be offered in evidence to support the conclusion that the private
enterprise system cannot do its job properly
under conditions of monetary instability. However, it should not be assumed that the various
Latin American countries have been relying entirely upon the decisions of private entrepren-
eurs to determine the optimum allocation of resources. To a greater or lesser extent, almost
all of those countries have relied upon their respective governments to influence the allocation
of resources in ways which, they believe, are
in the public interest and which private enterpre-
neurs will not, in fact, be willing to undertake.
Thus, such diverse activities as railroads, hydro-

electric power facilities, and petroleum exploration, mining and steel production have all come to
be considered as largely or entirely governmental
responsibilities in some Latin American countries.

The question of whether nations are wise to
turn such activities over to governmental officials
is worthy of separate consideration. At this point,
however, I wish only to emphasize that even governmental officials need the guiding light of prices
to help them determine where and how much to invest for any purpose as well as to ascertain their
production costs and to determine the proper price
to charge for their product. Yet, monetary instability has served to foster such a proliferation of
price controls, multiple exchange rates, rationing,
indirect taxes, and even governmentally determined
wage structures that it has frequently been impossible to determine the extent to which governmental
enterprises (and even certain private enterprises)
are being subsidized by the community at large.
And if the extent of an indirect subsidy is not known--
if, indeed, its very existence is sometimes not
known--how can the public determine the desirability
of that subsidy, or even the desirability of the existence of that enterprise?

Consider, for example, the case of a
government-owned petroleum company which
has been reporting operating "profits," but has
been depending upon preferential exchange rates
for its importation of goods and services and has
been drawing heavily upon the transportation services
of a government-owned railroad company which has
been reporting operating "losses." How can the public
determine whether the petroleum company has been
earning true profits unless there is a reliable method
of measuring the indirect subsidies deriving from the
preferential exchange rates and from the failure of the
railroad company to charge tariffs equal to the true cost
of the transportation services it is providing?

It is impossible to determine the extent of the
subsidy derived from the preferential exchange rates
because that determination depends upon a determina-

tion, first, of the "proper" rate of exchange, and
it is impossible to determine that rate for a country
experiencing inflation and balance-of-payments difficulties, with exchange controls. Likewise, while
a cost analysis of the services performed by a
railroad company is difficult in any country, chiefly
because of the large element of "overhead" cost,
such an analysis is particularly difficult when the
exigencies of monetary instability lead to frequent
and sharp switches in the volume and pattern of
railroad traffic. These difficulties are, of course,
further complicated when--as usually happens--the
public comes to accept railroad deficits as natural
and proper means of stimulating economic development, by providing "low-cost" transportation services, to industry and agriculture. For this comfortable acceptance of deficits helps reduce whatever
inducement the government officials managing
the railroad company might otherwise have to increase tariffs or to reduce operating costs, as by
discharging "excessive" employees.

(e) Severe social and political discontent are inevitable
companions of monetary instability. Almost everyone living in a climate of monetary instability has
somehow learned over the years to put up with it,
but few have come to like it.

The man whose income is relatively fixed has
learned that his monetary income will eventually be
adjusted so as more or less to compensate for the
inflation which has taken place during the interim
since his last increase, but he is certainly discon-
tented--and frequently violently so--during that
interim. He will naturally tend to adjust his
consumption standards to a level close to that
which he could afford at the time of the last increase of his monetary income, and he cannot
fail to be distressed as inflation chips away the
purchasing power of that income. When one takes
into account the low levels of per capita income in
all of the Latin American countries, when one
recognizes, in other words, that the great majority
of the people in that area are living at, or only
slightly above, bare subsistence levels, it will be

abundantly clear why the distress provoked by inflation has been a strong force for social and political discontent.

However, it is not only the fixed income groups
who suffer from inflation. The fact that prices increase at uneven rates during inflation means that
there is also a significant redistribution of monetary income among different people and groups during inflation. In fact, everyone is constantly
jockeying for position against everyone else during
the race against inflation.

As one of the more common manifestations of
such jockeying, almost everyone seeks to get into
debt as deeply as he can, even assuming heavy interest burdens, whenever he believes that the
rate of inflation will exceed the interest rate on
his debt and that his income (including any loan
proceeds) will increase along with inflation,
even though with some lag. Obviously, not everyone is able to get into debt on favorable terms,
inasmuch as lenders (commercial banks, mer-
chants selling goods on credit, real estate deal-
ers, etc.) are also aware of the inflation. Obviously, also, this kind of speculation frequently back-
fires, as individuals miscalculate and find themselves unable to meet the contracted payments.

Similarly, almost everyone tries to obtain pos-
session of whatever items (including foreign exchange) are considered most likely to increase in
value because of impending scarcities. In this
case also, however, speculation frequently back-
fires as individuals find that they have miscalcula-
ted the degree of scarcity or have even chosen to
hoard items which proved to be in surplus relative
to effective demand.

The strain of just trying to maintain one's relative income standing is severe. And needless to say,
the strain felt as one's income standing deteriorates
relative to that of his friends and business associates is even more severe.

The general social and political discontent is
especially aggravated by the fact that few people
understand the economic forces at work during
the inflationary process. Few people even understand the origins of the monetary instability from
which they are suffering. And failure to understand the broad and anonymous economic forces
at work usually leads to either of two explana-
tions for the evils associated with monetary instability: That the evils were created deliberately
by malicious persons who sought to derive personal benefit from them in some way; or that "the
economic system" is itself at fault. It is not
surprising, therefore, that history is so replete
with examples of the direct connection between
inflation, on the one hand, and social and political upheaval, on the other; witness, for example,
Russia, Italy, and Germany, during and after
World War I and China after World War II. I
believe that the conclusion is plain that monetary
instability is today one of the best allies which
Communism and Communists (and all other rev-
olutionaries) have anywhere.

I conceded early in this appendix that there has been
economic growth in Latin America since the end of World War
II. How, then, can I account for the fact of that growth in spite
of the monetary instability that has prevailed during that period?
The U.N.'s Economic Commission for Latin America (ECLA)
has estimated that during 1950-57 the gross national product of
Latin America increased by an average of 4. 4 per cent annually,
and that even on a per capita basis the annual increase averaged
2. 2 per cent. Private investment has taken place on a substantial scale, despite the fact that monetary instability has discouraged
savings and encouraged excessive consumption. Hydroelectric
power facilities and steel mills have been greatly expanded in
number and capacity, despite the fact that monetary instability
has discouraged large-scale investments directed toward mass
production, while encouraging small-scale investments designed
to obtain large profits quickly. The foreign exchange earnings
derived from exports increased greatly, and have remained high,
as compared with the prewar period, despite the fact that monetary instability has discouraged production for export purposes.
How account for these facts if monetary instability has in fact had
the effects summarized in the foregoing sections of this appendix?

I believe that the following factors, all related to international circumstances over which Latin America had little control, will adequately account for a substantial percentage of such economic growth as has taken place in Latin America since the end of World War II. Indeed, I believe that those factors having been cited, it will become evident that the failure of Latin America to have experienced greater growth has been a real tragedy, and that monetary instability has played the role of the villain in that tragedy:

First, much of the capital equipment importation into Latin America following the end of World War II was made possible by the great increase of its export earnings, as compared with prewar. According to the U. N. 's Economic Commission for Latin America (ECLA), Latin America's exports to the rest of the world yielded an annual average of $1,632 million during 1934-38, $5,290 million during 1946-51, and $6,754 million during 1952-55. It is important to note in this connection that this increase was caused almost entirely by the increase of the world prices paid for Latin American commodities rather than by an increase in the volume of Latin American exports. The annual volume of Latin American exports during 1946-51 and 1952-55 increased by only 24 per cent and 27 per cent, respectively, over that of 1934-38, while the annual value increased by 224 per cent and 314 per cent over the same periods.

It must be conceded that the tremendous postwar increase in Latin America's export earnings was in part offset by an increase in the foreign prices of the goods imported by Latin America. Thus, United States wholesale prices during 1946-51 and 1952-55 had increased by 83 per cent and 104 per cent, respectively, over 1937-38 prices. However, if the increased value of Latin American exports is adjusted for the increased volume of those exports, it is seen that the unit value of those exports increased during 1946-51 and 1952-55 by 161 per cent and 226 per cent, respectively, over 1934-38 prices. It is accordingly evident that the increase in the foreign prices of Latin America's exports permitted a very great increase of imports following World War II. Moreover, most of the Latin American countries have long applied their exchange controls and import controls, plus their tariff structures, so as to encourage importation of "essentials" as contrasted to "nonessentials." Accordingly, the increased export earnings have served primarily to facilitate the great expansion in the importation of the capital equipment which has been directed toward investment, plus the parts and raw materials needed to maintain that investment viable.

Second, there has been a large postwar movement of
foreign capital into Latin America. Thus, ECLA has estimated that during 1947-57 gross foreign direct investment
in Latin America totalled $5,289 million, exclusive of re-
invested earnings; gross long-term and net medium-term
loans by foreign businessmen totalled $893 million; net short-
term loans by private businessmen totalled $309 million;
gross loans (almost all long-term or medium-term) by
foreign governments or international lending institutions
totalled $3,280 million; and donations by foreign govern-
ments and international institutions totalled $420 million.
In all, foreigners provided $10,193 million, exclusive of re-
invested earnings, to supplement Latin America's export
earnings as a means of financing and supporting investment
during that eleven-year period.

The total inflow of such foreign capital amounted to
$8,623 million during the period, 1950-57, when the gross
national product was increasing at an average annual rate of
4.4 per cent, or a per capita rate of 2.2 per cent. To provide some perspective on this subject, it may be pointed out
that the average annual rate of capital inflow ($1,078 million)
amounted to 2.3 per cent of the estimated average gross
national product ($46.5 billion) and 13.1 per cent of the esti-
mated average total investment ($8.2 billion) of Latin
America.[3]

It would be much more difficult to demonstrate the quali-
tative contribution of the foreign capital inflow into Latin America
during the postwar period. However, some guidance on this
subject may be derived from examination of the estimates
by the U.S. Department of Commerce of the increase in the
book value of United States direct investments in Latin America
between the ends of 1946 and 1956. The total increase of $4,003
million (from $3,005 million to $7,008 million) is broken down as
follows: agriculture, $225 million; mining and smelting, $584
million; petroleum, $1,270 million; manufacturing, $1,116 million; public utilities, $172 million; trade, $423 million; and mis-
cellaneous, $213 million. Loans by the Export-Import Bank and
by the International Bank, on the other hand, have been predominantly in the fields of public utilities, transportation, and industry. While it would not be possible to demonstrate that such
capital inflows have been of special significance for the economic
growth of Latin America, I believe that most observers, including most Latin Americans, would agree that foreign investments and
foreign loans have contributed to that economic growth more con-

spicuously even than would be indicated exclusively by their
dimensions. The contribution made by the "know-how" of
foreign investors has been especially noteworthy.

Third, the postwar economic growth was promoted to a
relatively small (though not insignificant) extent by the forced
accumulation of gold and foreign exchange reserves by Latin
America during the war. Whereas those reserves had totalled approximately $800 million at the end of 1938, they had
increased to approximately $3,800 million at the end of 1945.
They subsequently declined to approximately $2,950 million
at the end of 1959. [4] The accumulation of reserves during
1939-45 was, of course, almost entirely the result of wartime exigencies. To some extent, the foreign exchange
savings which the war imposed upon Latin America represented a real loss to that area, in view of the decrease which
took place in the purchasing power of the dollar over that
period. Nevertheless, it should be recognized that the availability of large reserves helped promote postwar investment,
if only by permitting a somewhat greater importation of
capital equipment than would have been possible exclusively
by reliance upon current export proceeds and foreign capital
inflows. It seems likely also, though I don't know how to
prove it, that the mere fact that those reserves were known
to exist helped encourage some capital inflow, by providing
a degree of reassurance to foreign investors and lenders.

WILL THE EXISTENCE OF MONETARY STABILIZATION INEVITABLY LEAD TO ECONOMIC DEVELOPMENT?

I have gone to great length in trying to prove the soundness
of my conviction that monetary instability must inevitably retard
economic development. Fortunately, far less effort needs to be
devoted to my conviction that the prevalence of monetary stabilization would not be enough in itself to assure the economic development of Latin America. The principal reasons for this belief
may be summarized briefly as follows:

1. A few Latin American countries have actually been
    experiencing monetary stabilization, without having
    benefitted from economic development.

2. A significant rate of economic development re-
    quires a rate of investment which is beyond the
    savings capacity of most, or all, Latin American
    countries, except during periods when export
    earnings are especially high. The low average
    per capita incomes do not permit much savings,
    and the high rate of population increase tends to
    keep per capita incomes low even when gross
    national product is increasing at what might other-
    wise be a "satisfactory" rate.

3. Some governments may choose to achieve mone-
    tary stabilization by refraining from public ex-
    penditures which are fundamental to economic
    development everywhere, such as on education
    and roads.

4. Political conditions may be such in any country
    that foreign investors will be reluctant to enter,
    and potential domestic investors may not only
    avoid the risk of national investment, but may
    even seek to transfer their money abroad.

5. The current prevalence of monetary stabiliza-
    tion may not be sufficient to convince the public
    that such stabilization will long continue. Mone-
    tary instability has so long been the rule in most
    Latin American countries, in spite of the never-
    ending promises of government officials that such
    instability will be brought to an end and in spite of
    the many half-hearted efforts to do so, that few
    Latin Americans have any confidence in the likeli-
    hood of long-term stability. Accordingly, it is
    likely that individuals will continue to be reluc-
    tant to build up their savings or to invest in non-
    speculative enterprises unless and until they are
    somehow convinced that monetary stability will
    continue to exist not only for months, but for
    years into the future.

NOTES

NOTES TO CHAPTER 2

1. The appendix to this chapter (titled Appendix A and placed after Chapter 14) contains a summary of the understandings reached at Punta del Este plus a summary of the course which the Alliance has taken since then. Those who are already familiar with these subjects or who are not interested in their details will lose little by skipping over the appendix.

NOTES TO CHAPTER 3

1. The Winds of Revolution, (paperback ed. ; New York: Frederick A. Praeger, 1963).

2. Ibid. , p. 301. (paperback ed.).

3. The resignation of the Panel of Experts in April, 1966, and the transfer of its functions to the Inter-American Committee on the Alliance for Progress (which was created at the IA-ECOSOC meeting in Sao Paulo, Brazil, in November, 1963) has not significantly affected the substantive provisions of this part of the Charter of Punta del Este.

NOTES TO CHAPTER 4

1. A term applied to it for the first time, I believe, by Secretary of the Treasury Douglas Dillon in April, 1963, at the Bank's Annual Meeting, in Macuto, Venezuela.

2. A European observer at the meetings was so impressed that he told me that he had never heard the European members of the OEEC speak more frankly to one another, even after several years of experience during and after the Marshall Plan.

3. I am not one of those who believes that U. S. loans should necessarily decline as countries increase their ability to stand on their own feet. We may find it in our interest, as well as theirs, to help them grow even stronger and even more rapidly. We may well find it desirable to make our loan terms "harder" as the countries' needs for aid subsidies decline, though even this conclusion does not <u>necessarily</u> follow. In any case, we should recognize that strength alone does not necessarily preclude the need for loans. Even the largest and wealthiest of U. S. corporations maintain themselves in a constant state of debt; indeed, the most conservative of lending institutions welcome the opportunity to make new loans to them, at low rates of interest.

4. There will be no discussion here of the various economic advantages which the Alliance for Progress would derive from a greater volume of Free World loans and investments in Latin America. The other governments and the business organizations fully recognize their ability to provide those economic advantages. However, each government and each business firm will quite understandably make only such loans or investments as it considers appropriate in its own interests, and exhortations to do otherwise would be, and have been, useless.

NOTES TO CHAPTER 6

1. Springfield, Mass.: G & C. Merriam Company, 1963.

2. A New Deal for Latin America: The Alliance for Progress (Cambridge, Mass.: Harvard University Press, 1963).

3. Ibid. , pp. 98-99.

4. Secretary Gordon played an important role in implementatio of the Marshall Plan. Later he became Professor of International Economic Relations at Harvard Business School. In that capacity and as a consultant of the Ford Foundation he made a number of trip to Latin America during the 1950's. He was co-author, with Engelb L. Grommers, of United States Manufacturing Investment in Brazil (Cambridge, Mass.: Harvard University Press, 1962). Later, President Kennedy called him to Washington where he became one o the principal architects of the Alliance for Progress. He was U. S. Ambassador to Brazil between 1961 and 1966, when he became Assistant Secretary of State.

5. Gordon, A New Deal for Latin America . . . , pp. 99-100.

6. Ibid. , pp. 101-102.

NOTES TO CHAPTER 7

1. Quotation from The Uses of the University (Cambridge, Mass.: Harvard University Press, 1963), p. 126.

2. For a more extensive treatment of this subject, I commend The Voice of Latin America (New York: Harper & Brothers, 1961) by ex-Senator William Benton, with a foreword by Ambassador Adlai E. Stevenson. See especially Chapter 4, "Education--The Key to Latin America's Future."

3. Ibid. , pp. 120-21.

4. Ibid. , p. 122.

5. Ibid. , p. 126.

6. Ibid. , p. 125.

7. Ibid. , footnote, p. 73.

8. The General Theory of Employment, Interest, and Money (New York: Harcourt Brace, 1936), p. 383, as quoted in Kerr, op. cit. , p. 116.

9. Harlan Cleveland, Gerard J. Mangone, and John Clarke Adams, The Overseas Americans (New York: McGraw-Hill Book Company, Inc. , 1960). See especially pp. 191-305.

NOTES TO CHAPTER 8

1. I shall speak of economic departments in the following discussion primarily for illustrative purposes. It would be difficult to keep the exposition simple if reference were always made to each of the other departments which I believe should take similar measures. However, it is also true that I chose economics for my illustration because of my special concern about this subject, as described in Chapter 7.

2. At many points in this and the preceding chapter, I
have referred to "U.S. universities and foundations." My
failure to emphasize the contributions which U.S. foundations
can make to the success of the Alliance was primarily due to
the fact that I did not wish to dilute my emphasis upon the
role which I attribute to the universities, per se. There is no
doubt about the fact, however, that the foundations can also
be very helpful, as in encouraging the authorship and publication of books and articles pertinent to the Alliance.

NOTES TO CHAPTER 9

1. I am not referring here to the relatively few U.S. businessmen abroad who are owners of their own firms. While
speaking of them, however, I consider it worth pointing out
as very significant that they have usually been much more aggressive, and much more effective, in implementation of the
types of measures recommended here than that much larger
segment of the U.S. business community who represent U.S.-
based firms.

NOTES TO CHAPTER 11

1. The comprehensiveness of that coverage should not, however, be overstated. For example, on December 13, 1966, the
Washington Post and Times Herald printed the following complete
news item on page 12 as the last item of its "Around the World"
column: "A ten-nation meeting of the Latin American Free Trade
Association ended in Montevideo, Uruguay, with the delegates unable to reach agreement on implementing a program of regional
economic integration." The meeting in question was the culmin-
ation of a strong effort by several of Latin America's leading
statesmen to promote creation of a Latin American common
market, and the apparent failure of that meeting warranted full
explanation and analysis.

NOTES TO APPENDIX B

1. "A Positive Approach to Aid," Foreign Affairs, April, 1961.

2. I have noted instances (particularly for political offenses) where the courts have appeared to be extremely severe, by U.S. standards. On the other hand, I have noted instances of what appeared to be extreme leniency by U.S. standards. To cite one example, I remember the Brazilian case of a man charged with murder for having shot and killed his chief after a bitter argument. The defendant's attorney never brought the facts of the case into question. However, the defendant was acquitted on the ground that the hospital to which the victim was taken after being shot was a poor one, and that the victim's death was accordingly attributable to the poor hospital facilities!

NOTES TO APPENDIX C

1. Protectionism through the instrumentality of tariffs has, of course, been the traditional means of providing "temporary" shelter for "infant industries" in all countries, including the United States. However, the protectionism of tariffs is limited to the price differentials measured by the size of the applicable tariff rates. Protectionism through the instrumentality of exchange controls is usually much more complete inasmuch as the administrators of those controls can, at their own discretion, establish quantitative limits over the amount of any particular commodity which may be imported or over the amount of foreign exchange which may be spent on such importation. They can effectively prevent the importation of any commodity being produced locally, without regard for differences of price or quality.

2. To be sure, "capacity" is rarely fixed, in any absolute sense, e.g., a plant can be operated twenty-four hours, instead of eight hours, daily. In practice, however, capacity is fixed in Latin America by such circumstances as the operations of the advanced labor laws, which require special wage payments for extra-hour work, special bonuses to discharged employees, etc.

3.   Reference should be made to the fact that ECLA has
also estimated a gross capital outflow of $3,346 million dur-
ing 1947-57, of which $2,335 million took place during 1950-57.
In evaluating the contribution made by foreign capital to Latin
America's economic growth, the reader may choose--as ECLA
did--to subtract the gross outflow from the gross inflow, so
as to arrive at a net figure. I prefer not to do so, for the following reasons: (1) $790 million of the gross outflow represent-
ed the purchase of foreign-owned enterprises by the Argentine
and Brazilian governments in 1947 and 1948. In addition,
approximately $300 million represented investments abroad
by Latin Americans during 1947-57. In each of these cases,
the outflow was in no sense attributable to the decisions of
Latin American governments as to the proper disposal of
their foreign exchange availabilities. (2) While repayments of
foreign loans accounted for approximately $2,350 million of
the capital outflow during 1947-57 ($273 million of which was
during 1947-49), and such repayments may be ascribed to the
decisions of foreigners, I believe that it would be misleading
to subtract the full amount of that outflow when evaluating the
contribution made by the capital which entered Latin America
during that period. In my opinion, the balance-of-payments
approach is fundamentally defective for the purpose of such an
evaluation. Since all loans will presumably be repaid in the long
run, shall we conclude that no loan contributes to economic
growth? If a loan is utilized so as to provide cheap power or
transportation, or if it greatly expands a country's export capacity,
is the contribution of the loan to be considered as having been
zero when it is repaid?

4.   The general Latin American picture would perhaps be
more faithfully portrayed by the exclusion of Venezuela from
the over-all totals. The approximate totals for Latin America,
excluding Venezuela, were: 1938, $737 million; 1945, $3,550
million; 1959, $2,250 million.

ABOUT THE AUTHOR

Herbert K. May has been deeply involved in Latin American affairs for twenty-five years. He was a member of the U.S. delegation to the inter-American conference in August, 1961, at Punta del Este, Uruguay, where the charter which formally established the Alliance for Progress was written. He then became Chief of the Latin American Division of the U.S. Treasury Department in Washington, D.C. In May, 1962, he transferred to the State Department as Deputy Assistant Secretary in charge of economic relations with Latin America. While in that position he also served in the Agency for International Development as Assistant U.S. Coordinator of the Alliance for Progress. In his service with the U.S. Government (from October, 1942, to August, 1963) his positions have included, in addition, Fiscal Advisor of the Joint Brazil-United States Technical Commission (1948-49) and Financial Attaché of the American embassies in Manila, the Philippines, and Rio de Janeiro, Brazil. During 1964-66, he was director of a group of technical advisors to the government of Ecuador on fiscal and administrative reforms.

WESTMAR COLLEGE LIBRARY